CONSIDER HIM

Also by Catherine Campbell

God Knows Your Name (Monarch Books, 2010)
Broken Works Best (Monarch Books, 2012; 10Publishing, 2018)
Under the Rainbow (Monarch Books, 2013)
Rainbows for Rainy Days (Monarch Books, 2013)
When We Can't, God Can (Monarch Books, 2015)
Chasing the Dawn (Monarch Books, 2016)
Journey with Me (IVP, 2018)
God Isn't Finished With You Yet (IVP, 2022)

CONSIDER HIM

Listening, Learning and Leaning on Jesus

365 Daily Devotions

Catherine Campbell

INTER-VARSITY PRESS
SPCK Group, RH101, The Record Hall, 16–16A Baldwin's Gardens,
London EC1N 7RJ, England
Email: ivp@ivpbooks.com
Website: www.ivpbooks.com

First published 2023

British Library Cataloguing-in-Publication Data
A catalogue record for this book is available from the British Library.

ISBN: 978–1–78974–461–3
eBook ISBN: 978–1–78974–462–0

Set in Adobe Caslon Pro 10/13pt
Typeset in Great Britain by CRB Associates, Potterhanworth, Lincolnshire
Printed and bound in Great Britain by Clays Ltd, Elcograf S.p.A.

Produced on paper from sustainable sources

Dedicated
to
Mum,
who went to be with her Saviour during the writing of this book

and
also to
my friends – the 'Golden Girls',
who have consistently shown Jesus to me in their
friendship, love and prayers over many years.
You are truly a blessing in my life.

Acknowledgements

It takes only one person to write a book, but a lot of people are needed to see it through the publishing process and into the reader's hands. I am delighted once more to be published by IVP, and especially under the guidance of my editor, Joshua Wells. Thanks for your commitment and patience, Josh! Also, a big thank you to the sales and marketing team of the SPCK Group, who work diligently to inform both the trade and the public that the book is actually out there.

But, as far as I am concerned, the post-writing process begins closer to home. For nine books now, my husband Philip and friend Liz have been the first to read and to offer suggestions concerning the work in progress, as they check the grammar, biblical references and, in Philip's case, to make sure I write nothing heretical! They are kind in their advice, wise in their judgement, and encouraging when the writing road is tough. Thank you is never enough.

The amount of biblical reading, study and research required for each devotional of 370ish words is substantial. Thankfully, the twenty-first century provides us with more resources than at any previous time in our history. I have been blessed with access to a multiplicity of Bible versions and commentaries, to say nothing of what is now available from trusted online sources, to aid me in passing on to you the most accurate information possible. I have referenced quotations but apologize for any omissions, which I will happily amend in future editions, if informed.

I could not write what I do without the prayerful support of family and a few close friends. There are times when I am simply lost for words. It is especially at those times when your prayers release what God wants me to say next. I am indebted to you for praying, and thankful to God that I have you in my life.

Yet, to Jesus goes my highest praise. Thank you, Lord, for pouring Yourself into my life, and then onto the page, over the past year. At times I have simply been overwhelmed by Your presence, recognizing that my words can never be enough to communicate You to others. But I am eternally grateful that You have shown Yourself to me. You have my heart, Lord Jesus . . . always.

Introduction

I clearly remember the day, back in 2018, when I pressed the send button on my manuscript for *Journey with Me*. Following a little squeal of delight, I promised myself that I would never again write another 365-day devotional! It had taken eighteen months of blood, sweat and tears – I do not jest – and I vowed it would not be repeated. It took a further three years, and a lot of cajoling from readers of *Journey with Me* looking for a follow-up edition, before I even began to consider that I might write just one more 365. What you hold in your hands is the result of those considerations and much prayer.

I was overwhelmed by the way *Journey with Me* (awarded CRT Book of the Year, 2019) was received, and deeply humbled by what readers shared of how God had used the book in their lives. Covid-19 had done its worst, and my book *God Isn't Finished With You Yet* was completed. Its publication was slightly delayed, and during one of the products of the pandemic – a Zoom call – I was in conversation with my editor about what might come next. 'I'd love to write something about Jesus, but I don't think I could,' I said, quickly following on with a few other topic ideas. 'Well,' he replied, 'if you did another 365 you could combine a few of those ideas. We [IVP] would love you to do another 365.'

You can imagine my reply to that idea! 'It's too big a write. There's too much research. It's not easy to be both devotional and inspirational for 365 days!' But one of my main excuses was, 'I don't want to mess up a book about Jesus. It's too important – no, *He* is too important – not to get it right.' So, we prayed and agonized and prayed some more . . . and God worked in my heart until I believed that He and I could do this together. As I would consider His Son, He would guide and direct, and lend His Spirit for the task ahead. The rest is now history.

However, *Consider Him* is not a sequel to *Journey with Me*. It is not a 'part two'. While it is indeed a 365 that follows the same format of its predecessor, it has a central focus rather than an eclectic mix of all kinds of biblical morsels. *Consider Him* concentrates our minds and hearts on Jesus. For the next year we will look closely at God's Son, our Saviour, and reflect on Him – not merely on His thirty-three earthly years – but on the before, after, and all that is still to come, of Jesus. It is my prayer that your knowledge of Him will move beyond the intellectual; your wonder will translate into worship: your heart will be captured by His grace, and your love for Jesus will be catapulted to a new place.

So, as we listen, learn and lean on Jesus throughout the year, let's 'consider him who endured from sinners such hostility against himself, so that you may not grow weary or fainthearted' (Hebrews 12:3). We are on the Saviour's heart. Let's ensure He is first in ours.

My dad died during the writing of *Journey with Me* and then, while approaching the final stages of *Consider Him*, it pleased the Lord to take my mum to her heavenly home. She was an ardent supporter of my writing, but more than that, Mum prayed every day for me, and for my endeavours in serving Jesus. I already miss her dearly but rejoice that she is now seeing Jesus face to face . . . the One whom she loved so devotedly. No book can compare with the joy she is experiencing now.

Catherine Campbell (2023)

Catherine can be contacted via:
Her website: www.catherine-campbell.com
Facebook: www.facebook.com/catherinecampbellauthor
Instagram: @catherinecampbellauthor

January

1 January

Looking unto Jesus, the author and finisher of *our* faith,
who for the joy that was set before Him endured the cross,
despising the shame, and has sat down at the right hand
of the throne of God.

Hebrews 12:2, NKJV

Reading: Revelation 1:4–7

Happy New Year!

Did you sit up last night watching the clock hands slowly move past that magic moment when one year ends and another begins? Perhaps you cheered as fireworks exploded across the sky, signalling that the old had gone and a clean new sheet was unfurling before your very eyes.

Undoubtedly, there's something about change points that makes us want to reminisce over what's gone and focus on what might lie ahead. So, we resolve, plan and set goals to accomplish our dreams and to determine our focus for the incoming year. Problem is, it's so easy to become distracted.

The Coronavirus pandemic brought much change into our lives – not least in the world of communication. Media interviews are now frequently conducted via video link from people's homes. I have become fascinated by what lies behind the interviewee, especially what fills their bookshelves or their home décor – but it totally disrupts my focus from what I'm supposed to be engaging with.

The writer to the Hebrews encourages us to redirect our gaze ... to determine to make Jesus the One on whom we fix our eyes. We are to tighten our focus. Restrict our view. Refuse to be distracted by lesser things. There is much to be admired in all that surrounds the following of Jesus. The worship music can be awesome; the fellowship engaging; the programmes exciting; even the Bible teaching powerful, but it is Jesus who should command our focus.

Why? Because Jesus is 'the author and finisher' of our faith. Our life with God begins and ends with Him, as does everything in between. And I for one don't want to miss a thing in the year ahead because I'm looking in the wrong direction.

Heavenly Father, I want to see Jesus in a new way this year. Don't let anything distract me from focusing on Him. Amen.

2 January

Consider him who endured from sinners such hostility against himself, so that you may not grow weary or fainthearted.

Hebrews 12:3

Reading: Hebrews 12:1–3

'Consider him . . .'

Having decided to set our focus on Him, we are now invited to look deeply and see more clearly the One who is truly worthy of our attention: Jesus. The One we're told 'endured the cross, despising the shame', finished what He had come to do and 'is seated at the right hand of the throne of God' (Hebrews 12:2). And the same verse tells us that He did it all 'for the joy that was set before him'. The delight of fulfilling the Father's will (John 6:38); the fulfilment of redemption's plan (John 1:29); the opening of a home in heaven for those who trust in Him (John 14:2) was worth the agony as far as the Son of God was concerned. The present paled into insignificance compared with what was to come.

Hebrews 11 renders us spellbound as our minds engage with those often described as 'heroes of the faith'. In visual cameos we read of those who pleased God, and 'through faith conquered kingdoms, enforced justice, obtained promises, stopped the mouths of lions' (Hebrews 11:33). The chapter finishes with stories of a nameless heroic multitude, 'of whom the world was not worthy' (11:38).

Those listed had their lives taken cruelly from them. And while history blames Jesus' death on Jewish conspiracy and Roman execution, nothing could be further from the truth. Jesus made that clear when He said, 'I lay down my life that I may take it up again. No one takes it from me, but I lay it down of my own accord' (John 10:17–18).

One of the reasons given for His willing sacrifice is stated in our verse for today: 'that you may not grow weary or fainthearted'. This compassionate Jesus is the One we are encouraged to consider.

Have you entered this new year feeling weary and fearful? Then look to Jesus. The closer our gaze the more we discover that He has us on His heart.

Lord Jesus, I choose to make You the focus of my life this year. Show me Your heart, I pray. Amen.

3 January

[Cast] all your anxieties on him,
because he cares for you.

1 Peter 5:7

Reading: 1 Peter 5:6–11

Life demands so much from us. A great deal of this is both essential and time-consuming, determining where our attention is required. But when life's tough stuff hits it can prove overwhelming, allowing little time for anything else. In recent years we discovered that this can be a national experience as well as a personal one.

As we left 2020 you could almost hear the collective sigh of 'it's good to see the back of it' move in waves across the world when the clock struck midnight. The first year of what we thought was going to be over in a few short weeks had come to an end.

The horror named the Covid-19 pandemic had struck nation after nation, community after community, family after family. Devastation touched every area of our lives. Hospital staff worked heroically with the multitude of ill and dying. Scientists cooperated across political divides, while governments set rules of wartime proportions in an attempt to control this minuscule virus that was destroying lives and economies.

Thankfully, 2020 ended with a vaccine that has had an enormous impact on the virus, offering hope that 2021 would see its eradication. However, as I write, 2021 has also passed into history, and with it the knowledge that Covid-19 is likely to be with us forever in some form.

During the tight restrictions of those years, especially in the early days, I found Coronavirus was never far from my thoughts. It was easy to become weary and fearful, even to give houseroom to doubt.

But that's not how God intends for us to live. Nowhere in Scripture are we told we will never have worries. Perhaps you have carried deep pain over the timeline that stretched from last year to this, but Peter tells us what we are to do with those anxieties – cast them on to Jesus (1 Peter 5:7). And the more we get to know Him, the easier that becomes.

Lord Jesus, help me to get to know You better this year, and to trust You with what causes me to worry. Amen.

4 January

He existed before anything was created and
is supreme over all creation.

Colossians 1:15, NLT

Reading: Colossians 1:15–18

Our friend entered the dentist's waiting room and sat opposite a complete stranger. After exchanging the usual weather-related pleasantries, our friend opened his book. The man immediately asked what he was reading. On discovering a Christian theme, other questions followed, finally resting on, 'What church do you go to?' Our friend was rather surprised that the stranger knew so much about the church when he couldn't ever remember seeing him there. When the man began to wax eloquent about the pastor, our friend couldn't help but ask, 'Do you know the pastor?'

'Yes,' came the reply. 'I know him very well.'

Just then, a disembodied voice interrupted their conversation: 'Pastor Thomas [name changed] to room two, please. Pastor Thomas to room two.'

As he rose from his seat, an impish smile crossed our friend's face. It was hard to miss the jaw drop from the man who apparently *knew him so well.*

It begs the question: how well do I know Jesus? Is He more than the babe of Bethlehem to me? More than the miracle worker of Galilee? More than the teacher from Nazareth? Have I considered that 'he existed before anything was created' (Colossians 1:15), or that 'without him was not any thing made that was made' (John 1:3)? As I look at the stars piercing the night sky or see the first snowdrop push through the frozen earth, do I see His hand? From the terrifying swell of the untameable sea to the gentle breeze on a summer meadow; the rugged majesty of a mountain range to the simple beauty of a blade of grass; the first cry of a newborn baby to the final breath of a life well lived – can I see the creative signature of Jesus written across it all?

If only we would be brave enough to push aside our fears and see Jesus for who He really is – eternal Creator of the universe – we would never doubt that His power is sufficient for all we need.

Lord Jesus, open my eyes that I might behold Your greatness, and cause my heart to follow in faith. Amen.

5 January

And the scribes and the Pharisees began to question,
saying, 'Who is this who speaks blasphemies?
Who can forgive sins but God alone?'

Luke 5:21

Reading: Luke 5:20–26

We stepped directly from our air-conditioned coach into the scorching heat. We had just completed the thirty-mile journey north from Bethsaida to Caesarea Philippi in comfort – and in an hour. It probably took around ten hours for the disciples to walk that route, and I don't know how they walked so far in such heat. I'm guessing the conversation with Jesus on the journey distracted them somewhat. I couldn't help but wish I'd been on that particular tour, as the disciples had just seen Jesus feed the 4,000 (Mark 8:1–9); put the Pharisees in their place (8:11–12); and witnessed the blind man's sight restored (8:22–26) – to say nothing of the teaching they received along the way.

Now within sight of the slopes of Mount Hermon, and the source of the Jordan running close by, Jesus was the one asking the questions: 'Who do people say that I am?' (8:27). I'm sure there was a rush to get to tell Jesus something He didn't know. Little did they realize that this exercise was still about *their* education and not *His*.

'John the Baptist,' one said. 'Elijah,' added someone else. 'One of the prophets,' others chipped in (8:28).

Actually, 'Who is this man?' was the question on everyone's lips. Many, especially those who had personally encountered Jesus, had no problem in recognizing Him as no ordinary man (John 9:33). Yet, the things Jesus said, did, and claimed greatly disturbed the religious leaders, even provoking charges of blasphemy (Matthew 9:3) and working by Satan's power (Matthew 12:24)!

These very things, however, prove the opposite to be true. Or as John Piper put it, 'When you look at Jesus Christ, you are seeing God.'[1] The Pharisees' accusations against Jesus – 'Who can forgive sins but God alone?' (Luke 5:21) – have become our statement of faith. We know that 'Christ died for our sins in accordance with the Scriptures' (1 Corinthians 15:3). Jesus is God!

Lord Jesus, Your deity is not in question. May my response always be appropriate. Amen.

6 January

And he asked them, 'But who do you say that I am?'
Peter answered him, 'You are the Christ.'

Mark 8:29

Reading: Mark 8:27–29

The question was begging to be asked.

Jesus had only asked, 'Who do people say that I am?' to get the disciples to discuss the subject. Now, sitting around Him on the grass, it was time to make it personal. That's the thing about Jesus – His words, His teachings, His actions – He always makes them personal. As far as we are concerned, Jesus always requires a response.

The Barna Group survey commissioned by the Church of England, HOPE, and the Evangelical Alliance in 2015 concluded that 40% of adults in the UK didn't believe Jesus was a real person, while only 22% of people believe Jesus was God.[2]

The US 2020 Ligonier Ministries State of Theology Survey found 52% of people agree that Jesus was a great teacher but not God. More shockingly – 30% of those identifying as evangelical responded with the same answer.[3]

For Peter, who didn't have the Bible or a library of theologians to consult, his reply was both swift and accurate: 'You are the Christ' (Mark 8:29). Was this simply the impulsive response of the impetuous man we have come to know in the Gospels? I don't believe so. Peter's response grew out of what he had heard and witnessed in the short time he had been with Jesus. All of which fitted the One the Pharisees should have identified as the Christ from Isaiah 61:1, which foretold that:

- Jesus would teach in a way that no other man could (John 7:46).
- He would bring good news to the poor (Luke 4:18).
- He would treat the broken with compassion (Luke 7:11–15).
- Jesus would liberate those bound by evil spirits (Mark 1:23–28).

All this was fulfilled in Jesus from just one verse of Messianic prophecy! And this was the same verse Jesus used for His first sermon in the synagogue in Nazareth (Luke 4:16–21). Peter made no mistake ... Jesus is the Christ! How would we reply if Jesus asked us the same question?

Lord Jesus, You are no mere prophet, nor even an excellent teacher. You are the Christ, and I worship You. Amen.

7 January

THINK ON THIS

Jesus said to her [Martha], 'Did I not tell you that if you believed you would see the glory of God?'

John 11:40

- Read the verse through a number of times.
- Write it out, stick it on the fridge, have it on your phone.
- Meditate on the words, then respond in praise.
- Encourage someone by sharing this verse with them today.

8 January

And Jesus, aware of this, said to them,
'. . . Do you not yet perceive or understand . . .
Having eyes do you not see, and having ears
do you not hear? And do you not remember?'

Mark 8:17–18

Reading: John 14:7–11

My phone pinged. I had a good idea who it would be, having discovered a few minutes earlier that snow had fallen during the night. Barely enough to cover the ground, but no doubt enough to excite our two grandchildren.

I was right. And we laughed at the sight and sound of their enjoyment as the slo-mo video revealed the glee of each snowball successfully finding its target. But how did they manage to get enough snow for a snowball fight? They had literally scraped up every flake of snow in the garden, knowing full well that it would probably be gone by the time they returned home from school that afternoon. This is Northern Ireland after all, where the frequency and amount of snow is not guaranteed. So, our grandchildren made sure they didn't waste it.

The disciples had no idea how long Jesus would be with them. They were relishing the moment, but taking it all in wasn't easy. Jesus was challenging every part of them – body, mind and soul. Often, they just took things at face value, while Jesus, who knew His time with them would be short, wanted them to extend their understanding of who He was and what that meant for their lives. You can sense Jesus' frustration in the questions He asked in today's verse. Don't you understand? Can't you see? How can you not remember?

Hindsight, however, is a great thing. After Jesus had returned to heaven (Acts 1:9–11), the disciples began to remember what He had said and taught them (John 2:22). But while they were with Jesus, they often missed the point.

How privileged we are today to have God's word alongside an abundance of other resources all pointing to Jesus and what He wants us to learn.

Lord Jesus, forgive me for taking for granted what You have provided so that I might know You better. Please don't let me waste it. Amen.

9 January

And the Word became flesh and dwelt among us,
and we have seen his glory, glory as of the only Son
from the Father, full of grace and truth.

John 1:14

Reading: John 1

John is a superb wordsmith, a truth demonstrated in the first chapter of his Gospel. The beauty of the language used is superseded only by the life-changing content he shares. Powerful in its Christology, this Gospel differs from the others by opening with words that announce Jesus as the 'Word' (John 1:1).

John was writing from Ephesus, with the command of Jesus to 'go therefore and make disciples of all nations' (Matthew 28:19) still firmly embedded in his heart. But how could he reach the Romans and Greeks from purely Jewish thought? These Gentile nations would have no problem accepting Jesus as the Son of God – they already worshipped many gods . . . and their sons. But of course, Jesus was not some false deity to be added to the multitude they already had. Jesus, as the Word, was a concept understood by Jews and Gentiles alike.

The 'Word' is the English translation of the Greek word *logos*. If you said, 'Jesus is the Word' to a Jew, he automatically associated Him with God's power, especially in creation – 'And God said, "Let there be light"' (Genesis 1:1). The spoken word of God was the expression of His power (Psalm 33:9).

If you said, 'Jesus is the Word' – *logos* – to the Greeks, they would associate it with the mind of God – the One who brings order to the universe. And, to them, there is nothing more important than that.

John's heart was to reach the lost for Jesus, whether Jew or Gentile. Now, centuries later, this Gospel writer helps us to understand that Jesus is the Word – God's ultimate and final communication to humanity. And that the Saviour shows God's mind to us through redemption's plan, birthed in the heart of a loving Father. Then, in order to fulfil the Father's plan, Jesus *willingly* 'became flesh and dwelt among us' (John 1:14).

Lord Jesus, give me a heart like John's, that I might share Your love and grace with others. Amen.

10 January

'Men of Israel, hear these words: Jesus of Nazareth,
a man attested to you by God with mighty works
and wonders and signs that God did through him
in your midst, as you yourselves know . . .'

Acts 2:22

Reading: Galatians 4:4–7

Which section of the bookshop do you browse when you're looking for something to read? Having spoken to many bookshop managers, it appears that the majority of Christian men head to the theology or biography shelves, while most women go straight for the inspirational or fiction books. (Apologies if you feel labelled.)

To tell you the truth, the word 'theology' scares me. It comes across as academic, boring, complicated. A foolish perception, perhaps, as any dictionary defines theology simply as the study of God and how He relates to the world. God has given us the Bible as our textbook, and the Holy Spirit as our teacher, to show us who He is, revealing where Jesus fits into the eternal picture. That makes us students of theology!

I am, however, grateful for the wisdom and insight of those more knowledgeable than me. It is vital to understand that Jesus is more than the compassionate healer, more than the sum of thirty-three years. As we grasp the theology of Jesus – as the pre-existent Creator (Colossians 1:15), the Christ (Mark 8:29), the One who holds all things together by His power (Hebrews 1:3), co-eternal with the Father (John 10:30), the living Word (John 1:1) – it is essential also to recognise His humanity.

Jesus was a man – not some half-god, half-man creature of the X-Men variety, living between two worlds. The disciples who lived, walked, talked and ate with Jesus knew Him as absolutely human. There was nothing unnatural or abnormal about Him; rather, His humanity was crucial to make Him a suitable Saviour for humankind. The writer to the Hebrews explains, 'He [Jesus] had to be made like his brothers in every respect, so that he might become a merciful and faithful high priest in the service of God, to make propitiation for the sins of the people' (2:17). Forgiveness is only possible because Jesus is both God and man.

Lord Jesus, thank you for becoming a man in order that You might become my Saviour. Amen.

11 January

'See my hands and my feet, that it is I myself.
Touch me, and see. For a spirit does not have flesh
and bones as you see that I have.'

Luke 24:39

Reading: John 15:9–11

You will never hear a 'No' from me when the grandchildren say, 'Let's watch *Inside Out*, Granny.' The film tells the story of a little girl, Riley, through colourful caricatures of the emotions she experiences at a time of change in her life. The story reminds us that to be human isn't only to possess flesh and bones. We are also what we feel and think. Joy, Sadness, Fear, Anger and Disgust take on lives of their own in the movie to guide and protect the pre-teen. It's hard not to recognize them in us. Emotions are our daily companions, often more visible than we'd like them to be, yet every bit as real as flesh and bones.

We long that joy will wake us from our sleep and remain throughout the day; that sadness will be fleeting and prevented from delivering pain. We want disgust to be directed towards what dishonours God and all anger to be righteous. For fear to be transformed into trust.

After His resurrection, Jesus had to encourage the doubters to touch Him physically to prove He really was alive – more than that, he was still human. Something that had not been in doubt before the crucifixion. Jesus was a human being, like us. His bodily needs mirrored ours. He ate and drank (Luke 7:34); enjoyed friendship (John 15:15) and attended parties (John 2:2); slept (Mark 4:38); walked and talked (Luke 8:1).

And that wasn't all – Jesus also experienced every emotion we do. He toyed with His flesh as we do with ours. He was no stranger to exhaustion (Mark 6:31), disgust (John 2:16) and frustration (Matthew 17:17), to name a few.

As for joy, Jesus primarily found His in obedience to the Father (Psalm 40:8, NLT). And He was a joy-spreader! You can't spread it unless you have it in the first place. Wherever He went, people were left rejoicing, amazed and praising God because of Jesus' acts of kindness and healing (Mark 2:12). He was magnetic – people enjoyed being around Him.

Thank you, Jesus, that in You we receive the joy of an abundant life. May we follow Your example and spread it around today. Amen.

12 January

Jesus wept
John 11:35

Reading: John 11:30–44

Were there ever more precious tears shed? Did God's bottle (Psalm 56:8) ever become a receptacle for a more priceless liquid? Than the tears of sadness from the One whose hands flung the stars into space?

What could possibly have made God the Man cry? Didn't Jesus know when He set out for Bethany that it would end with the miraculous? Didn't He know that His friend Lazarus, who had died, would be raised to life again; that Mary and Martha's sorrow was only temporary? Of course He did. But it didn't stop the Saviour from feeling the pain He observed when He arrived with the grieving family. His tears were not of weakness, but of deep sadness, perhaps because Mary and Martha felt He had let them down (John 11:33), but more likely because He empathized with their grief (Hebrews 4:15). Face to face with heart-breaking sorrow, Jesus wept.

Seven hundred years earlier, Isaiah had prophesied that the Messiah would be, 'a man of sorrows and acquainted with grief' (Isaiah 53:3). He wouldn't merely be an observer. The prophet spoke with sincerity of the coming King as One who would personally experience all the horrors of this fallen world – not only through the pain of others, but particularly through His own. Jesus wasn't given a free ride in the emotion stakes. Black as well as gold were the brushstrokes used across His life, just like ours. He was fully human.

Through the years I have been asked how I can trust in a God who has allowed so much pain in my life. Despair, anger, sadness and even disappointment with God, during the twenty years we cared for our disabled daughters, were the emotional battles I fought. The frustration of not understanding what God was doing in my life, or theirs, often shook me, but through His word I've heard the whispered promises of His presence – that I would never walk alone through the heartache (Isaiah 43:2) – alongside encouragements to trust His heart even when I couldn't see His plan.

The God who weeps is the One we can trust.

Man of Sorrows, thank you for bearing my griefs and carrying my sorrows. I don't deserve such love. Amen.

13 January

But when the Helper comes, whom I will send to you
from the Father, the Spirit of truth, who proceeds
from the Father, he will bear witness about me.

John 15:26

Reading: Matthew 3:13–17

The Trinity is fundamental to the message of the Bible. The prefix 'tri' meaning 'three', and the word 'unity' meaning 'as one', combine to explain the three distinct persons of Father, Son and Spirit, brought together as one in the Godhead; their separate identities never working apart from each other, the blending of each nature fulfilled in the actions of the others.

The word 'trinity' is not mentioned in the Bible, but the evidence is right there from Genesis 1, where we first read of the persons of the Godhead working in co-operation with creation. In the beginning, *God* created the heavens and the earth' (Genesis 1:1), and 'He [*Jesus*] was in the beginning with God' (John 1:1). 'And the *Spirit* of God was hovering over the face of the waters' (1:2). Clarity is further given as to three persons in one when we read of plurality in verse 26, 'Then God said, "Let *us* make man in *our* image, after *our* likeness"' (italics throughout this paragraph mine).

When my knee-replacement surgery was planned, I investigated the surgeon online. His handsome features and kind eyes weren't important, but his curriculum vitae was. I didn't want a jack-of-all-trades doing a mediocre job on my painful joint. I wanted a specialist in knee surgery to perform the operation – someone who could be trusted to do the job right.

Jesus wasn't merely another 'man sent from God' like John the Baptist (John 1:6). He was, and is, the second person of the Trinity, as today's readings show. The Father planned redemption (1 John 4:14), while the Son brought it about by His death on the cross (1 Corinthians 15:3), and the Spirit seals the promise in us that we are born of God (Ephesians 1:13).

Jesus' curriculum vitae surpasses all others. He is who He says He is. At the very least, that should drop us to our knees in awe and worship.

Lord Jesus, You alone are qualified to save my soul from sin. I bow in adoration that You should love me and give Your life for me. Amen.

14 January

THINK ON THIS

[Christ Jesus] who, though he was in the form of God, did not count equality with God a thing to be grasped, but emptied himself, by taking the form of a servant, being born in the likeness of men.

Philippians 2:6–7

- Read through these verses a number of times – including out loud.
- Write them out, stick them on the fridge, have them on your phone.
- Meditate on the words, then respond in praise.
- Be a doer ... Serve someone with an act of kindness today.

15 January

Nathanael answered him, 'Rabbi, you are the Son of God!
You are the King of Israel!'

John 1:49

Reading: Hebrews 1:8–9

'He's on his way!'

Pride welled up in me as I looked along the row of children sitting in their specially designed pushchairs waiting to meet our future king. Each one profoundly disabled, yet each wonderfully brave in how they faced the challenges of every day . . . our daughter Joy among them. They were unaware of the status of the man who moved towards them, gently ruffling hair and stroking small hands.

These children were involved in a campaign to bring a children's hospice to Northern Ireland, something Prince Charles asked about when he stopped in front of us. Joy's hand had closed tightly around his finger as the prince listened to me sharing our dream. I was surprised at his tenderness towards the children. And even more shocked a week later to discover that the Prince of Wales had nominated the Northern Ireland Children's Hospice Project the beneficiary of his annual golf charity event at Wentworth Golf Club. The name of the event? 'Tee-off for Joy'!

Our future king had remembered the children . . . and even the name of one little girl!

The first chapter of Matthew's Gospel sets out the evidence for the kingly line of Jesus, all the way from King David. The Magi asked King Herod where they would find the one born king of the Jews (Matthew 2:2). Mary was told by the angel, 'The Lord God will give to him the throne of his father David' (Luke 1:32). Even the Roman governor, Pilate, asked Jesus, 'Are you the King of the Jews?' (Matthew 27:11). Yet none of them knew what kingship – Jesus style – was all about (John 18:36).

Could the lepers Jesus healed (Luke 5:12–13), the demon-possessed He delivered (Matthew 8:16) or the dead He raised to life (Luke 7:15) ever have thought that the man who touched them with such compassion was none other than the King of kings (Revelation 19:16)? Or that they, too, could be part of Christ's kingdom (Luke 23:42)?

King Jesus, I gladly offer the throne of my heart to You. Reign in me. Amen.

16 January

'My kingdom is not of this world . . . For this purpose
I have come into the world – to bear witness to the truth.'

John 18:36–37

Reading: John 18:33–37

Queen Elizabeth II had six palaces and castles across the UK that she called home. Buckingham Palace, with 775 rooms, is the official residence of the monarch. Windsor Castle was by far Queen Elizabeth's London favourite, with 1,000 rooms. Sandringham House, where she hosted her family for Christmas, is estimated to have between 100 and 200 rooms. Balmoral Castle, the monarch's Scottish summer retreat has fifty-two bedrooms alone, while the official Scottish Palace of Holyrood boasts 289 rooms. Hillsborough Castle in Northern Ireland is more of a grand country house than its title suggests. Quite a tally of grandeur – now inherited by her eldest son, King Charles III.

The building of grand palaces is not a modern tradition. Herod the Great, the Rome-appointed king of Israel, was a master builder. Apart from the reconstruction of the temple in Jerusalem, the Herodium – Herod's Palace, the Masada Fortress and the Antonia fortress – which included magnificent palaces, were all structures created by this brutal king.

If living in grandeur was a sign of position, a way for kings and rulers to display their wealth as evidence of their power, what about Jesus? Some who followed Jesus thought He was about to defeat the Romans and remove their puppet Herodian kings. They believed His lack of wealth would be short-lived – the kingdom would soon be His (Luke 19:11). In fact, the opposite was true. Jesus was homeless – 'the Son of Man has nowhere to lay his head' (Matthew 8:20). He and His disciples stayed in the homes of people willing to give them food and lodgings (Luke 10:7). They weren't wealthy men.

Jesus – a king? Really? Yes, but His 'kingdom is not of this world' (John 18:36), and we who follow this King look for 'a building from God, an eternal house in heaven, not built by human hands' (2 Corinthians 5:1, NIV). And when we enter there, we shall fall 'before the throne, saying, "Worthy are you, our Lord and God, to receive glory and honor and power"' (Revelation 4:10–11).

Lord Jesus, create in me a humility like Your own. Amen.

17 January

But the angel said to him, 'Do not be afraid, Zechariah, for your prayer has been heard, and your wife Elizabeth will bear you a son . . . And he will turn many of the children of Israel to the Lord their God.'

Luke 1:13–16

Reading: Luke 1:8–23

Twice a year, Zechariah travelled from his home in the Judean hills to Jerusalem to perform his duties at the temple. But this was one year he'd never forget.

Yahweh is silent for 400 years and then chooses to speak to me! And now it is I who cannot speak. How could I have been so foolish? Lost in his thoughts, and then forced into silence, Zechariah couldn't respond to the excited chatter of his priestly travelling companions as they discussed what happened on that once-in-a-lifetime day when he was chosen to burn the incense offering at the daily sacrifice. He had gone into the Holy Place alone; stayed longer than expected; and returned looking shocked and unable to speak. *Surely Zachariah has seen a vision,* they concluded (Luke 1:21–22).

Later, sitting together with his wife, the old priest tried to explain, using a writing tablet, the sequence of events . . . filling in the gaps of what others had told her. Elizabeth's eyes brimmed with pride as Zechariah signed to her how he had placed the incense on the hot coals. Gasping, her hands shot to her mouth as the word 'angel' appeared. But Zechariah wasn't finished. *He said we will have a son!*

Elizabeth rocked back on her heels, laughing and crying at the same time. *And that's not all.* Zechariah continued writing. *He will be special – he is to prepare the way for the Messiah* (1:17). And the woman who thought God had said 'no' to her fervent prayers for a child bowed in worship; the silent prayers of her husband joining hers in praise to the God of heaven.

'Why can you not speak?' Elizabeth asked, her hand stroking Zechariah's cheek.

Disbelief, he wrote. *I dared to question God's messenger.*

Lord Jesus, forgive me when doubt and disbelief are my response to Your Word. Help me to walk in the truth You give me. Amen.

18 January

'And you, child, will be called the prophet of the Most High; for you will go before the Lord to prepare his ways, to give knowledge of salvation to his people in the forgiveness of their sins.'

Luke 1:76–77

Reading: Mark 1:1–8

It was a different Zechariah who next opened his mouth, after having it closed in rebuke by the angel Gabriel in the temple (Luke 1:20). The elderly priest had plenty of time to consider the words of God's messenger concerning the son who would soon break God's prophetic silence to the nation. As Zechariah wrote the name 'John' – given by the angel – on the writing tablet, he was rewarded for his obedience (1:63–64). Only this time his words erupted in Holy Spirit-inspired prophecy (1:67–79). Zechariah and Elizabeth's newborn son was to be the first living prophet since Malachi 400 years before.

Remarkably, John's coming had been prophesied 700 years earlier by Isaiah as the one who would 'prepare the way of the LORD' (Isaiah 40:3–5).

Historically, there were always people in Israel claiming to have a word from the Lord. But the Bible has its own tests for authenticity. People were not to believe every utterance because someone dared to declare it as the word of, or from, the Lord. Instead, Moses gave strict instructions: 'When a prophet speaks in the name of the LORD, if the word does not come to pass or come true, that is a word that the LORD has not spoken; the prophet has spoken it presumptuously' (Deuteronomy 18:22). A prophecy had to be 100% accurate! Much later, the apostle John wrote, 'Beloved, do not believe every spirit, but test the spirits to see whether they are from God . . . every spirit that confesses that Jesus Christ has come in the flesh is from God' (1 John 4:1–2).

John, called the Baptizer, was undoubtedly God's prophet as he prepared the way for the coming Messiah, while preaching repentance for sin (see today's reading). We are living proof that he was no fake.

Lord Jesus, not everyone speaks truth. May I be like the Bereans 'examining the Scriptures daily to see if these things are so' (Acts 17:11). Amen.

19 January

'And blessed is she who believed that there would be a fulfilment of what was spoken to her from the Lord.'

Luke 1:45

Reading: Luke 1:39–45

Who God choses to be part of His plan never ceases to amaze me.

The man sent to prepare the way for the coming of God's Son was born of humble, ageing parents in rural Judea. We aren't even told the name of their hometown. Yes, John's father was a priest, and his mother was a daughter of the priestly tribe of Aaron (Luke 1:5), but they were hardly high up on the ecclesiastical ladder. Apart from attending the temple in Jerusalem for what was required of every Jewish male (Deuteronomy 16:16), Zechariah completed a week of priestly service there twice a year. The rest of the time he faithfully spent serving the local community.

But what set Zechariah and Elizabeth apart from everyone else was explained by Luke: 'And they were both righteous before God, walking blamelessly in all the commandments and statutes of the Lord' (1:6). Only a few others are described in the Bible as blameless. The short list includes Noah, of whom it is written, 'Noah was a righteous man, blameless in his generation. Noah walked with God' (Genesis 6:9). And he was the man God chose to prepare humanity for judgement. Then there was Job, defined as 'blameless and upright, one who feared God and turned away from evil' (Job 1:1) – the person God used to teach us about suffering and the response of faith in a sovereign God.

It is no surprise, therefore, that the couple God chose as parents to John the Baptist were also described as both righteous and blameless (Luke 1:6). Blameless is not the same as sinless, but rather speaks of character beyond reproach – exactly what God could use.

Today's verse concerned Mary, the mother of Jesus, but the same could easily have been said of Elizabeth. She also believed that God would fulfil the promise made to her. They were both women of faith – open to God's will, whatever the cost.

Lord Jesus, You see my heart, I want to follow You wherever that might take me. Amen.

20 January

He was in the wilderness and preached that people should be baptized to show that they had repented of their sins and turned to God to be forgiven.

Mark 1:4, NLT

Reading: Matthew 3:1–12

'Repentance' is not a word any of us like. Where forgiveness brings delight, repentance is painful – our sin is exposed and acknowledging it isn't enough. We need to do something about it. True repentance means we need to own up, seek God's mercy, and determine, with God's help, to change our direction in obedience to His word. Repentance means action – not merely a silent prayer to make us feel better.

We have no information as to how long John's godly parents lived after his remarkable birth, but we know that John lived an ascetic life after he left the family home (Luke 1:80). When the time came for John to engage with the public, his message and demeanour had a magnetism unheard of since the time of Elijah (John 1:21). The people flocked to see and hear this strange-looking prophet who didn't mince his words when he preached a message of repentance and of judgement to come (Luke 3:9).

'Repent,' John would shout, 'for the kingdom of heaven is at hand . . . Bear fruit in keeping with repentance' (Matthew 3:2, 8). If you were serious about repentance, he taught, then you should help the poor, feed the hungry, treat others honestly and be content with what you have (Luke 3:10–14). The penitent then publicly declared they were leaving their old, sinful ways behind, and were preparing for the arrival of God's kingdom by submitting to baptism.

Today we prefer to hear sermons on forgiveness and God's mercy rather than on sin, judgement and repentance. We don't like to feel uncomfortable, or to make others feel that way. I can't help but wonder, would John address us as he did the Pharisees and Sadducees (Matthew 3:7, 9)? Have we become comfortable with our Christian heritage at the expense of preaching the whole counsel of God – including repentance?

The rugged man of the wilderness would eventually pay the ultimate price for delivering God's message (Mark 6:27).

Lord Jesus, forgive me for worrying about what others say. Make me fearless. Amen.

21 January

THINK ON THIS

For I am not ashamed of the gospel, for it is the power
of God for salvation to everyone who believes,
to the Jew first and also to the Greek.

Romans 1:16

- Read through this verse a number of times – including out loud.
- Write it out, stick it on the fridge, have it on your phone.
- Meditate on the words, then respond in praise.
- Take steps to allow God's word to change you: perhaps . . . repent, forgive, love.

22 January

'Prepare the way of the Lord.'

Luke 3:4

Reading: Luke 2:25–38

The usual greeting went unsaid as Simeon reached the little family; two young pigeons now held firmly in the man's hands – the sacrifice required for the mother's purification rite. Simeon's eyes focused intently on the tiny boy in the young woman's arms.

Is Simeon up to his old tricks again? some of the passers-by wondered. However, the couple didn't seem at all perturbed by the elder's interruption of what was a very important day for them, presenting both mother and firstborn son at the temple. It wasn't their first experience of strange intrusion into their lives.

Simeon's hands trembled. He stared deeply into the baby's eyes, bright with the charm of infancy, while the little one's hand grasped Simeon's finger. The old man chuckled, the baby smiled. Oh, how long he had waited to see that smile! Then, glancing towards the parents, Simeon lifted the baby out of his mother's arms and nestled him against his own heart. Tears of joy ran down the creases of his cheeks. Holding the young child close, Simeon blessed God for this moment, surprising the baby's parents with his words.

'Sovereign Lord.' Simeon's eyes lifted from the baby to the sky above. 'Now it's time for me to die in peace.' The baby's mother, Mary, looked wide-eyed at her husband, Joseph. 'For now I have seen Your salvation with my own eyes, just as You promised,' the old man continued. 'The salvation – declared by the prophets and promised for all people – is now here.' And Simeon's eyes shifted back to the wriggling bundle he held, 'Yes, Lord, *this* salvation will bring light even to the Gentiles, and honour to Your people Israel, who gave Him life.'

Mary and Joseph could hardly believe what they were hearing, and now Simeon turned to address them. 'Listen carefully,' he said, his bony fingers resting on their shoulders, 'this child will be the ruination of many in this land, bringing down the proud and arrogant ... but He will also exalt others beyond what could be imagined.'[4]

Thank you, Lord, for the example of those who waited and believed. Give me a faith like that. Amen.

23 January

'Every valley shall be filled, and every mountain and hill
shall be made low, and the crooked shall become straight,
and the rough places shall become level ways.'

Luke 3:5

Reading: Acts 13:23–25

'How many sleeps until Daddy comes home?'

This was a frequent question in our home when our son was little. Having a dad who was an itinerant evangelist meant he wasn't always there to tuck him up at night. So, Paul used the number of sleeps without his dad as his measurement of time until the great homecoming happened. It also meant that I had this little 'starfish' spread out across my bed many a night! Yet, on the plus side, seeing the excitement on his little face each morning when another 'sleep' had passed was worth my edge-of-the-bed existence . . . especially when he learned subtraction and could work out for himself how many sleeps were left. He was a boy who waited eagerly for his dad's promise of, 'I'll be back soon,' to be fulfilled. Paul learned early in life that his father was a man of his word. Daddy always came home.

Our heavenly Father's promise of a messiah stretched back as far back as the garden of Eden (Genesis 3:15), with more details given in the many prophecies of Isaiah 700 years before Christ's birth, for example in Isaiah 7:14, 9:1–7, 25:9–10, to say nothing of Isaiah 53. However, unlike our son's dad, the heavenly Father didn't say exactly when our Messiah would come – only that He would. For centuries, those who faithfully believed God's word waited for the promise to be realized – John the Baptist and Simeon among those who got to meet Jesus face to face. John even observed a little of what the prophet Isaiah meant about the levelling of life's mountains and valleys, as Jesus transformed lives.

I don't think Paul counted the sleeps until his daddy came home because he felt insecure; rather, because he missed his presence. Life was better when he was there . . . and anyway, Mummy couldn't fix things the way Daddy could. He was worth waiting for. How much more so is Jesus.

Father, I can always trust Your promise, even if it involves waiting. Keep me patient.
Amen.

24 January

Jesus increased in wisdom and in stature
and in favor with God and man.

Luke 2:52

Reading: Deuteronomy 11:18–21

'Alexa! Tell me a joke!'

I don't know who laughed more: our six-year-old grandson in response to the joke told by his great-grandmother's new piece of technology, or us at him laughing! Laughter is contagious – especially that of a child. It's also a sign of happiness from a position void of fear. And there's plenty of research to prove that happy children go on to become satisfied adults, especially if the child's happiness comes from the security of loving and affirming parents.

We know very little about Jesus' childhood. Much has been speculated, but the Bible is strangely silent about His life between the escape to Egypt (Matthew 2:13–14) to the beginning of His public ministry when He was around thirty. Yet one thing we can be sure of is that, because of what we know of Mary and Joseph's character, Jesus was brought up in a loving home. This child had a mother who was obedient to God's word (Luke 1:38), and an adoptive father who is described as 'just' (Matthew 1:19).

Jewish family life revolved around the home and the synagogue. Jesus lived in a simple home in a small town. Growing up, He learned carpentry and stonemasonry from his father, which was especially useful as Nazareth was close to the growing city of Sepphoris.

Alongside providing the daily necessities of life, Joseph understood his spiritual responsibility to teach his family God's word: 'You shall teach them diligently to your children, and shall talk of them when you sit in your house, and when you walk by the way' (Deuteronomy 6:7). My guess is that many a spiritual conversation was had between father and son as they walked to work . . . and many a laugh too.

There is nothing strange about the silence surrounding Jesus' early life. He had growing up to do . . . just like our children. He needed a loving family and spiritual guidance . . . just like our children. And like Joseph, we also need to step up to the plate as we teach and care for children, in whatever role that might be.

Father, may future generations hear about Jesus from me. Amen.

25 January

'Did you not know that I must be about
My Father's business?'

Luke 2:49, NKJV

Reading: Luke 2:41–50

Boys will be boys!

The Jews loved to party, and the temple festivals were not to be missed. While the adult males in the family were obligated to attend the three feasts of Passover, Tabernacles and Pentecost (Exodus 23:14), the whole family often travelled together to Passover. Jesus' family was no different. Perhaps a chore for some, for the children it was an adventure and a holiday rolled into one. There was a lot of fun to be had on the journey as friends and families met up.

Yet Jesus knew how special this particular year in Jerusalem was for Him. Now twelve years old, this would be the last Passover He would attend as a child. The next year He would be included with the men in the sacrificial rites. Fun and games were okay on the journey, but something deep inside His adolescent frame told Him He still had much to learn. So engrossed was Jesus in listening to and questioning the teachers in the temple that He missed the family group leaving for home (Luke 2:46). And worse still, they hadn't missed their son, believing Him to be with others in the extended family.

Panic ensued as Mary and Joseph spent three days searching for the Son whom God had entrusted to their care. But this incident was about more than a missing child. It was about that child discovering His identity, and a reminder to His parents of who He was. 'Did you not know that I must be about My Father's business?' (Luke 2:49, NKJV) was Jesus' reply to His parents' rebuke. The words were not a prepubescent rant, but rather an awakening to the depth of His spiritual responsibility and where His focus should lie.

As I picture the scene of this gangly twelve-year-old, eager to learn, I am humbled. Do I rush eagerly to open my Bible? Do I relish time spent with Him above all others? Do I seek His will above all else? Shouldn't I be about my Father's business?

Lord Jesus, I want to sit at Your feet . . . to be Your willing student. Amen.

26 January

But if anyone has the world's goods and sees
his brother in need, yet closes his heart against him,
how does God's love abide in him?

1 John 3:17

Reading: James 2:15–17

Brrr . . . it was cold last night! Hot water bottle at my feet and wrapped in a warm duvet, I could hear the wind whip the trees beyond our garden fence. Grateful that our little corner of the UK hadn't suffered like other places under the ferocity of Storm Eunice – we still had light and heat. I cuddled down, thanking God for the comfort of a good home and a loving family to share it with. But sitting at His feet is not just about enjoying what He gives.

From the time Jesus started synagogue school aged five until He sat listening to Israel's finest teachers at twelve, He learned the compassion of His heavenly Father, evident in the Law. God's children were to care for the poor (Deuteronomy 15:11); they were to treat the refugee like one of their own (Leviticus 19:34); they were to act with kindness and justice to all (Micah 6:8).

Compassion . . . it ran right through Jesus' life the way the name of a seaside town runs through a stick of rock. We read repeatedly in the gospels how Jesus responded when He met those in need, and the word compassion was always in the mix (Matthew 9:36, 14:14; Mark 1:41, 6:34, all NKJV). But one word stands out in all these stories. Jesus didn't just *feel* compassion for those He met – He was *moved* with compassion. He acted on what He saw – and did something about it.

As the wind continued howling, my heart turned in prayer for those clutching each other for warmth on some freezing mountain, or scraping parched land for food for their children. However, feeling sorry for those in need isn't enough. 'So also faith by itself,' James says, 'if it does not have works, is dead' (2:17). Action is needed.

God of compassion, may my life be moved to act when I see a brother or sister in need. Amen.

27 January

And behold, a voice from heaven said,
'This is my beloved Son, with whom I am well pleased.'

Matthew 3:17

Reading: Matthew 3:13–17

Jesus cut a lone figure as He walked towards the Jordan, John's words piercing the air as He came closer. 'You brood of vipers! Who warned you to flee from the wrath to come?' Stifled chuckles rippled along the edges of the Baptist's congregation as the self-righteous teachers received a verbal slapping for their hypocrisy. They wouldn't be dipping beneath the water today, or any day. This baptism thing was only for sinners, a category they were happy to count themselves out of.

Momentarily lifting His eyes from the water, John, the preacher-baptizer, stepped back, shocked. *Could it be Him? No, He doesn't need to be baptized . . . and certainly not by me!*

John's silence suddenly stilled the crowd, people standing aside to make a path to the water for the stranger. He didn't look any different from them. He certainly wasn't a Pharisee or a Sadducee. His clothes were ordinary – dusty from the journey. Simple sandals covered His feet, a water bottle and whittling knife hung from His belt, a thin blanket draped over one shoulder.

Shedding both blanket and belt, the man stepped into the river, the Baptist almost falling back into the water at His approach. Briefly, the two men engaged in quiet conversation. Lifting his hand in protest, it looked as if the Baptizer was refusing the baptism request. 'The Baptist is saying that he needs to be baptized by the other man,' someone whispered. Finally, John dips Jesus under Jordan's cold water, but before anything more could be said the skies part. Mesmerized, the crowd watch what could have been a scene from their childhood stories of the exodus. God was speaking, and a dove-like Spirit was resting on the man coming out of the water!

The startled crowd dispersed as the Son, whom God had just affirmed, fastened His belt. And both Jesus and John knew that the time of preparation had finished. The Father's business was going public.

Thank you, Father, that Your love is no secret, and Your power is available for the task ahead. Amen.

28 January

THINK ON THIS

But Peter and the apostles answered,
'We must obey God rather than men.'
Acts 5:29

- Read through this verse a number of times – including out loud.
- Write it out, stick it on the fridge, have it on your phone.
- Meditate on the words, then respond in praise.
- Encourage someone by sharing this verse with them today.

29 January

How impossible it is for us to understand
his decisions and his ways!

Romans 11:33, NLT

Reading: Habakkuk 3:17–19

Some of what God does doesn't make sense from this side of eternity.

This morning (at the time of writing) we learned that a teenager we'd been praying for had passed into the presence of his Saviour. We had never met, yet his name was often on our lips in prayer. We had grown fond of this seventeen-year-old who was standing on the edge of manhood, yet for the past two years had battled cancer. A short time before his diagnosis he had trusted the Lord for salvation and had been on fire for Jesus since that day. His father followed his son in faith soon after. Life was good . . . until the cancer train crashed into their lives.

What followed was pain and treatment . . . good news dashed by bad . . . hope cracked by disappointment – each seemed set on repeat like some old record player. And prayer, lots of prayer, offered by people from near and far. His church family met frequently, while his friends in the youth group learned some tough lessons of what it means to follow Jesus – that an easy road is not promised. The age-old unanswerables were asked. 'Why?' was top of the list, especially, 'Why did God not heal him?' The theological responses, though never adequate, may be helpful down the line, but for now, love, compassion and a sense of presence are what's needed, especially for those who will miss him most.

Having lost two of our own three children, my husband and I have sat where these parents are sitting now. We fought for the health and life of our daughters, just as they fought for their son's. We filled what seemed like oceans with our tears, as they have and will continue to do. There are no words, but there is empathy . . . and the knowledge obtained over the years that God has not left them – whatever lies their grief may tell them. In the valley, God is still God . . . and in Jesus He has shown Himself willing and able to lead us through.

Jesus, lover of my soul . . . leave, ah! leave me not alone, still support and comfort me.'[5]
Amen.

30 January

You must live as God's obedient children.
Don't slip back into your old ways of living
to satisfy your own desires.

1 Peter 1:14, NLT

Reading: 1 Peter 1:13–17

Jesus was thirty years old when He stepped out of the River Jordan (Luke 3:23). Carpentry was now behind Him, while the more important business of changing the world lay ahead. The Father's public affirmation at the Jordan baptism was the final commissioning of Jesus to the purpose for which He was born . . . 'For the Son of Man came to seek and to save the lost' (19:10). But why wait until He was thirty? Did He ever become impatient to get on with things more important than window shutters? Highly unlikely.

The age of thirty was seen as the peak of maturity and strength, and only men between thirty and fifty were eligible for spiritual service (Numbers 4:3). While His work was far greater than any other undertaken previously, Jesus remained subject to God's instruction. Then, when the time came, He was ready. There would be no slipping back to the familiar family building business.

For Jesus it was all about obedience. Something He took seriously . . . right to the very end, 'by becoming obedient to the point of death, even death on a cross' (Philippians 2:8).

It's easier to obey when you're happy with what's being asked of you, or if you respect the person who's asking. Few of us like to be told what to do. Our sinful nature bristles against submitting to another's command or wishes. Yet Christ has left us the ultimate example of obedience to the Father's will – not to the demands of a tyrant, but rather to a loving Father who works *all things* together for our good (Romans 8:28).

Too often we seek thrills in the Christian life rather than the experience of God Himself, gained through obedience. 'To listen to one word and go out and obey it,' comments Elisabeth Elliot, 'is better than having the most exalted "religious experience", for it puts us in touch with God Himself – it is a willed response.'[6]

Rarely do our own desires satisfy.

Lord, I want to be in touch with You. Teach me obedience. Amen.

31 January

'For I have come down from heaven,
not to do my own will but the will
of him who sent me.'

John 6:38

Reading: John 6:37–41

As I write, the world is reeling from the news that Russia has invaded Ukraine . . . this without provocation, it seems, for no other reason than that one man wants control of what doesn't belong to him. Like a spoilt child wanting his own way, Putin is causing death and devastation for selfish ambition, thinly veiled by what he calls peace-making. His will trumps that of millions, while the oppressed respond in ways of which Putin knows nothing.

Last night a missionary couple from Northern Ireland requested urgent prayer for the Ukrainian city where they have been based for the past eight years. Their message included these words: 'We are not leaving . . . how can we? We would like to turn our Gospel Hall into a place of shelter for those in need.' I was deeply moved by their commitment, especially by the words that ended their call for prayer: 'We are not any braver than you – but confident we are where God would expect us to be.' I felt I was looking into the face of obedience. God hadn't changed His call – and they hadn't changed their response. What will the outcome be? I do not know, but these dear people believe passionately 'that the Most High rules in the kingdom of men' (Daniel 4:17, NKJV).

Against this difficult benchmark of obedience, Jesus stands above all others. He had only one goal in mind – one reason to get up in the morning – to do the Father's will. Jesus already knew what that would involve, and yet still He chose to follow the path of obedience that eventually ended at the cross. What necessitated such costly obedience? 'For this is the will of my Father,' said Jesus, 'that everyone who looks on the Son and believes in him should have eternal life, and I will raise him up on the last day' (John 6:40). Our eternal destiny was the motivating force behind the Son's obedience to the Father. Amazing love!

Lord, may my love for You be seen in all I do. Amen.

February

1 February

He is the radiance of the glory of God and the
exact imprint of his nature, and he upholds
the universe by the word of his power.

Hebrews 1:3

Reading: Romans 1:20–25

You don't often hear the word 'glorify' these days. It doesn't sound very fashionable. Yet it is part of our nature; an activity we all engage in daily – like when we chant and wave our team's colours at a football match, sharing in their glory when they score. Marking that 'X' on polling day to endorse the political party we choose to honour, or getting carried away at a concert. It's all part of this glorification habit we think we don't engage in. Even the way we speak of our children teeters on its edge.

To glorify someone simply means to bestow honour and admiration, to the point of public praise. Unfortunately, those we hold up highest often fall hardest. Glory is frequently temporary. We are all flawed human beings. What we attain is quickly forgotten by others.

Not so with Jesus.

The writer to the Hebrews explains that God's glory – the attributes of holiness, power, justice, love, faithfulness and so on – literally shone from Jesus. Worshipping the Father wasn't difficult for Jesus. No one knew the Father like the Son. His very nature was imprinted on Jesus' soul. The honour, position and praise Jesus gave the Father was demonstrated through His obedience in doing the Father's will, and in making Him known everywhere He went.

What an example Jesus gives us. Our calling is to point others to God's glory, for Christ in us to be the attraction. 'In the same way,' Jesus tells us, 'Let your light shine before others, so that they may see your good works and give glory to your Father who is in heaven' (Matthew 5:16). What we do is not to impress others. It is of far more importance. Our aim is to initiate praise for the only One worthy to receive it.

John the Baptist's attitude of, 'He must increase, but I must decrease' (John 3:30), is one we need to emulate, for it will surely point others to Jesus.

Lord, may my praise only ever be directed towards You. Amen.

2 February

'Behold, the Lamb of God,
who takes away the sin of the world!'

John 1:29

Reading: John 1:35–42

Andrew was a seeker. Not merely looking for a messiah to rid his people of the Romans, but actively seeking the One promised in the Scriptures as *the* Messiah (Isaiah 49:6, NLT). Lately, his search had taken him away from fishing to learn from the weird preacher/baptizer of the Jordan River – a fearless man, unafraid to speak about judgement for the unrepentant. John's teaching both excited and frightened Andrew. One topic in particular grabbed the fisherman's attention. The Baptist preached that the Messiah was already born and would come after him (John 1:26, 27), something Andrew was determined not to miss.

But was Andrew prepared for how John introduced the Messiah when Jesus walked along the river that day? 'Behold, the Lamb of God, who takes away the sin of the world!'

'Lamb of God!' 'Sin-bearer!'

This had no resonance of expected power – neither of military commander nor of kingly authority. *God's man was to be God's Lamb!* Andrew knew more about fish than lambs. However, he was fully aware of the importance of a lamb to the Jews. Didn't he attend Passover at the temple with his family every year? Hadn't they watched the lamb they'd brought sacrificed – its blood caught in a basin, then tossed onto the altar as an atonement for their sin (Hebrews 9:22)? Hadn't Andrew tasted for himself the roasted lamb, reminding him of Israel's readiness to flee from Egypt's tyranny centuries earlier? Yes, yes and yes!

But how could this teacher be the 'Lamb of God'? How could a man take away 'the sin of the world'? Andrew's head was spinning. He had so many questions. So many things he didn't understand.

But Jesus knew exactly what John meant, for one Friday He would:

- be led like a lamb to the slaughter (Isaiah 53:7) – the innocent for the guilty (1 Peter 3:18);
- shed His own blood to make us holy (Hebrews 13:12, NLT);
- die to restore our relationship with the Father (Romans 5:10).

Lord Jesus, I am overwhelmed by Your great love – that You were willing to become the 'Lamb of God' for me. Thank you. Amen.

3 February

For because he himself has suffered when tempted,
he is able to help those who are being tempted.

Hebrews 2:18

Reading: Luke 4:1–13

Life demands more than mountaintop experiences. Its challenges require strength usually honed in tough places.

Who would have thought that the exhilarating start to Jesus' ministry, beautifully affirmed by the Father, would have changed so quickly? His clothes were barely dry before 'the Spirit immediately *drove* Him out into the wilderness' (Mark 1:12, emphasis mine), where Satan tempted the Saviour for forty days. Jesus didn't just happen to lose His way and survive to tell the tale of living in a hostile environment. The Spirit led Him into it. Why?

If Jesus was ever going to be able to 'understand our weaknesses', He had to face 'all of the same testings we do' (Hebrews 4:15, NLT). More importantly, if He was to take on the role of our High Priest – interceding on our behalf before the Father – He had to come through the temptations 'without sin' (4:15). After all, if the 'Man' Jesus had been given an easy ride in this world, how could we have identified with Him . . . or He with us?

Satan didn't only tempt Jesus on three occasions during those forty days. There was so much more. Everything around Him produced a desire to flee. The desert environment; the wild animals (Mark 1:13); the sense of being all alone. The wondering when was it all going to stop. Jesus felt all the things we feel when we're alone in our wildernesses.

But then He wasn't alone. Those few words at the end of Mark 1:13 remind us that 'the angels were ministering to him'. Nor are we alone. Whatever our wilderness experiences, God provides 'ministering spirits sent out to serve for the sake of those who are to inherit salvation' (Hebrews 1:14). There are angels about!

It's easy to become confused and discouraged by the places into which the Spirit sometimes leads us. But 'the LORD directs the steps of the godly . . . Though they stumble, they will never fall, for the LORD holds them by the hand' (Psalm 37:23–24, NLT).

Father, thank you that I never face life alone. Hold my hand, Lord. Amen.

4 February

THINK ON THIS

As a father shows compassion to his children,
so the LORD shows compassion to those who fear him.

Psalm 103:13

- Read through this verse a number of times – including out loud.
- Write it out, stick it on the fridge, have it on your phone.
- Meditate on the words, then respond in praise.
- Be a doer . . . Serve someone with an act of kindness today.

5 February

When he saw the crowds, he had compassion for them,
because they were harassed and helpless,
like sheep without a shepherd.

Matthew 9:36

Reading: Mark 6:30–34

Do sheep really need a shepherd? Surely they wouldn't come to much harm left to their own devices. It seems the opposite is true. In fact, we are told that sheep require constant, watchful care if they are to remain healthy and stay away from danger, to say nothing of finding pasture and water. Wool becomes long, matted and dirty – a perfect home for disease-bearing parasites – while uncared-for hooves make walking painful, never mind how easily they get lost and fall prey to predators. Without a shepherd for any length of time, sheep are not just a sorry sight, but are in danger of losing their lives.

It is this very picture Jesus paints in our minds when He steps off the boat and sees the crowds. 'They were harassed and helpless' (Matthew 9:36). No one was speaking truth to them; no one, it seemed, was concerned for their suffering. Worse still, there had been no one equipped to help with their greatest need – salvation from sin. Is it any wonder that when Jesus saw the multitude He had compassion on them? He refused to look away. He didn't try to save Himself from the anguish of others by avoidance or excuse.

St Augustine explains that compassion is 'but a kind of fellow-feeling in our hearts for another's misery, which compels us to come to his help by every means in our power'.[7] This feeling is demonstrated when we: 'Remember those in prison, as if you were there yourself. Remember also those being mistreated, as if you felt their pain in your own bodies' (Hebrews 13:3, NLT).

Compassion doesn't remain at a distance. It enters the crowd and walks with them; talks with them; touches them; feeds them and weeps with them . . . just as Jesus did.

> Let me look at the crowd as my Saviour did,
> Till my eyes with tears grow dim;
> Let me look till I pity the wandering sheep
> And love them for love of Him.[8]
> Amen.

6 February

Moved with compassion, Jesus reached out and
touched Him. 'I am willing,' he said. 'Be healed!'

Mark 1:41, NLT

Reading: Mark 1:40–45

It was now or never. Habit forced the leprous man to cover his mouth as he ran after Jesus, shouting, 'Unclean! Unclean!' at a trader as he rushed into the city. The noise stopped Jesus and his men long enough for the leper to catch up with them and fall at Jesus' feet.

For some reason he didn't need anyone to tell him which of the men was Jesus – his heart told him. Before this Man he felt more unclean than he had ever felt in his life, but courage rose for the briefest of moments and he dared to speak, ignoring the furore that was developing around him.

'If you are willing, you can heal me and make me clean.'

Then it happened. Jesus bent over and touched the deformed, diseased and dirty leper.

No one had touched the man in years – not a handshake, no kiss of greeting, no friendly clap on the back, no contract agreed by the slapping of a sandal into the palm of his hand. No human contact of any kind – only in his memory. And nowhere in his memory had he ever felt such a touch!

'I am willing. Be healed!'

Five simple words – only five. Yet these were most beautiful words the leper had ever heard, spoken with such unrivalled compassion that he thought his heart would burst with their tenderness. The rivulets of tears coursing down his dirty cheeks didn't stop him looking into the eyes of God. He was no longer a leper!

Rising from the ground he saw toes on his feet, unblemished skin on his hands. He could feel his nose – eaten away by disease – rise up onto his face once more. Even the stench of death had disappeared. Able to stand straight, with strength and vigour now filling his frame, the man's cries of delight and praise reached every corner of the marketplace.

He was no longer a leper! Now he could do the unthinkable – he could go home![9]

Compassionate Saviour, teach me to love the unlovely as You do. Amen.

7 February

'Whoever has seen me has seen the Father.
How can you say, "Show us the Father"?'

John 14:9

Reading: John 14:8–11

Some say that God's compassion begins in the New Testament. That Jesus shows us a side of God's nature not seen previously. I beg to differ ... strongly. Yes, the New Testament is very different in many aspects, but the Old Testament clearly evidences God's compassion for humanity, and especially for the Jewish nation – His chosen people.

When Jesus was trying to prepare His disciples for His earthly departure, Philip asks Jesus to show them the Father so they would be assured an entrance into the Father's house (John 14:2), the place Jesus was preparing for them. Jesus' response was clear, 'Believe me that I am in the Father and the Father is in me' (John 14:11). *We are one and the same,* Jesus declared. *You see me, you see the Father.* The Father's character dwells within the Son – the epitome of compassion.

Still need evidence?

- God cares for the poor, and commands they be looked after
  (Deuteronomy 15:11).
- If someone in poverty requests a loan, they are not to be charged interest
  (Exodus 22:25).
- God demands justice for the widow, the orphan and the refugee
  (Deuteronomy 10:18).
- The Lord provided to enable the poor to gather grain at harvest-time
  (Deuteronomy 24:19).
- Those who withhold justice from the poor shall face the judgement
  of God (Deuteronomy 27:19).
- As for our sin ... God, 'does not deal with us according to our sins,
  nor repay us according to our iniquities. For as high as the heavens are
  above the earth, so great is his steadfast love toward those who fear him'
  (Psalm 103:10–11).

Let's never forget that 'the Lord your God is indeed God. He is the faithful God who keeps his covenant for a thousand generations and lavishes his unfailing love on those who love him and obey his commands' (Deuteronomy 7:9, NLT). Compassion beats the heart of both Father and Son.

Merciful God, thank you that no struggling heart escapes Your notice. May my hands and feet deliver Your love to those in need. Amen.

8 February

For I am not ashamed of the gospel,
for it is the power of God for salvation to everyone
who believes, to the Jew first and also to the Greek.

Romans 1:16

Reading: Matthew 4:12–17

Good news always spreads fast, even in an era without phones or social media. At first it was the reports of miracles that sent the crowds in search of Jesus. Trapped by poverty and disease, the desperate sought help from anywhere and anyone who might be able to help them. And this new rabbi didn't merely preach repentance like the Baptizer . . . He was healing people and actually making them well again! Many a day's work was left undone to go in search of this Man.

However, Jesus' compassion went further than how He felt and what He did about the broken bodies brought to Him. Even the dead He raised to life would one day have to die again. Jesus not only cared about how they lived on Earth, but about their destiny when this life was over. The grave was not the end, as the Sadducees taught (Acts 23:8). There was an afterlife, a heaven, a hell, a resurrection. The people seeking Jesus undoubtedly needed so much more than His physical touch. They needed to hear the truth from the One who described Himself as 'the way, and the truth, and the life' (John 14:6).

First-century Jews were overloaded by rule-led religiosity. The Law of Moses was given to teach them how to live before a holy God, but it had been twisted and added to by the Pharisees, crushing the people on a daily basis.

Conversely, the gospel was liberating. Jesus' message did not add to their burden. It relieved them of it. Years later, Paul explained that the gospel was the very power that God used to save us from our sin – a salvation He had made available to everyone, whatever their race (Romans 1:16).

Let's not allow religiosity to be the thief who comes to steal and kill and destroy in our lives. Instead, let's accept Jesus' offer of abundant life (John 10:10).

Saviour, my works could never match Your forgiveness, for the law is powerless when faced by such grace. Amen.

9 February

Then Jesus said, 'Come to me,
all of you who are weary and carry heavy burdens . . .'

Matthew 11:28, NLT

Reading: Matthew 11:25–30

'How's things?'

The paediatrician's question disturbed the silence in the dimly lit side ward, where I sat holding our daughter's little hand through the cot sides. Joy hadn't opened her eyes in more than forty-eight hours. There wasn't much to say.

'She's weary,' was the only response I could muster.

In an unexpected move, the doctor kissed her own two fingers and transferred the affection to her tiny patient's forehead. 'Oh Joy,' she whispered, 'you are so brave.' After thirteen years of treating our precious child there was nothing else her expertise could do, so instead she honoured her with a rare show of emotion.

Joy's little body was tired of fighting. The weariness of disability and disease was draining for her. Truth be told, it was wearying for her mother too. Three months later Joy heard the Saviour's invitation to 'Come' as she lay in my arms. I knew it was best for her struggling body and whispered to her that it was okay to go. His embrace would do more for her than mine ever could. Only Jesus could lift the burden that had become too heavy for Joy to bear.

Few of us ever get to avoid being weary – to feel life's difficulties, the pain of both body and soul. Each of us carries different burdens. Those hearing Jesus' invitation to come to Him were dog-tired of what had been laid on them by others. Roman taxes, temple taxes, religious legalism, poverty and, for many, sickness and rejection. Scanning the crowd, Jesus recognized their struggle – situations they couldn't possibly handle by themselves.

Just as Jesus invited those people to come to Him with what was wearing them down, so He asks us today to bring our pain, our very lives, to Him. Only His shoulders are wide enough to hold what we struggle to carry by ourselves. I know. I've run into His arms many times and felt His strength carry what I could no longer carry by myself.

Listen for His voice . . . He is still calling!

Lord Jesus, thank you for willingly carrying my burdens. May I only ever run to You. Amen.

10 February

'. . . and I will give you rest.'

Matthew 11:28, NLT

Reading: Isaiah 40:28–31

Sleep and children can be strange bedfellows. For some there seems no serious reason for their night-time manoeuvres, while for our daughters their medical conditions required round-the-clock supervision. The result was a period of almost twenty years of broken sleep, much of which rendered me a daytime zombie. After Cheryl and Joy died, it was a long time before I was able to sleep through the night.

A good night's sleep often changes our perception of the situation that caused the sleeplessness in the first place, which is why you should never make important decisions when you are tired.

However, just as to be weary is different from being tired, so requiring sleep is different than needing rest. Similar is not the same. Jesus knew that, and often spoke beyond what seemed obvious to the actual cause. For the weary who accepted His invitation to come to Him, Jesus was promising rest, not the opportunity for a nap.

No one knew the meaning of rest more than the One who had spent six days speaking the universe into creation (Genesis 2:1–3).

The Greek root of the word 'rest' means 'to put an end to something', or 'to cause to stop'. When the Trinity had finished creating, they 'put an end to it' – they had finished. 'God saw everything that he had made, and behold, it was very good' (1:31) – so they rested, giving us the sabbath. We 'put an end to' – rest – from the work of the previous six days, recuperate and celebrate Him.

The crowd receiving Jesus' initial invitation to come to Him were overwhelmed by the expectations of twisted leaders and perverted law. Religion was demoralizing, sucking the life out of them. The rest Jesus was offering put an end to the must-do-better, never-acceptable mentality wearying them, enabling them to put their trust in Him.

Legalism is still the blight of the church today. Jesus says we need to 'put an end to it' . . . to stop working at who we think we should be. Satisfying rest is only found in trusting Him completely.

Lord, I am weary of trying. I come to You for rest. Amen.

11 February

THINK ON THIS

So then, there remains a Sabbath rest for the
people of God, for whoever has entered God's rest
has also rested from his works as God did from his.

Hebrews 4:9–10

- Read through these verses a number of times – including out loud.
- Write them out, stick them on the fridge, have them on your phone.
- Meditate on the words, then respond in praise.
- Take steps to allow God's word to change you: perhaps . . . repent, forgive, love.

12 February

'Take my yoke upon you. Let me teach you.'
Matthew 11:29, NLT

Reading: Matthew 23:1–5, 23–26

At first, Jesus' invitation seems so appealing. 'Come to me ... and I will give you rest' (Matthew 11:28). Yet what comes next could hold you back from running into His arms. He's talking about taking on a yoke. Surely yokes were for working, not for resting? Rural Jews understood the analogy well. Hadn't they felt like a beast of burden often enough? And didn't they know exactly how it felt to be controlled by others, including by painful means? They'd watched enough donkeys struggle through hard ground trying to plough a straight furrow with the weight of the yoke pressing them down to know exactly what the rabbi from Nazareth was talking about.

Growing up with carpentry, Jesus knew that the best yokes were carved to fit individual animals. Moulded across the shoulders, they rubbed less and caused less pain. The animal could also work for longer than with the usual heavy, rough beam. Better yokes made the burden easier to handle. His listeners understood that as well, except that Jesus wasn't speaking about wood.

He was offering a different spiritual yoke from that which the Pharisees hypocritically taught as essential for salvation. And Jesus wasn't afraid to call them out on it: 'They tie up heavy burdens, hard to bear,' he said, 'and lay them on people's shoulders, but they themselves are not willing to move them with their finger' (Matthew 23:4). How different these so-called teachers were from Jesus. They wouldn't lift a finger to help others, yet Jesus Himself became the burden-bearer, stooping down to lift the needy up, and eventually going to the cross to carry the guilt of their sin.

'Let me teach you,' Jesus says (Matthew 11:29, NLT). *Yoke up with Me. Walk alongside Me. Watch what I do. How I react, love, forgive and show grace to others. Let Me take the load when the burden grows heavy. Let's do life, with all of its difficulties, together.* This is His invitation to us all.

Teacher, I want to learn from You, to be yoked together with You – walking by Your side on this difficult journey of life. Amen.

13 February

'Because I am humble and gentle at heart,
and you will find rest for your souls.'

Matthew 11:29, NLT

Reading: Philippians 2:5–11

Who would you list as the top-five greatest influencers in your life? My guess is they were strong people who worked longer and harder than anyone else; achieved more than others ever said they would; made a name for themselves; perhaps had a rags-to-riches story. They were beautiful, strong and independent, and didn't let anyone get in their way. You might even say they deserved everything they achieved. Perhaps you believe that if you worked as hard, looked as good, and had the same breaks and as much money as them, you could be just as successful.

Now for the reality check. In all honesty, who has made the greatest impact in your life? Your parents, who sacrificed their money and dreams to set you up for yours? That teacher who believed in you, encouraging you not to give up? The school dinner lady, who always remembered your name as she added extra chips to your plate? Your friend, who stood by you when you messed up? Your grandfather, who was never too busy to listen? Your grandmother, whose constant encouragement – and cooking – brought you joy?

When Jesus calls us to come to Him, He never sets out a stall of greatness . . . yet He was greater than all. He never wagged a finger at our failure, but opened His arms wide to receive us as we are. He never set a list of requirements to meet before He could accept us. Jesus never put a price on the forgiveness He offered or expected us to earn His approval. Instead, He paid for it Himself with His own blood.

The only requirement Jesus sets if we want to experience this promised rest for our souls is that we are weary, heavily burdened . . . and willing to come.

To be lowly, humble, gentle and kind is not weakness. It is strength . . . in its purest form. This is Jesus, and I, for one, am willing to come.

Gentle Saviour, thank you for the strength of Your love for me. Create in me a heart like Yours. Amen.

14 February

Put on then, as God's chosen ones,
holy and beloved, compassionate hearts,
kindness, humility, meekness, and patience.

Colossians 3:12

Reading: Luke 6:31–36

The coffee shop was busy. Always a positive first impression when you've been given a recommendation from someone. Standing in the queue gave us time to observe more than the array of mouth-watering home-baked goods on offer.

An interesting whiteboard hung behind the servers. *Good idea*, I thought. *You can pre-order . . . avoid the wait*. But the more I read, the less I understood. 'Soup and sandwich', 'Coffee', 'Tea' . . . I understood. It was the '£5' and '£10' written multiple times that puzzled me. So, when the friendly server finished taking my order, I had to have my curiosity satisfied.

'It's a pay-it-forward board,' she explained. 'Customers pay for something extra. We write it on the board, and if someone can't afford to buy food, they can ask for an item from the list.' The young woman went on to say that people rarely ask, so the staff have the joy of telling someone who appears to be in need of encouragement that their bill has already been paid. How kind is that?!

Kindness acts in response to compassion. One without the other produces emptiness for potential givers and receivers. Acts of kindness have become a popular way to prepare for Easter rather than the practice of self-denial usually associated with Lent. Yet, if we're honest, they are often dependent on our situation at the time.

Jesus' kindness was always pay-it-forward, always sacrificial. His compassion wasn't determined by suitable circumstances or sufficient finance. Jesus met need wherever He encountered it, even when He was grieving (Matthew 14:13–14), tired (John 4:6–15) or hungry and wanting time alone (Mark 6:32–34). What the Saviour felt in His heart He acted on – free of charge – paid in full for us by His love and kindness.

Lent rarely shares the date with St Valentine's Day, yet it is more than appropriate when it does, because 'Love is . . . kind' (1 Corinthians 13:4).

Lord Jesus, forgive me when I make kindness hard work. Fill my heart with Your love, which automatically prompts me to act with compassion. Amen.

15 February

He heals the brokenhearted and
binds up their wounds.
Psalm 147:3

Reading: Mark 1:32–34

I worked for a number of years in a coronary care unit. Every patient I nursed had a broken heart – physically broken, that is. While not all of them had exactly the same problem, they each had a heart damaged by disease, and sometimes by nature itself. But what was true of all was that every one of them needed healing or they would die. Sadly, no matter how hard we tried, there were some we couldn't mend.

That is not true of Jesus. 'He heals the brokenhearted' . . . every single one!

This time, however, I'm not speaking of the blood pump positioned in the centre of the chest, but the part of us that makes us who we are. The seat of our emotions. The centre of our being. And it's very fragile.

It's easy to see that we live in a broken world, damaged by 'man's inhumanity to man',[10] but it's the things that happen closer to home that cause the greatest personal heartache:

- Broken bodies . . . damaged by disease.
- Broken marriages . . . destroyed by infidelity.
- Broken lives . . . spoiled by sinful practices.
- Broken hearts . . . crushed by the cruelty of others.
- Broken faith . . . cracked by disappointment and disbelief.

Yet, however irreparable the breakage seems, we have a Master Craftsman who specializes in putting the broken pieces of our lives back together again. The broken of body and soul rushed to find Jesus on His travels across Israel (Mark 1:34), often going to great lengths to meet Him. They were rewarded by the miracle of His physical touch; a touch still available to us today through the Holy Spirit. Both equally effective, both requiring a willingness to bring what ails us to Jesus for His healing. Right now, He waits for us to:

Pick up the broken pieces and bring them to the Lord
Pick up the broken pieces, trust in his holy word.
He will put them back together and make your life complete
Just place the broken pieces at the Savior's feet.[11]

Healing Saviour, I bring the broken pieces of my life to You, asking that You bind up my wounds and make me whole again. Amen.

16 February

'For my yoke is easy to bear,
and the burden I give you is light.'

Matthew 11:30, NLT

Reading: Psalm 119:1–5

The scorching sun reflected off the golden statues lining the way to the Buddhist temple. The haunting mantras of 'boy novices' met us at the foot of a mountain of stone steps leading to the largest Buddha in that part of Thailand. No longer would these children experience the joys of childhood. Instead, they would live out the rest of their lives in the spartan surroundings of a monastery, under the tutelage of severe teachers. They would learn that desire is the root cause of all suffering and death, only to discover that desire can never be satisfied. Suffering will only end when a person rids himself of desire by following the Eightfold Path ... a complicated journey of gaining wisdom, enlightenment and eventually nirvana. Not heaven, but a blissful state of non-existence that requires no further rebirth.

The platform surrounding the Buddha was empty apart from us and one very elderly man. *How did he manage to climb the steep steps?* Silently, we watched his twisted hands spinning one prayer wheel after another, while reciting a mantra, in an attempt to bring merit and purification to his soul. Perhaps, tormented by the lie of reincarnation and the terror of what form that would take, he had forced himself out of his armchair to the foot of the Buddha again. *How many thousands of times has he done this before?*

Since time immemorial, religions of all kinds have crushed their followers under the weight of what is expected from them as they search for 'rest for [their] souls' (Matthew 11:29).

Following Jesus makes no such demands. He carried the burden we were meant to carry by taking on the punishment for our sin, thus making us right before God (1 Peter 2:24). Through his indwelling Spirit, He also supplies the power we need to live in the way He asks of us, to say nothing of what we learn from Jesus yoked with us.

What mercy! His burden is indeed light.

Thank you, Jesus, for carrying our burdens, empowering us to make the journey with You. Amen.

17 February

Then Jesus told his disciples,
'If anyone would come after me, let him deny himself.'
Matthew 16:24

Reading: Matthew 16:24–28

Self-denial! Whatever happened to, 'For my yoke is easy, and my burden is light' (Matthew 11:30)? No, it's not a contradiction. Jesus *did* speak of 'yokes' and 'burdens'. Not that they would disappear, but rather that they would be lighter than those pressed on us by others. Added to which, He promises His strength and His presence for the journey.

Self-denial has little to do with giving up chocolate, or whatever, for Lent … however good that might make us feel. Neither are Christ's words a public call to an ascetic lifestyle, forgoing everything we enjoy. Yes, there are times when abstinence – from food, in particular – is an essential component of a spiritual disciple. But that is not what Jesus is teaching in this verse. It is all about how this new life with Him is to be lived, and the rewards it delivers.

'If any of you wants to be my follower,' the NLT puts it, 'you must give up your own way' (Matthew 16:24). *I must have first place in your life,* Jesus is saying. *The universe does not revolve around you!* That will come as a surprise to some.

My desires, my goals, my habits, my money, my relationships – everything that gets in the way – must be submitted humbly to His will, just as Jesus submitted His will to the Father (Luke 22:42).

Paul shows us what living for Christ looks like. 'Yes, everything else is worthless,' he tells us, 'when compared with the infinite value of knowing Christ Jesus my Lord.' In fact, he goes on to say that he has 'discarded everything else, counting it all as *garbage*, so that [he] could gain Christ and become one with him' (Philippians 3:8–9, NLT, emphasis mine).

God's path is the complete opposite of the direction the world wants us to take. Denying ourselves – changing the habits of a lifetime – isn't easy, but it is worth it, especially when the result is to become more like Jesus in every way.

Jesus, I want to follow You. Help me to release whatever needs to go in my life. Amen.

18 February

THINK ON THIS

'You shall love your neighbor as yourself.'
Matthew 22:39

- Read through this verse a number of times – including out loud.
- Write it out, stick it on the fridge, have it on your phone.
- Meditate on the words, then respond in praise.
- Encourage someone by sharing this verse with them today.

19 February

And when the Lord saw her,
he had compassion on her and said to her,
'Do not weep.'

Luke 7:13

Reading: Luke 7:11–17

The station concourse groaned under the weight of the crowds meeting the train that had just pulled in. Held aloft, placards waved at those disembarking shouted the words, 'I have one room – enough for three people!' 'Two rooms for a family of four to six!' The message bearers stretched the length of the platform – hundreds of them! And written across those cards was – 'FREE! For as long as needed!' The wave of cardboard surely created a breeze of love to those arriving.

The train had travelled from Kyiv. Its passengers were displaced families fleeing the war in Ukraine. The placard wavers were people, moved by what they had seen in the media, willing to give up their privacy, homes, food and money to help complete strangers who had lost everything. Some people had travelled hundreds of miles to be there for the train's arrival. The city? Berlin!

And I wept at the sight of such humanity . . . such compassion.

When Jesus walked towards Nain, He was about to meet a stranger; one deeply acquainted with pain and loss. The words 'and she was a widow' (Luke 7:12) seem like a throwaway remark to us today. But not so for those who owned the description. No husband meant no income; no security; no identity, and often no food. Unless, that is, you had another male relative. This woman had a son – just one. He held not only her heart but her future security . . . and then he died.

The sight of this woman walking behind her son's coffin touched Jesus deeply. He said, 'Do not weep' (Luke 7:13), as He walked towards her. Astonishment undoubtedly spread through the crowd when He then proceeded to put His hands on the coffin. *What is He doing? Doesn't He know He is rendering Himself unclean?* (Numbers 19:11). Jesus knew exactly what He was doing – miraculously giving life back to the dead, and returning a son to his mother, who so desperately needed him (Luke 7:14–15). Jesus counted His compassion worthy of the cost.

Lord Jesus, help me to make compassionate choices, whatever the cost. Amen.

20 February

The crowds were astonished at his teaching,
for he was teaching them as one who had authority,
and not as their scribes.

Matthew 7:28–29

Reading: Mark 1:21–27

During the Christian conference season, crowds of believers head off to hear 'top' preachers from home and overseas. There's something exciting about gathering with thousands of other worshippers, and of having the opportunity to hear powerful Bible teaching. Unfortunately, there are times when the hype around the speaker is greater than the reality. Publicity may present the man, but it's the Spirit within the man that delivers the message.

Jesus was a crowd-puller who didn't need a publicity agent, and He wasn't there to please the crowd. Mind you, the majority who heard Him teach originally came for the miracles, but ended up amazed at what came out of the Nazarene's mouth. 'No one ever spoke like this man!' (John 7:46) was the report given by the officers who had been sent to arrest Jesus, yet returned without their prisoner (7:32, 45). He was a master communicator in a land filled with teachers, amid a people whose history was replete with messages from God spoken to them through both patriarchs and prophets. Then, silence! God had stopped communicating ... until Jesus came on the scene.

Whether He taught in the cities and villages (Matthew 9:35); by the sea (Mark 4:1) or on mountain slopes (Matthew 5:1); in synagogues or the temple (John 18:20); as He travelled (Luke 13:22) or sat in people's homes (Luke 10:38), one thing was certain: Jesus' teaching amazed everyone who heard it (Mark 1:27). He communicated at every level, whatever the intellect of the listener, using stories to simplify complicated doctrine, and the age-old method of debate with the curious and those who thought themselves more knowledgeable.

Many hung on Jesus' words for days – at times even forgetting to eat (Matthew 15:32)! Yet, at the edge of every congregation stood the critics, so concerned about protecting 'truth' that they missed God breaking the silence ... missed hearing that God's kingdom had come at last ... missed recognizing the Messiah they had long prayed for.

Teacher, save me from self-righteous cynicism. Instead, teach me to recognize Your voice. I dare not miss a word. Amen.

21 February

For I have not spoken on my own authority,
but the Father who sent me has himself given me
a commandment – what to say and what to speak.

John 12:49

Reading: John 12:44–50

How often have you heard the following words? Or worse still, said them? 'Go and make something of yourself!' 'Make your mark!' 'Make sure they remember your name!' The celebrity culture of today's society tells us that if nobody knows your name, you must be a nobody. After all, who wants to play second fiddle when you could be leader of the orchestra?

The Pharisees wanted to be noticed in their day too. They cut quite the figure standing in the marketplace in their long robes embellished with long fringes. Their dress and the leather pouch of Scriptures tied to their left arm and forehead announced to the common people, *I'm more righteous than you* (Luke 18:11). But they embellished more than their clothing. One wonders if they wanted to show even Moses up with their addition of an extra 613 laws! Personal backslapping was a frequent habit – one they hoped didn't go unnoticed.

But Jesus was not that man. Glory-grabbing was not His thing. Rather, He was the Teacher who only ever delivered Someone else's material, spoke Another's words, taught commands not His own. Second fiddle was perfect as far as the Saviour was concerned. After all, there's no harmony without it. Jesus made sure the glory went to His Father ... the One who wrote the script Jesus taught from ... the One who gave Him the authority to speak as He did. If not, Jesus would only ever have been known as the clever 'son' of Joseph (Luke 4:22).

Obedience and humility were the twin tracks on which Jesus' life ran. Proclaiming the gospel of the kingdom was His priority (Matthew 4:23) – God's purpose for His life (Luke 4:43). It was essential for the people to hear the message the Father had given to His Son: 'Repent, for the kingdom of heaven is at hand' (Matthew 4:17). Jesus' agenda was not His own.

Humble Teacher, forgive me for the times I have placed my agenda before Yours. May I willingly accept Your authority over my life. Amen.

22 February

'The Spirit of the Lord is upon me,
because he has anointed me
to proclaim good news to the poor.'

Luke 4:18

Reading: Matthew 12:17–21

The home crowd is never easy! Soon after His baptism, Jesus' first big teaching challenge was at Nazareth synagogue, in front of people who knew Him ... or thought they did. Their children had played with Jesus when He was growing up. Many had work carried out by the carpentry business of Joseph and Sons – honest workers, but hardly teachers of the law.

Word of what had happened at the Jordan river had, however, reached these people in their back-of-the-woods town, so when Jesus was handed the scroll of the prophet Isaiah that Sabbath Day, they leaned forward in anticipation. Isaiah 61 – a favourite passage, from a favourite prophet – which spoke about the long-awaited Messiah. What could be better?

Jesus read it well. Good start. In fact, Joseph's 'son' had them eating out of His hand, as every eye was fixed on Him (Luke 4:20). Nods of approval followed His words (4:22), until the young rabbi diverted from the passage – at first confusing, then shocking His listeners.

'The Scripture you've just heard has been fulfilled this very day!' He said (4:21, NLT). While they were absorbing Jesus' announcement – that He was the One anointed by God to do what they were expecting of God's Messiah – Jesus continued. He was on a roll! Attributing the prophecy as realized in Himself – 'I am the Messiah' – the former carpenter didn't hold back, going further in His interpretation of Isaiah 61 than any other religious expert had.

Yes, the Messiah would 'bring good news to the poor' (Isaiah 61:1), but it wouldn't stop at the poor of Israel. By the time Jesus reminded His audience of God's past merciful dealings with the Gentile nations (Luke 4:25–27), their praise had turned to disgust. They would rather the poor be left as such, than God stretch His kindness to the hated beyond their borders.

Jesus' revolutionary teaching had begun. God is not prejudiced – not then, not now. His message is for everyone ... whatever their race, status or financial situation.

Lord, may I reflect Your 'no borders' policy by sharing the good news with everyone. Amen.

23 February

'He has sent me to proclaim liberty to the captives
and recovering of sight to the blind,
to set at liberty those who are oppressed,
to proclaim the year of the Lord's favor.'

Luke 4:18–19

Reading: Psalm 146:5–9

Jesus was neither timid nor arrogant when He taught. Right from the age of twelve, when His parents found Him debating with teachers in the temple, through to His preaching as a thirty-year-old in Nazareth's synagogue, Jesus amazed His listeners. His astonishing knowledge and delivery were not simply to impress; His oratory neither highbrow nor condescending. Rather, Jesus' anointing by the Spirit at His baptism gifted Him with all He needed for what lay ahead.

His mandate was to a ministry of proclamation and deliverance, and He wasn't going to waste time trying to debate who He was before getting to it. His life presented His case. You were either for Him or against Him – you either believed or rejected His message. When His own townsfolk attempted to kill Him, He simply moved on (Luke 4:28–30).

It is easy, with the benefit of hindsight, to be horrified by the actions of Nazareth's religious. Yet, in many ways I can't help but wonder how we would have reacted if we had been in that congregation on that particular Sabbath. We are also very protective of biblical truth – often stubbornly – especially when it comes to our interpretation of it. But are our hearts attuned to the Spirit, such that we would not miss the Messiah in our midst, while defending what we so firmly believe?

Yes, Jesus was embarking on the remarkable! He had good news to bring to those who had none; freedom to offer those in captivity; deliverance for the oppressed . . . and even sight for the blind! And His words did not speak only of the spiritual. Jesus did change hearts, restore man's relationship with God through repentance and forgiveness, and set people free from life's oppression. But He also fed the physically hungry (Matthew 14:19–20), spoke truth to those oppressed by Pharisaic law (Mark 12:38–40) and even healed the blind (Luke 18:41–43)!

Jesus' teaching was never separate from action. The action proved that what He said was true.

Help me to follow Your example, Lord. To bring salvation's message to the needy, and to back it up with action. Amen.

24 February

'He has anointed me . . . to proclaim
the year of the Lord's favor.'
Luke 4:18–19

For the law was given through Moses;
grace and truth came through Jesus Christ.
John 1:17

Reading: Titus 2:11–14

Grace. The most beautiful word in the English language. The subject of millions of books, articles, songs and sermons. Jesus' commission to deliver grace rounded off his mission mandate in Nazareth's synagogue.

'The year of God's favor' was ushered in with Jesus' arrival, heralding the age of grace. Centuries of trying to respond to God's holiness through adherence to the Law of Moses produced only one result: failure. Nothing we do, think, say, pray or give could ever deal with the problem of sin (Romans 3:23) or release us from the judgement rightly ours. But God had a masterplan – a costly one, but one that demonstrated His heart and nature more than anything else had done previously.

The masterplan? God chose to bless us rather than curse us. He chose grace, giving us what we don't deserve and lacing it with mercy by holding back the punishment we are due. He '*sent* His Son to be the Savior of the world' (1 John 4:14, emphasis mine). And Jesus chose to go at the Father's command, saying, 'For this reason the Father loves me, because I lay down my life that I may take it up again' (John 10:17).

What's even more remarkable is that 'God shows his love for us in that while we were still sinners, Christ died for us' (Romans 5:8). What abundant grace! Think of it:

- God showed His love . . . when I thought only about myself;
- God showed His love . . . when I refused to believe His Word;
- God showed His love . . . when I wanted nothing to do with Him;
- God showed His love . . . when I rejected His Son.

No matter how long the list, Christ covers it completely with one crimson word: GRACE! It is why He left the grandeur of heaven; the accolade of angels; the companionship of Father and Spirit. He came to lift the lid on grace.

God of grace and love, I am unworthy of the least of Your blessings, yet thankful that You have poured Your mercy on me, a sinner. Amen.

25 February

THINK ON THIS

And God is able to make all grace abound to you,
so that having all sufficiency in all things at all times,
you may abound in every good work.

2 Corinthians 9:8

- Read through this verse a number of times – including out loud.
- Write it out, stick it on the fridge, have it on your phone.
- Meditate on the words, then respond in praise.
- Be a doer . . . Serve someone with an act of kindness today.

26 February

So that being justified by his grace we might
become heirs according to the hope of eternal life.

Titus 3:7

Reading: Titus 3:3–7

Grace didn't appear like magic overnight. The New Testament is not where God decided to act differently. Jesus, our guardian of grace, was not suddenly unleashed when He arrived on earth.

Actually, the Old Testament overflows with God's grace. His mercy repeatedly held back judgement from a rebellious, undeserving people. Grace allowed the expulsion of Adam and Eve from the garden of Eden instead of their deaths (Genesis 2:17, 3:23). Grace kept a remnant of people alive on the ark when the earth faced annihilation in the flood (7:23). Grace delivered the children of Israel from slavery in Egypt (Exodus 3:7). On and on we read of God's faithfulness and grace to humanity in the Old Testament.

But the sacrifice for our sin problem would only ever be a temporary fix – it needed to be continually repeated (Hebrews 10:11) . . . until God made good on His promise. One day a Saviour would be born who would crush Satan's head, even though He Himself would be bruised in the process (Genesis 3:15). That event would usher in God's age of grace; a period of time when God's forgiveness would be offered to humankind through the one-time sacrifice of His Son (Hebrews 10:12).

But grace is for a limited time. It stretches from Calvary to our death, or to Christ's return, whichever comes first for us. Paul says, 'Behold, now is the favorable time; behold, now is the day of salvation' (2 Corinthians 6:2). After that it will be forever too late. God's mercy will end and judgement will take its place. Let's make sure we don't neglect this amazing gift of grace (Hebrews 2:1–3).

Grace is like a piece of spiritual elastic. It stretches beyond God's forgiveness, throughout our lives, and into the promise of eternal life with Him (John 14:2). Jesus is the joy-giver as well as the grace-giver (17:13). And still it stretches on, for as C. S. Lewis once said, 'Joy is the serious business of heaven.'[12]

All this because of grace!

Heavenly Father, thank you that Your grace has reached my heart, and fills me with inexpressible joy. Amen.

27 February

His mother said to the servants,
'Do whatever He tells you.'

John 2:5

Reading: John 2:1–12

'Someone messed up big time!' the young servant said, as his pail splashed into the well yet again.

'Ssshh, they'll hear you. Just get on with it . . . there's only one more jar to go.'

But the lad couldn't hold his tongue. 'I don't know how they think they're going to fool the guests with water for the next four days!'

'The lady is a family member. So, when she says, "Jump!" you say, "How high?" Running out of wine at a wedding! They'll be a laughing stock if word gets out. Keep going. A week's work is hard to come by.'

'I can't wait to see what her son is going to do with all this water,' the boy chuckled.

'His problem,' was the curt retort as they made their final trip back to the storehouse. 'We've done what He asked, just as she said.'

Water splashed from the final water pot, now filled to the brim and standing tall beside the other five. Swiping the sweat from their brows the lads looked towards the woman's son. The Man smiled at them, no hint of anxiety as He pointed towards a jug and cup sitting by the pots and said, 'Now draw some out and take it to the master of the feast.'

In went the jug and out came what they had just put in it. Nervously, the servants approached the master of ceremonies, expecting a clip on the ear for serving him water instead of wine! Then it happened. Shakily pouring it into the master's cup, the servant tried not to look . . . but he couldn't miss it. The wine, that is! The wine he was now pouring into the cup . . . from the water jug! For once in his life, he was speechless! And the host was stunned by the quality of the wine he didn't know they had.

Across the room the lads saw the Man. No fanfare. No fuss. He simply smiled, acknowledging that they had done as He had asked. Think what they would have missed if they hadn't.

Holy Spirit, may I learn to listen closely to Jesus and always do what He asks. Amen.

28 February

And Jesus said to her,
'Woman, what does this have to do with me?
My hour has not yet come.'

John 2:4

Reading: Exodus 20:12

Like many others these days, we are blessed to have family members whose first language is not English. Communication, especially at the beginning, was always rich, often funny, and created a more careful listening on our part. English is not a giving language. Certain phrases do not transfer easily and can actually mean the opposite of their literal translation.

That's what causes a bit of problem with this verse and Jesus' interaction with His mother. Many have looked at it as a sign of disrespect, even rudeness, on Jesus' part. Not so. Jesus knew the fifth commandment better than most. He knew of the sacrifice the girl from Nazareth had made the night the angel came to tell her she would bear God's Son (Luke 1:26–38).

I have no doubt that Jesus loved His mother. In the original language, the term used here for 'woman' is more correctly translated as 'ma'am'.[13] This is the same word used from the cross when He tenderly handed her into the care of John (John 19:26). Jesus wasn't being rude; rather, He was respectfully reminding His mother that He was a man now. However, I can't help but wonder if Jesus had a twinkle in His eye as He said, *Ma'am, what's this got to do with Me?* (my paraphrase).

Jesus had lately left the family home to begin His ministry, and had arrived at the wedding in Cana with three recently acquired followers. Things were only just beginning. He was acutely aware of being on His Father's timetable, hence the 'My hour has not yet come' response given to His mother's request. Yet, Jesus was also aware of the disgrace His relatives would face if word got out that – for whatever reason – they'd run out of wine!

Compassion was the motivation behind what some see as a trivial miracle. However, kindness is never trivial in God's eyes. And the episode of water into wine was certainly something Jesus' travelling companions would never forget. Nothing is wasted in our lives.

Heavenly Father, teach me to recognize the legitimate sidesteps to take while still following Your plan. Amen.

March

1 March

And he appointed twelve (whom he also named apostles)
so that they might be with him and he might
send them out to preach.

Mark 3:14

Reading: Luke 6:12–19

Team building has become big business. Courses, seminars, away days, and mentorships are all available to help you build a successful team that will increase your business's productivity. Add some events to increase individual strengths within your workforce, while teaching each one how to work together with others, then set the mantra of 'only being as good as your weakest link' on repeat, and you have a team.

Jesus didn't go on a course before He chose His team. He went up a mountain to pray . . . all night (Luke 6:12)!

Remarkably, Mark doesn't record the job Jesus wanted to train the disciples for – to preach (Mark 3:14) – first. Instead, He uses a little phrase that could easily be passed over – 'so that they might be with him' – before getting to what some might see as the important stuff.

Was Mark only speaking about the mentoring of a team that would increase Jesus' productivity in getting the message out? Could He have been speaking about multiplying the number of people healed by training the twelve to do miracles? Or was Jesus setting up a rabbinical school of His own, wanting His name and teaching quoted in all the important places? Well, if He did, He wasn't much good at choosing a top team! Fishermen, a tax collector and a Zealot – hardly quality material for any of the above.

In Genesis we read that God made man in His own image (Genesis 1:26). Much debate has surrounded exactly what this means, but for sure, God is a relational God – not only within the Trinity, but also in His desire for relationship with us (3:8).

Jesus the Man had that same wish running through His veins. He knew the importance and power of friendship. Salvation would always, only, be through Him (Acts 4:12), but the companionship of these men was essential for the difficult days ahead, as well as for the continuation of His mission on earth. Jesus wanted them to be with Him.

Lord Jesus, thank you that even today You desire our company. May I not be so foolish as to miss Yours. Amen.

2 March

And Levi made him a great feast in his house,
and there was a large company of tax collectors and
others reclining at table with them.

Luke 5:29

Reading: Luke 5:29–35

Life with Jesus is never boring.

The most ridiculous response I get from people when I talk to them about Jesus goes something like this, 'Being a Christian is boring! You can't do this . . . and you can't do that. Christians have no fun!'

No fun? They don't know what they're talking about. My love for Jesus began when I gave him my heart, aged fourteen. I've been many things since then, but never bored! It's sad that some Christians equate a godly life with an ascetic one. Being a Christian is a serious matter, but it is also filled with joy (Psalm 144:15, NLT).

To those who think the opposite, 'fun' is often an activity engaged in but rarely remembered the next day. It may also be embarrassing, and even damaging, if they do happen to recall it. And no, I'm not so foolish as to say there's no enjoyment in the 'big night out'. What I am saying is that there is lots to enjoy in following Jesus . . . and afterwards you get to both remember and savour it.

The disciples learned early on that following Jesus was demanding and self-sacrificing (Mark 8:34). They were ridiculed (Luke 9:40), exhausted (Matthew 26:43), even hungry at times (Matthew 12:1). But they were also amazed (Mark 10:24) and fulfilled as they travelled with Jesus (John 3:22). They even attended the odd party (Luke 5:29)!

Imagine what it must have been like for the disciples to spend day after day with the physical Jesus. To eat, drink, debate, walk and laugh with the One they came to know first as Teacher (John 13:13), then as Messiah (Matthew 16:16) . . . and who called these ordinary men His friends (John 15:15). That's real living! Something we, too, can experience through faith in Jesus . . . day after day.

Lord Jesus, You came that I might have life in all its fullness. There is joy in serving You, Jesus, and delight in being in Your presence. Thank you for the privilege. Amen.

3 March

THINK ON THIS

A man of many companions may come to ruin,
but there is a friend who sticks closer than a brother.

Proverbs 18:24

- Read through this verse a number of times – including out loud.
- Write it out, stick it on the fridge, have it on your phone.
- Meditate on the words, then respond in praise.
- Take steps to allow God's word to change you: perhaps . . . repent, forgive, love.

4 March

'Whoever does not bear his own cross
and come after me cannot be my disciple.'

Luke 14:27

Reading: Luke 14:27–33

'Always buy quality, Son,' my husband's tiny grandmother used to tell him. 'Anything of value is worth the cost.'

Following Jesus is the most valuable thing any one of us will ever do, but it does involve a cost. Jesus made that clear to those who followed Him, especially to the twelve men He chose to be His closest companions. Salvation was purchased on our behalf by Jesus (Romans 5:15) – a free gift. But it was not cheap by any means, having cost Him His life (5:6). Neither is commitment to following the Saviour cheap – then or now.

Jesus isn't interested in mere hangers-on; those who just listen and agree with His teaching. His involvement is with those who are 'doers of the word', as one of Jesus' closest disciples wrote after His death (James 1:22). Of the hundreds who followed Him, Jesus chose only twelve to impart His richest teaching, which included the tough messages of true discipleship.

The twelve may be thought of as ordinary men – even uneducated – and with fishermen, a tax collector and a revolutionary among them, it's not hard to see why. Yet, in many ways they were anything but ordinary, each one willing to pay the cost of following Christ (apart from Judas the betrayer). When Jesus said, 'So therefore, any one of you who does not renounce all that he has cannot be my disciple' (Luke 14:33), He was actually asking for *everything* from them!

There would be no financial reward for their commitment, and few of life's comforts on their mission. Persecution was to be expected, along with imprisonment for some (Luke 21:12) and eventual martyrdom for ten of the original twelve disciples. But God is no man's debtor. Nothing given up for Christ will ever go unnoticed or unrewarded (Matthew 19:27–30), but as pioneer missionary C. T. Studd reportedly said: 'If Jesus Christ be God and died for me, then no sacrifice can be too great for me to make for Him'.[14]

Thank you, Jesus, that You thought the cost worth it to die on the cross for me. Take my all, and let Your light shine through me. Amen.

5 March

Jesus looked at him and said, 'You are Simon
the son of John. You shall be called Cephas'
(which means Peter).

John 1:42

Reading: Luke 5:1–11

No night-time catch meant nothing with which to feed the family, and no money to pay the taxman. It was a discouraged group of fishermen, cleaning nets which had caught nothing, that saw Jesus arrive beside the lake.

Jonah's son Simon had recently met Jesus after responding to his brother Andrew's claim that he had found the Messiah. It was an unusual introduction; brief and to the point. Remarkably, Jesus knew his name. But the first thing the Man did was change Simon's name. From then on, Simon was to be called 'Cephas' – Peter – meaning 'stone'.

He'd heard of others who had changed their name before ... usually because of some life event, or patriarchs whose names were changed by God, such as Abram to Abraham (Genesis 17:5) and Jacob to Israel (35:10). But after meeting Jesus that day he'd gone back to fishing – no change there – so the new name hadn't made much sense to the fisherman from Galilee. Until now.

With the shallow water lapping over his feet, Simon strained to hear what Jesus was saying while continuing the tedious job of washing his nets. Soon the rabbi was also up to His ankles in water. As the crowd pushed further forward, Jesus – still teaching – got into Simon's boat. Simon had never thought of his boat as a pulpit before! Sermon over, Jesus told the fisherman to go fishing one more time. Imagine – a carpenter rabbi telling an experienced fisherman what to do!

'Master, we toiled all night and took nothing!' Simon protested, slightly frustrated. 'But at your word I will let down the nets' (Luke 5:5). The result? A catch so large that two boats almost sank trying to get it on board (6–7)! Suddenly there was no query over Simon's name change. For in the fisherman Christ chose as His first disciple (Mark 3:16), Jesus had seen the potential of stone-like quality – strength and stability. The change had begun. There was much more to come.

Lord Jesus, as Your disciple may the name 'Christian' always clearly identify me to others, and may I wear it with pride. Amen.

6 March

And when they had brought their boats to land,
they left everything and followed him.

Luke 5:11

Reading: Matthew 4:18–22

Witnessing a miracle would certainly tip the balance in the belief stakes!

Like Simon Peter, James and his brother John had strained their muscles as well as their understanding when the nets bulged and almost broke the day Jesus told them to try again for a catch. Fishing is unpredictable at best, and these men knew this lake better than most. They'd fished it since boyhood, and there was no visible shoal when their fishing partner was asked by the rabbi to push back out into the water. But then Jesus was no ordinary rabbi.

James and John had seen this Man before . . . they had likely heard John the Baptist speak of Him. They might even have been at the Jordan that day the heavens opened (Matthew 3:17), and had undoubtedly heard Andrew, Simon Peter's brother, speak excitedly of Him (John 1:41), as he seemed to be doing to everyone. But Jesus had disappeared after the baptism, so the would-be followers headed home again. There were fish to catch, families to feed and taxes to pay.

Jesus always sees beyond the obvious. He knows us. Sees our hearts.

The disciples were frequently called ignorant, unschooled, even common (Acts 4:13). The educated religious had no time for shepherds, fishermen and the like. They associated outward dirt with inward sin, but Jesus saw straight through their hypocrisy. 'You can make the outside look as clean as you like but I see the wickedness of your heart' (my paraphrase of Luke 11:39).

The brothers may have had dried blood and guts on their skin, and probably smelled of fish when Jesus met them, but it was their hearts He saw. These brothers were spiritual men. They were messiah seekers . . . God's Messiah, that is. What they'd heard of Jesus, and from Him, was almost enough . . . and then came the miracle of the fish! Confirmation, if any were needed, that Jesus was indeed the One they had been waiting for.

When He called for them to follow Him they left everything – without hesitation.

Lord, I don't always get it right, but You see my heart. You know that I love You. May my following always be close. Amen.

7 March

Jesus answered him, 'Because I said to you,
"I saw you under the fig tree," do you believe?
You will see greater things than these.'

John 1:50

Reading: John 1:43–51

I confess to having a few television crime series that I like to watch. Good story-lines are obviously key to my enjoyment, but it's the team that keeps drawing me back. The different personalities, their personal strengths and weaknesses, and the backstory that brought them together draws me in. I'm fascinated to see how they gel together to accomplish their goal. How so? Each member believes in the team dynamic and purpose, and has complete trust in its leader.

Some of Jesus' team of twelve had connections. There were three pairs of brothers and several fishermen among them. For about six of them, however, we know very little. Yet, while observing them through the Gospel writers – three of whom were disciples themselves – we see not a ragtag team of fools, but a group of men devoted to their teacher. While Jesus' formal call came to them all at the same time (Mark 3:13–19), many had already chosen to follow Him.

It was different for Philip. He was the only one of the twelve Jesus 'found' (John 1:43). He went looking for Philip! Yet, in spite of this fact, we know very little about Philip's specific function within the team, as he's mentioned on only a few occasions.

One important thing Philip did was immediately go and tell his friend Nathanael – the next to follow Jesus (John 1:45). While sceptical at first (1:46), the man whose name meant 'given by God' went to meet Jesus and was astounded that He not only knew his name, but was able to tell him what he had been doing before Philip got to him (1:48). That was enough! He believed and followed Jesus.

Jesus' team was coming together, and He wasn't interested in those best qualified. No job description for what He needed had been written! He called men willing to learn; men with obedient hearts and, above all else, faith in Him.

Lord, You see my heart. I am willing to follow You wherever You lead. Amen.

8 March

Jesus said to him, 'Have you believed
because you have seen me? Blessed are those
who have not seen and yet have believed.'

John 20:29

Reading: John 11:11–16

Some things just can't be undone, no matter how hard you try. After years of building a reputation of quality work and a 'Mr Nice Guy' persona, Will Smith will forever be remembered as the actor who slapped a comedian at the Oscars . . . in front of millions!

Thomas, one of the chosen twelve, dubbed with the nickname 'Doubting Thomas' over his disbelief of Jesus' resurrection, has also provided us with a phrase that equates a person with doubt. Yet, Thomas was more than the sum of that one-liner recorded in John 20:25. He had a truth-seeking nature (14:5) and a courageous heart, rallying the others to go into Bethany with Jesus after Lazarus had died – in spite of the rumoured plan to kill Jesus that was circulating (11:16). He also confessed his mistake and followed it with a declaration of resolute faith (20:28).

We don't always get it right, do we? But Jesus is forever willing to draw alongside and speak firmly but lovingly into the questions we have. We need to ensure that our faith-filled responses shout louder than our questions.

Peter, Andrew, James, John and even Thomas are the names we remember easily, with Peter, James and John taking the top spots of the trusted 'inner circle'. Although equally called by Jesus, there are disciples who have remained in obscurity, with little recorded in the gospels about them.

James, known as 'the Less' or 'the Younger' so as not to confuse him with the other James, and Thaddaeus, are two in particular. Just because we do not have much information about them does not make them any less as disciples. Neither will Jesus' promise to them fail. They, along with the others, will be appointed thrones in the future kingdom (Matthew 19:28), to say nothing of having their names inscribed on the foundation stones of the New Jerusalem (Revelation 21:14).

Quiet service may be unseen by others, but God sees . . . and He rewards.

Lord, human accolades are unimportant. It's Your smile of approval on my life and service I long for. Amen.

9 March

For we are God's fellow workers.

1 Corinthians 3:9

Reading: Matthew 9:8–13

Let's face it, we are all different. Within any group you'll find varying opinions, likes and dislikes. Yet, there has to be some common ground for the group to stay together. Among the twelve there were definite disparities that, under other circumstances, would never have kept this group together for those three years with Jesus. He wasn't merely the common ground; Jesus was their hope, their freedom.

Matthew (also known as Levi) worked for the Romans. As a tax collector, he held one of the most hated positions in the country. Despised by his own, he wasn't exactly loved by the Romans either. They regarded the likes of Matthew as a necessary evil . . . especially as he was also a Jew. Matthew was probably disowned by his family, while his companionship was reduced to those of similar employment (Matthew 9:10). Matthew loved the rewards of his job . . . until he met Jesus.

Simon the Zealot had revolutionary politics flowing through his veins. He had devoted his life to the sect's mission to remove the Romans from Israel by every means possible. That was, until the trained fighter met Jesus. Following Jesus was a different revolution altogether, but he hadn't reckoned on sharing life with a tax collector! Surely Jesus knew that adding Matthew to the group would cause trouble?

And Judas? Where did he fit in? We read of no redeeming qualities in this man – anywhere! He even stole from the very moneybag with which he had been entrusted (John 12:6). And after three years in the company of Jesus, it was clear that he loved money more than he loved the Saviour. His treachery even stretched to putting a price on Jesus Himself (Matthew 26:15).

What were these three misfits doing in the group Jesus planned to use to change the world? Twenty-five per cent of His team? Not so. Jesus knew what He was doing. Watch and wait. Apart from Judas, these men continued in their commitment and devotion to the One who would change their lives, transforming them into 'God's fellow workers'.

Thank you, Lord, that You see beyond what others do, and as You change us You afford us the joy of working together with You in the Father's plan. Amen.

10 March

THINK ON THIS

And the world is passing away along with its desires,
but whoever does the will of God abides forever.

1 John 2:17

- Read through this verse a number of times – including out loud.
- Write it out, stick it on the fridge, have it on your phone.
- Meditate on the words, then respond in praise.
- Encourage someone by sharing this verse with them today.

11 March

'I, yes I, am the LORD,
and there is no other Savior.'

Isaiah 43:11, NLT

Reading: Romans 12:1–2

Jesus didn't have a disciple mould. These men didn't fit some pre-design of what makes the perfect disciple. There was no 'right' candidate. Jesus called followers with a dependence on God, whom He could trust to continue His mission after He returned to heaven. Teachability and a willingness to leave behind any desire for worldly wealth or recognition were the essential criteria.

We should beware the mould-makers within the Christian church today. Jesus isn't calling clones, but those whose dependence rests fully on Him. Faithful, selfless, grace-filled kingdom builders.

Back then, the Jews had a huge 'messiah-shaped' mould. If a messiah were genuine, he first had to rid them of the Roman occupiers and free the nation from tyranny. Then he was expected to deliver an abundant life of wealth, plenty and happiness to his people. At first, Jesus seemed to fill the brief with His healings and mesmerizing new ideas. But many turned away once He started talking about sacrifice (John 6:60). *This can't be the Messiah. He would liberate us, not expect us to make more sacrifices.* What they didn't comprehend was that the true Messiah was offering an altogether different liberation – a liberation of soul that would last forever.

Jesus was unique. Born in a stable, not a palace. The Son of God . . . and a teenage virgin. A carpenter by trade. He neither looked, nor lived, like a king or a conqueror. Frequently maligned and misunderstood, He ministered for three short years: healing the sick, feeding the poor . . . even raising the dead! His teaching shocked the educated and amazed the unschooled. His compassion was unparalleled. His life sinless, His love unrivalled. His death obscene and His resurrection mystifying.

The world had never seen His like before . . . nor has it since.

'All the armies that ever marched, all the navies that ever sailed, all the parliaments that ever sat, all the kings that ever reigned, put together, have not affected the life of man on this earth as much as that one solitary life.'[15]

Unique Saviour, may my life only ever be shaped by You, my path only directed by Your Spirit. Amen.

12 March

And they were astonished beyond measure,
saying, 'He has done all things well.'

Mark 7:37

Reading: Acts 10:35–38

Carrot or stick? Some preachers major in stick wielding, while others only ever dangle the carrot. Neither approach is right on its own. Towards the end of his life, Paul reminded the elders at Ephesus that he 'did not shrink from declaring to [them] the whole counsel of God' (Acts 20:27). God's message contained love, mercy, compassion, peace ... and judgement. The latter theme was not the only sermon to be preached, but neither was it to be ignored. God's word is to be taught in all its fullness, for while salvation is our greatest need, we also hunger for so much more.

Jesus was no entertainer, but He could hold a crowd's attention better than anyone (Mark 12:37). People thronged to Him everywhere He went. Yet, among the myriad of faces He scanned, He saw desperation etched there. He felt their thirst for truth; identified the emptiness of their lives; sensed their need for rest in a demanding world.

For those looking back into the face of that one Man, they saw understanding, concern ... and – a first for them from a teacher – love. And as His voice carried across the crowd, they heard truth laced with compassion. Somehow when this man spoke, hearts shrivelled by the dryness of law-filled commands swelled once more with hope: His words were an unexpected oasis in a desert place.

At every table, over every crowd, in every synagogue, in each face ... and in every heart down through the centuries, Jesus speaks.

As the 'bread of life' (John 6:35), He feeds those who are always hungry for what will make them happy, yet are never satisfied. As the 'living water' (4:10), Jesus is the only One who can slake our thirst in a world that offers much and delivers little. What He gives makes us new (2 Corinthians 5:17), changes our desires and fills what we didn't notice was empty in the first place.

Then, never stingy, Jesus adds the cherry on top: peace for our restless hearts in this hurried world (Philippians 4:6–7). He really does do things well!

Soul Satisfier, help me to gaze on Your face, and accept the fullness You offer. Amen.

13 March

And the twelve were with him,
and also some women . . . who provided for them
out of their means.

Luke 8:1–3

Reading: Mark 15:40–41

Recently we watched a docudrama about the Apollo 11 space flight, in which Neil Armstrong and Buzz Aldrin were shown landing and walking on the moon on 21 July 1969. They spent two hours outside the lunar module, and a total of twenty-one hours – including seven hours of sleep – on the moon's surface. The world watched, spellbound.

My heart, however, went out to Michael Collins, orbiting the moon alone in *Columbia* while his colleagues got to do the exciting part. He knew his role was essential to the mission – he had to get them home again – but I wonder if he wished he'd been down there, bouncing in zero gravity and having 650 million people watch him do it.

Little that is great ever happens without others working in the background, out of sight, and rarely the recipients of praise or accolade. Nasa estimated that more than 400,000 people worked on the Apollo 11 mission, including engineers, scientists, technicians and factory/company staff of all grades. Each individual role was important in landing the *Eagle* on the moon's surface and maintaining *Columbia* safely in orbit. Yet, in the mix of the great unknown were three women in a world of white males: JoAnn Morgan, Margaret Hamilton and Mary Jackson (NASA's first female African–American engineer).

The twelve are undoubtedly 'big' in the story of the Gospels. We could probably remember some of their names, but it's easy to forget that there were a few women in the background making life bearable by their endeavours. They 'orbited', if you like, while Jesus and the disciples got on teaching and healing. But their service was important to the Saviour. It ensured that everyday menial tasks didn't get in the way of spiritual business, which, in turn, transformed the menial into acts of spiritual significance.

Ever wish you had something more important to do for Jesus? Remember, the One who matters sees all we do for Him. 'You are precious in my eyes, and honored, and I love you,' He says in Isaiah 43:4. That's accolade enough for me!

Lord, the glory is all Yours. I need only to please You. Amen.

14 March

And he said to them,
'The Son of Man is lord of the Sabbath.'
Luke 6:5

Reading: Luke 6:6–11

'Come and stand here,' the visiting rabbi said, beckoning Dan to the front, beside Him. *What does He want?* Dan wondered, his cheeks flushed with embarrassment. But the rabbi's tone was not aggressive; not at all how others spoke to him – as if having a withered hand made him something of a freak.

Just minutes earlier he'd wished he hadn't come. The presence of so many strangers at synagogue had forced him to sit in the front row – in full view of everyone! That's when he'd noticed the Pharisees . . . far too many of them. *Why are they here?*

Every day since Dan's accident things had got worse. Joints had swollen while flesh had wasted. Pain was the glue that kept it attached to his arm, rendering more than his hand useless.

He hadn't heard a word the visiting rabbi had spoken, except that now He was calling for him to stand in front of all these people! Yet, something compelled Dan to rise and walk toward the Man. The atmosphere instantly electrified – Pharisees were standing by, as if waiting to pounce! Dan didn't like it but, in the time it took for him to cross the floor his eyes met the rabbi's and he wasn't afraid any more.

'Is it lawful on the Sabbath to do good or to do harm?' the rabbi asked, His eyes fixed on the Pharisees. 'To save life or destroy it?'

Dan was trembling. Then, when the rabbi said, 'Stretch out your hand,' Dan attempted to move it, just as he'd tried numerous times before. But this time was different! His fingers tingled, not with pain but with feeling. His hand moved upwards, now obedient to his commands. Immediately, Dan held the healthy hand straight out in front of him, the noise of cheering quickly interrupted by furious, finger-pointing Pharisees. 'Sabbath breaker!' they yelled, venting their disgust towards the rabbi who had just healed his hand and transformed his life!

What's wrong with them? Dan thought, waving his hand in triumph. By the time Dan turned to thank his Healer, Jesus had gone . . . but He would never be forgotten.[16]

Lord of the Sabbath, teach me to respect Your Day by always prioritizing grace over law. Amen.

15 March

For the law was given through Moses;
grace and truth came through Jesus Christ.

John 1:17

Reading: Colossians 2:20–23

You can imagine the conversation as Jesus and the disciples made a quick getaway from the synagogue towards Galilee. They had left pandemonium behind instead of a celebration of the miraculous. The talk among the disciples was hardly harmonious either, with their many differing religious and political opinions.

Why did Jesus heal the man on the Sabbath? Couldn't He have waited one more day?

Why doesn't He give the Pharisees a wide berth? He's stirring up a hornet's nest!

Before you know it, we'll be on the Romans' radar! We can't risk their attention before Jesus has time to plan His overthrow.

Do you think we really have broken the Sabbath?

They had much to learn on their journey with Jesus.

The Pharisees had done such a good job of asserting their self-appointed authority over the Jews that the people feared the consequences of not doing what they said. Instead of encouraging devotion to Yahweh, these so-called religious leaders were breaking the backs and hearts of God's people. But the hundreds of additions they had made to God's Law, and especially the thirty-nine relating to 'work' on the Sabbath, was something Jesus could not overlook. Only public confrontation could inform the Pharisee and the people of the lies being perpetrated!

Legalism wasn't right in Jesus' day, neither is it now. It portrays a false appearance of outward spirituality, but it is genuine, inward change that God desires. Let's not be the 'Pharisee' at the door of our churches, checking whether our brothers and sisters in Christ are doing things 'right' – according to us!

'You, then, why do you judge your brother or sister?' Paul says in Romans 14:10 (NIVUK). 'Or why do you treat them with contempt? For we will all stand before God's judgment seat'.

Lord, may my devotion be pure, untainted by self-righteousness and filled with love for You. Amen.

16 March

And he said,
'He who has ears to hear, let him hear.'
Mark 4:9

Reading: Matthew 13:34–35

We think we know what is good for us. But Jesus knows exactly what we need.

The crowds following Jesus came for miracles. Jesus taught them truth. The people wanted better lives. Jesus told them how they could live forever (John 11:25). They wanted liberation from the Romans. He preached freedom from sin (John 8:36). His listeners asked for judgement for others. Jesus told them to deal with the 'plank' in their own eye first (Matthew 7:3, NIVUK). They called for a new kingdom. Jesus announced that the kingdom of God had come (Luke 17:21).

Jesus saw narrative as key in delivering profound truth – essential for spiritual life – to those truly listening. He painted pictures in their minds that sat alongside His teaching. These everyday scenes required the listener to become involved in the story – to see themselves in the characters and situations portrayed.

Yet, a parable is much more than 'an earthly story with a heavenly meaning', or an illustration to let the light in, or to help the less learned among us with the difficult stuff. Spreading colour and shade across life's canvas caused the serious to deliberate, while the frivolous miracle chasers didn't bother to seek understanding for the things that would outlive a sickness cured. This preaching tool used by Jesus would sort the true followers from those who would tag along for their own selfish aims.

But Jesus kept turning up as thousands journeyed to find the One they thought could give them what they believed they needed. All the while, Jesus knew that within the multitude were those seeking truth and peace with God. At the same time, He couldn't ignore His heart of love for the broken. Compassion could never be tucked away, allocated only to non-teaching days.

Jesus is always the complete package. He still meets need wherever He finds it. He will never stop calling sinners to repentance – until the day of grace comes to an end. And He will continue to paint pictures across our minds from His word, drawing us into an ever-closer relationship with Him.

Lord Jesus, give me ears to hear and a heart to respond. Amen.

17 March

THINK ON THIS

'For truly, I say to you, many prophets and righteous
people longed to see what you see, and did not see it,
and to hear what you hear, and did not hear it.'

Matthew 13:17

- Read through this verse a number of times – including out loud.
- Write it out, stick it on the fridge, have it on your phone.
- Meditate on the words, then respond in praise.
- Be a doer . . . Serve someone with an act of kindness today.

18 March

And he answered them, 'To you it has been given
to know the secrets of the kingdom of heaven,
but to them it has not been given.'
Matthew 13:11

Reading: Matthew 13:10–17

When those fishermen cast their nets into the sparkling waters of the Sea of Galilee for the last time, could they ever have dreamed of sitting around a campfire, miles from the sea, listening to the rabbi speak to them of 'kingdom' matters? Did Matthew ever imagine deliberately committing himself to a group where he'd often be looked on as the odd man out? Or did Simon the Zealot and the others conceive that their life's work would be changed beyond recognition by someone they had only just met?

Or you? When career, friends, money, achievement or entertainment were what got you up in the morning, could you ever have thought, in your wildest dreams, that a Man who lived more than 2,000 years ago would become your Saviour? Your companion? Your life-giver? Your polestar? Your protector? Your present? Your future? And . . . your Teacher?

When you open your Bible each day, do you feel like one of the twelve? Do you hear Him speak? Feel His love for you? Recognize His nearness? Sense His pleasure . . . or, occasionally, His loving rebuke? Does your pulse ever quicken? Do your eyes ever moisten? Does everything else slip away apart from His presence?

The twelve often looked at Jesus across a crowd, but then had the privilege of sitting around the fire with Him; eating and laughing *with Him*; asking the questions crowding their minds; having their knowledge increased and their love expanded . . . each and every day.

Along with other believers, we too listen across the crowd to someone else speaking His words. But we also own the privilege of time alone with the Saviour . . . to hear His voice, feel His joy, experience His closeness . . . and to present our lives and offer our worship to Him day after day.

Welcome to the world of the disciples. In this world His presence is our most prized possession; His teaching our greatest balm and infallible guide. It is the place where we discover that He is the 'revealer of mysteries' (Daniel 2:47).

Lord Jesus, may I be prepared to give up everything to sit around the fire with You. Amen.

19 March

'But blessed are your eyes, for they see,
and your ears, for they hear.'

Matthew 13:16

Reading: Matthew 13:18–23

'Ssh . . . don't tell anyone! It's a secret!'

Secrets range from the harmless – 'There's going to be a surprise party' – to the threatening – 'Tell, and you will suffer!' Often used as a weapon of power, insistence on secret-keeping can lead to devastation and destruction, especially in the lives of children. We shouldn't teach our children to keep secrets. Conversely, we sometimes withhold information, recognizing that, if released, it may cause enormous hurt. Some things are better left untold, but great wisdom is needed in this area. The 'can-you-keep-a-secret?' game treads too often on dangerous ground.

Jesus had secrets. However, his secrets were not for keeping, but for telling. He made partial disclosure of them in the parables He told to everyone within the sound of His voice. But He demystified their deeper meaning to those closest to Him (Matthew 13:11). Away from the multitudes of the curious, Jesus took time to explain truths to the disciples that until then had been hidden – truths they needed to know about His kingdom. Truths essential for the task they would inherit when Jesus was no longer with them. Truths now written in the Bible for us.

Those truths were so foreign to anything the disciples had heard before that it often took a while for the coin to drop. Even after Jesus' death they forgot that He'd told them He would rise again (Luke 24:6)! Although we have so much more than those first disciples had, we too are frequently slow to appreciate what lies behind Jesus' words. Such are the treasures available to us that at times it's hard to take it all in. He is indeed the revealer of mysteries. Some obvious, some just beneath the surface. Some deep enough to require digging on our part.

Yet, just as we praise our children for each new achievement, so Jesus encourages every person who sees and believes, and who listens and hears (Matthew 13:17). The effort is always worth it!

Teacher of mysteries, thank you for Your patience as I seek to learn more from You. Amen.

20 March

'You will be sorrowful,
but your sorrow will turn into joy.'

John 16:20

Reading: John 16:20–24

Teaching is about more than transferring what the teacher knows into the minds of the students. Some things are hard to teach, others even more difficult to learn.

Jesus didn't shy away from the tough stuff. He taught us the truth about: sin (John 8:34); judgement (Matthew 10:28); sacrifice (16:24) and persecution (10:22). And yet, He softens His words with the encouragement of His presence, and offers hope in spite of heartache. Life is empty without encouragement. Hope unexpressed makes God appear unconcerned, distant in our darkest times. Jesus understood the frailty of the human psyche. He knew that living in a fallen world is made easier when encouragement is present. That's why He laced His more difficult words with the golden thread of loving cheer.

'I have said these things to you, that in me you may have peace,' Jesus said to the disciples during their difficult conversation about His impending death. 'In the world you will have tribulation. *But take heart*; I have overcome the world' (John 16:33, emphasis here, and below, mine).

To the woman who had suffered for years with haemorrhaging, He tenderly said, '*Take heart*, daughter; your faith has made you well' (Matthew 9:22).

'*Take heart*; it is I,' Jesus spoke to the terrified disciples struggling with the stormy waves. 'Do not be afraid' (Mark 6:50).

And I especially love the one that is prefaced by the words, 'Jesus stopped and said, "Call him."' Previously rebuking blind Bartimaeus, those around him then said, '*Take heart*. Get up; he is calling you' (Mark 10:49).

Is there anything more comforting than hearing the words, '*take heart*' or '*fear not*' from the Saviour's heart to ours? In the darkest of days and the most fearful of nights they give us hope to go on ... reminding us He is near, loving us and working all things together for good (Romans 8:28).

And sometimes He asks *us* to be *His* encouragement ... to be the people who might say to another struggling soul, '*Take heart*. Get up; he is calling you.'

Lord Jesus, thank for the times You have cheered my heart even when hope seemed gone. Help me to share Your comfort with others. Amen.

21 March

And he called the twelve together and gave them power
and authority over all demons and to cure diseases,
and he sent them out to proclaim the
kingdom of God and to heal.

Luke 9:1–2

Reading: Luke 9:1–6, 10

We all learn in different ways. Personally, I have a strong dislike for writing seminars that include a practical component, requiring attendees to participate actively in what they've been learning. I go to absorb as much as I can from the expert, so having a go is a waste of time for me – I can't suddenly create from a snappy writing prompt. However, there comes a time, when – as one sportswear company puts it – you 'Just do it!'

Jesus was the consummate teacher. By word and example, He trained the disciples for a life without His physical presence, even though they didn't recognize it at the time. This was no one-hour seminar. The time had come to get out there, as Christ's ambassadors, 'to proclaim the kingdom of God and to heal' (Luke 9:2).

To us they still looked a bit 'green', but Jesus had prepared them well, explaining their task clearly. They were to address the physical and the spiritual needs of their listeners with healing and the gospel. Founder of the Salvation Army, General William Booth, reportedly replied to critics of his work among the poor by saying, 'It is impossible to comfort men's hearts with the love of God when their feet are perishing with cold.' Both reponses are needed.

Specific instructions as to how the disciples were to conduct themselves enabled them to cover as much ground as possible. So much to do . . . so little time to do it! Every detail was important. But most important of all was that they were supernaturally enabled through the 'power and authority' (9:1) given to them by the One sending them, who had Himself repeatedly demonstrated both.

Jesus never sends us to do His work or a specific task, or simply to live each day for Him, without His equipping and enabling. He doesn't set us up to fail. The time is too short, and there are still so many people to tell.

Lord, one day You will return. May I keep spreading the word! Amen.

22 March

'If I have told you earthly things and you do not believe,
how can you believe if I tell you heavenly things?'

John 3:12

Reading: John 3:1–7

One thing was certain – Nicodemus knew where to find Jesus. In fact, there was little the ruler of the Jews didn't know about Him. No one had disturbed the Sanhedrin as much as this Man, not even John the Baptist. Nicodemus needed to meet Jesus for himself. To sort truth from fiction. To look the Man in the eye and hear what He had to say.

Nicodemus 'came to Jesus by night' (John 3:2). Darkness provided privacy for the debate this 'teacher of Israel' (3:10) wanted when he arrived unannounced and alone at the place where Jesus was staying. But for the first time in years Nicodemus found himself the pupil, disarmed by the profundity of what a former carpenter from Nazareth was saying.

Jesus quickly brushed aside the Pharisee's flattery (3:2) and got straight to the point. Nicodemus was interested in religion, while Jesus wanted to introduce His visitor to regeneration . . . to lift him from his comfort zone of law into the nitty-gritty of kingdom theology. And there was no issue more basic than how to enter the kingdom of God.

'Unless one is born again he cannot see the kingdom of God' (3:3).

What a spiritual grenade that was! And yet, Jesus' words always engage our minds. He wants us to think . . . to challenge our preconceptions, especially about spiritual life. Nicodemus appeared not to understand the 'born again' thought, even though he knew of the concept from Gentiles who had converted to Judaism. They were called 'newborn' children, as they had entered a new life within a new nation. *But was Jesus saying that only Gentiles could enter God's kingdom on earth?* That was Nicodemus's problem. His thinking was earth-bound. He believed God's Messiah would only ever be human. King David's royal successor, only a man like himself.

Raising the old barricade of rejection simply because of a lack of understanding often results in missing the miraculous. At least Nicodemus stayed. He was still listening.

Lord, there is much that I do not understand, but I want to stay at Your feet and keep listening. Amen.

23 March

Jesus answered him, 'Are you the teacher of Israel and
yet you do not understand these things?'
John 3:10

Reading: John 3:8–21

Imagine the conversation in the room below the roof where Jesus and Nicodemus were in discussion. *Why has the most senior Pharisee in Jerusalem come to see Jesus . . . alone? And why isn't Jesus speaking harshly to him, as He did to others?* Then it came, much to the delight of the listeners, a rebuke – something about Nicodemus not understanding what Jesus was saying . . . and him the top man (John 3:10)! Yet still no significantly raised voices.

Whatever was happening downstairs, the rooftop conversation continued. Jesus had much to tell Nicodemus. The Pharisee appeared to know little of God's plan to redeem humankind through new birth, brought about by the Spirit and not the law. 'Humans can reproduce only human life,' Jesus said, 'but the Holy Spirit gives birth to spiritual life' (3:6, NLT). As a cooling evening breeze blew across the roof, Jesus continued: 'Just as you can hear the wind but can't tell where it comes from or where it is going, so you can't explain how people are born of the Spirit' (3:8, NLT).

And still the Pharisee couldn't understand (3:10)! Or was it that Nicodemus *wouldn't* believe (3:12, NLT)? Was his mind closed? Did pride get in the way? Could the most religious man in the holy city not bring himself to admit that his eternal salvation depended only on believing in the Son of Man (3:15)? That all his law-keeping . . . and law-making . . . counted for nothing? That God was not at all impressed by his religiosity? Or could it be that the intensity and expression of God's love, explained by Jesus (3:16) – actually embodied in Him! – was too much for the teacher to take in?

Nicodemus, still groping in the darkness of salvation by works, was afraid to let in the light (3:21). As he disappeared back into the night, Jesus knew it wasn't the last he would hear of Nicodemus.

'You *must* be born again' (3:7), whether you believe it or not.

Lord Jesus, thank you for the day I was born again, trusting in You alone for my salvation. Amen.

24 March

THINK ON THIS

'Say to the daughter of Zion,
"Behold, your king is coming to you,
humble, and mounted on a donkey,
on a colt, the foal of a beast of burden."'

Matthew 21:5

- Read through this verse a number of times – including out loud.
- Write it out, stick it on the fridge, have it on your phone.
- Meditate on the words, then respond in praise.
- Take steps to allow God's word to change you: perhaps . . . repent, forgive, love.

25 March

And the disciples simply replied,
'The Lord needs it.'

Luke 19:34, NLT

Reading: Luke 19:28–40

Donkeys may be sentient beings, but I doubt that on this particular day the donkey knew how important it was in God's plan. This beast was about to have its identity changed. Once Jesus sat on its back it wouldn't be called a colt again. Its never-before-ridden-on status was now history. Remarkably, the young donkey behaved impeccably, submitting to its Creator. That day the Lord *needed* a donkey to enter Jerusalem – no victory parade on a white steed for Jesus . . . that would come later (Revelation 19:11). The young animal was *needed* to send a message to the authorities and the people. *I am King!* Jesus was declaring. *I bring peace . . . the kind that comes only through me* (John 14:27).

The people must have understood the prophetic symbolism (Zechariah 9:9), or why else would they have shouted, 'Hosanna to the Son of David! Blessed is he who comes in the name of the Lord!' (Matthew 21:9)? Solomon's coronation took place on the donkey of his father, King David (1 Kings 1:32–35), setting the precedent in the nation's history. Unlikely as it might seem, monarchs and donkeys do go together.

Jesus is King! And He *needed* a donkey for the proclamation, just as He *needed* a big fish to set rebellious Jonah back on course (Jonah 1:17, 2:10 – 3:1–3) and *needed* ravens to keep Elijah alive (1 Kings 17:4).

However, *needed* is a strong word. It gives the impression that some things can't happen without us. As humans we have a deep desire to feel needed; that our lives should have purpose . . . individually unique, yet deeply satisfying.

Does the holy, all-sufficient God of the universe *need* me? No. He doesn't. He has no limitations or deficiencies. Yet, He chose to clothe Himself in flesh and come to live among us to demonstrate His love in the most ghastly fashion – death on a cross. He also chose to leave the business of continuing His work on earth to us, with the help of His ever-present, power-giving Holy Spirit.

Does Jesus *need* me? No. But He chooses to love me and use me. That meets my *need*.

Self-sufficient One, I choose to give myself to You. Only You can satisfy. Amen.

26 March

Look carefully then how you walk . . .
making best use of the time,
because the days are evil.

Ephesians 5:15–16

Reading: Matthew 21:12–19

The clock was ticking.

The crazy celebration of Palm Sunday had flowed into Monday with a busyness that belied what was about to unfold. Jesus lived every day of His short three-year ministry with passionate determination, yet what He packed into those last few days was remarkable. Jerusalem was bursting at the seams with around 2 million Passover pilgrims, as well as just about every religious leader in Israel. The temple was the place to be, and Jesus was right there in the middle of it.

Had He ever been more public? There was no rushing away from the crowds. No seeking solitude. No telling the blind and lame He had healed not to tell anyone. Jesus had things to say, miracles to perform, lives to change.

Friday was coming.

The disciples looked on nervously while Jesus took on the religious elite – no time for political correctness. Tables flew into the air and stallholders chased rolling coins, while the religious mafia – under the guise of temple service – boiled with indignation. Hands on daggers, the temple guards held back as the crowds noisily sided with Jesus. They knew He was right. God's house was not the place for legalized theft! But the chief priests and elders of the people had dared to think that the temple was their domain. Jesus put them right. This house of prayer belonged to His Father and was not a place where robbers could hide (Matthew 21:13).

The clock ticked on, Monday sliding into Tuesday. With barely a night's sleep, Jesus headed back to the temple. It appeared the religious elite had spent all night constructing a list of loaded questions to trap Him and restore their pride. They would have been better off sleeping! His answers left the crowd astonished (22:33), the Sadducees bewildered (22:34) and the Pharisees silenced (22:46). But silence wasn't golden . . . it was crimson red!

Friday was coming.

Lord Jesus, help me not to fritter away the time You have given me to spread the truth and share the gospel. The clock is ticking. Amen.

27 March

And he said, 'Truly, I tell you,
this poor widow has put in more than all of them.'

Luke 21:3

Reading: Luke 21:1–6

These days you can travel the world without leaving your living room. Television introduces us to countries we can only dream of visiting. Programme makers even point out the best places to visit if you choose to take a short city break. They also include which church or cathedral you simply must not miss. Unfortunately, it's not so that you can enjoy worship or fellowship with other believers. What they don't want you to miss is the architecture!

After all the teaching they had been receiving from Jesus, the confrontations they had witnessed with the religious elite and the near-riot caused by the table-turning escapade of the Master – to say nothing of the countless miracles performed over the previous two days – some of Jesus' disciples thought it more important to discuss the temple architecture!

Jesus had only just spoken to the disciples about a little woman most people in the crowded temple hadn't even noticed. He had watched her drop her two last small coins into the offering box. Yet, it was the memorial plaques adorning the temple walls, framed by majestic stonework (Luke 21:5), that stole the men's attention. They pointed out the wealthy donors to the temple. Jesus identified the biggest giver of all. The person who had given everything she had (21:4). Her name would never make it onto a plaque, but it was written on the Saviour's heart. Surplus givers (21:4) didn't impress Jesus the way this poor widow had. It was always all or nothing for the Saviour.

Something He was only too aware of. Friday was coming.

Later that evening, in the plainer surroundings of a friend's home, another woman gifted the Saviour with everything she had, anointing Him with expensive perfume – an act severely criticized by those still unwilling to learn the lesson of surrender (Mark 14:3–10). It's all or nothing for Jesus. Don't you love Jesus' response to the critics: 'She has done what she could' (14:8)? Better than any plaque on a temple wall!

It was Wednesday. Friday was coming.

Holy Spirit, teach me what is truly important. May it always be 'all for Jesus'. Amen.

28 March

'But the time is coming – indeed it's here now –
when you will be scattered, each one going his own way,
leaving me alone. Yet I am not alone
because the Father is with me.'

John 16:32, NLT

Reading: Luke 22:39–53

Jesus had been the guest at many meals. For His final meal on earth, He was the host. Peter and John were sent to set things in order. The lamb – purchased, then sacrificed at the temple courts – was now roasted, tantalizing Jesus' guests as they arrived at the upper room loaned for the event. Wine, bitter herbs and bread waited on the low table for the celebratory Passover feast to begin.

But the usual excitement associated with the annual Passover commemoration was mixed with something they couldn't quite define. Jesus had said so much over the past few days that their brains were throbbing with information they hadn't always understood. Then Judas almost upended the table in his sudden rush to leave. He had been acting strangely of late, but Jesus' comment about betrayal had obviously disturbed the group's treasurer.

The men were relieved when Jesus decided they should go to Gethsemane. All this strange talk of betrayal, denial and abandonment had taken its toll. Time in the garden was sure to bring peace to them all . . . perhaps even some rest. They were so tired!

Peter, James and John jumped when they felt Jesus' hand shaking them awake. *What have we missed?* 'Could you not watch with me one hour?' (Matthew 26:40). Jesus' disappointment was not hard to miss. *But wait, is that blood dripping from his forehead?* Try as they might, they couldn't keep their eyes open. *Asleep when He needed us most.* Suddenly, it was too late to pray.

'See, the hour is at hand,' the Master sighed over the sleepy three, 'and the Son of Man is betrayed into the hands of sinners' (26:45). This time it was more than Jesus' words that brought His closest disciples to their feet. Striding towards them was Judas . . . followed by a mob. They had come for Jesus! Just as He had said.

And Friday was almost here!

Forgive me, Jesus, for the times I've slept when I should have been praying . . . for the times I didn't listen carefully enough to what You were saying. Amen.

29 March

When Jesus had received the sour wine, he said,
'It is finished,' and he bowed his head and gave up his spirit.
John 19:30

Reading: John 19:16–30

Would I have run and left Jesus alone in Gethsemane? I hope not. But I can choose to walk that worst of all days with Him today in contemplation and worship.

Friday had arrived.

4:00 to 6:00 a.m. Jesus illegally tried at night by Annas, Caiaphas and the religious assembly (Luke 22:66–70), helped along by the testimony of liars (Mark 14:56).

6:00 to 8:00 a.m. Jesus was bounced between Pontius Pilate and King Herod for interrogation (Luke 23:1–25). Neither could find fault, but both were too cowardly to release Him.

8:00 to 8:30 a.m. Mocked, humiliated, beaten beyond recognition and unjustly condemned to die, Jesus carries His cross with the help of Simon of Cyrene – a stranger pulled from the crowd – to Golgotha (Luke 23:26).

9:00 to 9.30 a.m. Jesus is nailed to a Roman cross, His body hanging naked for all to see. Spittle is running down His skin, His beautiful brow torn by the long thorns of a mock crown.

9:30 to 11:00 a.m. Watching Jesus' physical suffering was not enough for His torturers. Their vicious taunting continued, insulting the One who ought to have received their praise (Matthew 27:39–44).

11:00 a.m. to noon Jesus speaks grace from the cross – pleading forgiveness for those who crucify Him (Luke 23:34), promising eternal life to the penitent thief (23:43) and lovingly arranging the care of His mother after His death (John 19:26–27).

Noon to 3:00 p.m. Creation did what man had not and bowed to its Creator. The temple curtain tore from top to bottom; the sun stopped shining; the earth shook; the graves gave up their dead. And for three hours Jerusalem trembled in inexplicable darkness (Matthew 27:51–54).

3:00 p.m. The cup of suffering was as nothing compared with the cup of separation Jesus drank. The howl of the forsaken rent the air as the Father turned away from His Son, unable to watch as Jesus bore our sin on His body on that cross.

'It is finished' (**bold type** mine) marked the end of this day of all days, 'and gave up his spirit' (John 19:30).[17]

What can I say, Lord? I'm so thankful that Sunday is coming! Amen.

30 March

Joseph of Arimathea . . . took courage and
went to Pilate and asked for the body of Jesus.

Mark 15:43

Reading: John 19:38–42

No matter how film-makers romanticize Jesus' death with haunting music and special lighting, there was nothing sanitary about that place of execution. Roman crosses silhouetting the countries of their occupation were commonplace. The sights and sounds of torturous deaths forever seared the minds of those who witnessed such horror.

And yet, in those dark hours when God hid His eyes from the central cross, something was happening in a nearby garden. Two old friends were hurriedly making plans. Accustomed to debating the religious legal matters of the nation, Joseph of Arimathea and Nicodemus were meeting in the dark for the last time. Joseph had secretly followed Jesus (Mark 15:43), Nicodemus perhaps having spoken in whispers to his friend of his own night-time meeting with Him (John 3:1–2). But pride and fear of what might happen to their positions and future income had held back any open witness for Jesus.

Now that Jesus was breathing His last, yards from where they stood, they could no longer keep quiet. Rapid communication with Pilate and a hurried gathering of linen and burial spices took place (John 19:38–39) when the Man they both believed to be the Messiah 'gave up his spirit' (19:30). What had they missed by their silence? Or did God allow it in order that His Son's body could be looked after in death?

No one of lesser position or means could have done what this pair did. The King of kings could have been unceremoniously dumped in a mass grave . . . but the Father had other plans (Isaiah 53:9). Plans that included two fearful people speaking up at just the right time.

It touches me deeply to imagine John lowering the body of his Lord from the cross into the arms of these two religious statesmen. Of the blood, shed for them, seeping into their rich robes, while their tears of regret washed the Saviour's filthy face.

Then, on that 'Day Between', as Joseph and Nicodemus quietly awaited the judgement of their peers, their hearts knew God's peace . . . for the first time. And Sunday was coming!

Heavenly Father, thank you that it's never too late to do the right thing. Amen.

31 March

THINK ON THIS

'He is not here, for he has risen, as he said.'

Matthew 28:6

'Death is swallowed up in victory.'
'O death, where is your victory?
O death, where is your sting?'

1 Corinthians 15:54–55

- Read through both passages a number of times – including out loud.
- Write them out, stick them on the fridge, have them on your phone.
- Meditate on the words, then respond in praise.
- Encourage someone by sharing these passages with them today.

April

1 April

'Truly, I say to you, wherever this gospel is proclaimed
in the whole world, what she has done will also
be told in memory of her.'

Matthew 26:13

Reading: Matthew 26:6–13

I had missed my lift home after a nightshift in cardiology. Now I was missing sleep because the bus was crawling between stops. I guessed this bus was a regular for many of the early morning travellers, something I became acutely aware of when the bus stopped yet again. Only this time I could feel my fellow travellers react differently, placing bags on empty seats beside them or moving to the aisle seat, rendering it occupied. The actions piqued my interest, and then my heart sank.

The latest addition to our temporary travelling community bounced on board, greeting the driver loudly. As he passed all the 'occupied' seats, he smiled widely at each person, rarely engaging as the bag-movers looked embarrassingly out the window. Their actions played on my exhaustion. As the young man reached my seat, I returned his happy greeting with a smile and a deliberately loud 'Hello', hoping he hadn't noticed the rogue tear dropping off my chin. But he didn't sit beside me. Instead, he walked past to take a seat at the back of the bus, where he sat alone, as he probably did every morning.

While each of us travellers could hide our backstories, the young man's features wrote his as clearly as the text on this page. He was 'different'. He had Down syndrome. And too often 'different' translates into judgement, misunderstanding and prejudice.

And I cried, my sadness deepened by the recent medical diagnosis our own first child had received – a diagnosis that had proclaimed her 'different'. Was this what her future held? Would people bristle at her approach? Look away? Move their bags?

Jesus wouldn't have moved seats on the bus.

One woman who had experienced disgust, rejection and discrimination all her life – where to be a Gentile, a dog or a woman rendered you worthless – was praised by Jesus . . . something her critics would never forget. History has seen to that.

Lord Jesus, thank you for demonstrating that everyone deserves to be loved and respected. Help me to learn the lesson. Amen.

2 April

And all his acquaintances and the women
who had followed him from Galilee stood
at a distance watching these things.

Luke 23:49

Reading: John 20:1, 11–18

Mud sticks. Unfortunately, it's often flung at the wrong wall!

Coming from a town notorious for its brothels does not make every female resident a prostitute. Neither should the position of a person's story in the biblical text cause connections to be made that are ill-founded. Yet both have labelled Mary Magdalene with an unproven reputation as an immoral woman. Yes, Mary was from Magdala – a town infamous for prostitution; yes, Mary was introduced in Luke 8:2 after the unnamed woman of Luke 7:37. But the links are tenuous, and assumptions are often wrong. Mud has been thrown at this woman for too long.

Since her healing–deliverance, Mary Magdalene had followed – no, devoted – her life to Jesus (8:1–3). She left behind the comforts of her own home to live in tents or sleep on other people's floors . . . to bake bread, wash clothes, shop, cook, erect tents. She endured inuendo, abuse and rejection as she accompanied men, none of whom was her husband or father. But she deemed it all worth it because she witnessed miracles of body and soul as diseases were defeated, demons expelled, hearts changed . . . and women respected.

Where Jesus was, you would find Mary Magdalene. She was *always* serving, *always* listening, *always* learning. Mary was always there.

> Not she with traitorous kiss her Master stung,
> Not she denied Him with unfaithful tongue;
> She, when Apostles fled, could daggers brave,
> Last at the Cross, and earliest at the grave.
> (Author unknown)

And when cruel men mocked, flogged and crucified her Lord, Mary was there. Last at the cross (Matthew 27:56). Last at the burial (27:61). First at the empty tomb (John 20:1). First to see the risen Christ (20:16–18)! Her devotion had been worth it.

Lord Jesus, thank you for showing such grace to Mary Magdalene . . . and to me. May I serve You with the same devotion and selfless love. You are worthy of no less. Amen.

3 April

When Jesus saw his mother and the disciple whom
he loved standing nearby, he said to his mother,
'Woman, behold, your son!'

John 19:26

Reading: Luke 2:48–51

My husband and I have been blessed with three children. We have also watched our two daughters suffer during their short lives, and then die. Children shouldn't die before their parents. It isn't right.

Mary, the mother of Jesus, watched her Son die. He didn't die of some unfortunate disease. He didn't have a fatal accident. He was murdered. No sudden stabbing in the dark of night, though. No blow to the head. No robbery gone wrong. Mary's boy was slowly executed, but not for any crime He had committed (Luke 23:14–15). Yet, in horror she followed the crowd to the place of execution, as her precious boy struggled to find the strength to carry the crossbeam of Rome's instrument of death.

I wonder, did she stop her ears as the hammer blows punctured the limbs she had once washed as a baby? Did she cover her eyes, so she didn't have to see the bruised, battered and pierced face she had smothered with her kisses? How did the legs that chased Him as a child hold her up through those long hours? Were her hands tightly held against her broken heart that had so recently almost burst with pride for the Man her boy had become? Was her mind confused as the words of the angel echoed in her mind – 'He will be great ... and of his kingdom there will be no end' (1:32–33)? Or in the cruel scene before her, did she recognize the fulfilment of Simeon's words (2:34–35)? Was this the sword's piercing of which he spoke?

In spite of the horror, Mary was there. She had been there at His birth and throughout His childhood; loved Him, then released Him to the ministry of the Father; journeyed with Him; and now ... here she was at the cross, watching Him die.

And her heart swelled once more as she heard Him say, 'Woman, behold, your son!' (John 19:26). Even on the cross He was thinking of her.

Jesus, thank you for Mary's devotion to You. Keep me near the cross, Lord. Amen.

4 April

'Away with him,' they yelled.
'Away with him! Crucify him!'

John 19:15, NLT

Reading: Mark 14:53–58

The ancient Egyptians used drowning and impalement. The Romans favoured crucifixion. The French had Madame Guillotine. Methods of execution show the depravity of leaders who thought themselves better than those they deemed guilty. For most, though, execution had to involve humiliation. And if you ever doubted the darkness of the human heart, think on the crowds who chose to watch these public spectacles. It was no different for Jesus.

Crowds are fickle. Made up of organizers, followers, the inquisitive, the foolish and the few bystanders who couldn't get away, one thing is always certain: the one who shouts the loudest grabs all the attention and, more often than not, gets his way.

The crowd who spread palm branches to welcome their King into Jerusalem on Palm Sunday shouted their Hosannas loud enough to be heard ... heard by the Pharisees, that is (John 12:19). From then on, the Pharisees knew Jesus had to go.

The crowd at Jesus' trials consisted of the Jewish elite (Mark 14:55), strangely backed by those they ordinarily wouldn't have given the time of day. But then money shouts even louder than the crowd. And lies are cheap!

The crowd around the cross included the treacherous, the mocking, the executioners ... even the curious. Still shouting. Still mocking. 'Ha! Look at you now ... Well then, save yourself and come down from the cross!' (Mark 15:29–30, NLT).

Yet, mixed among the cold and the cruel were those who loved the Man on the middle cross. While disciples watched from a distance (Luke 23:49), some of the women bravely pushed through the crowd, accompanied only by John (John 19:25). Close enough to hear every word, observe the agony and count every drop of blood that fell, they stayed.

But they didn't shout. They couldn't shout. It was too late to protest. Too painful to watch. Yet unthinkable to leave Jesus alone. Their presence said more than any protest could. They were the gold reflected in the dark crowd at Calvary.

Lord Jesus, I cannot imagine what You suffered there for me. May I always stand out from the crowd and be the gold in our dark world today. Amen.

5 April

'For truly, I say to you, whoever gives you
a cup of water to drink because you belong to Christ
will by no means lose his reward.'

Mark 9:41

Reading: Luke 22:24–27

Nothing given to Jesus, or done for Him, is ever wasted: our love; our devotion; our time; our money; our relationships; the risks we take . . . even our very presence.

Mary, the mother of James the Less, and Salome, mother of James and John, also followed Jesus from Galilee to the cross (Luke 23:27–28). Part of the background team, they happily avoided the limelight. Yet, Jesus elevated the mundane, everyday work of women to the role of spiritual service. Imagine how they felt when Jesus said that a cup of water given in His name would not go unrewarded (Mark 9:41). They could do that! Simple service mattered to Jesus.

The Master wasn't setting up a business – there were no frontmen, no spiritual celebrities. Everyone had an important role in building His kingdom. Committed service was the important thing for Jesus. Whether He sent the disciples out to preach (Mark 6:7), or the women to tell those same disciples that He had risen from the dead (Matthew 28:10) or simply to cook a meal for hungry men (John 12:2), each was of equal value.

Jesus wasn't only Creator, King and Messiah. He was also the perfect servant – even going as far as to wash the dirty feet of the disciples (John 13:2–5). Nothing was beneath Him.

I've seen polished floors dirtied by church worshippers. Tables full of beautiful food consumed in no time. Fancy furniture left scuffed after a children's club. Hours spent childminding to encourage lone parents. Savings emptied to fund mission trips. Sleep interrupted to pray for the broken.

Not all service for Jesus happens in a pulpit.

And what we give to Jesus He sanctifies. What He sanctifies He fills. What He fills He uses for His glory, and for the benefit of others and the building of the church. Jesus isn't so interested in what we can do for Him, but rather in what lies behind it. Duty or love? For the women at the cross the answer was simple.

Lord, give me a servant heart . . . full of love for You. Amen.

6 April

'This Jesus, delivered up according to the definite plan
and foreknowledge of God, you crucified and
killed by the hands of lawless men.'

Acts 2:23

Reading: Matthew 27:19–26

Imagine if they'd had major incident reviews back then. I wonder what conclusion
it would have come to.

- **How did it start?** 'One of His own turned Him in,' a scribe shouted.
  'We paid him well for his information,' another added.
- **Where was Jesus arrested?** 'Gethsemane.' 'He knew He was guilty,'
  someone interjected. 'He didn't even put up a fight.' 'After one of His men
  sliced off my ear, Jesus put it back on,' Malchus said. 'Sshh, Malchus, that's
  not relevant at this enquiry.'
- **Who brought formal charges?** Silence. 'The charges came later . . . after
  His arrest,' someone eventually offered. 'Jesus was a blasphemer – we had
  to do something.' 'But you were His judges,' the chairman replied. 'You
  can't bring charges and then sit in judgement.'
- **When did the accused's trial take place?** 'We worked all night to get it
  sorted,' a Pharisee answered smugly. 'It had to be over before the Sabbath.'
  'But it's illegal to hold a trial at night – the accused had no opportunity to
  call witnesses on his behalf,' said the exasperated chairman. 'The Mishnah
  clearly states that capital offence trials cannot be concluded in one day,
  yet you took only nine hours . . . in the dead of night!'
- **Where did this trial take place?** 'In Caiaphas' house, then the Romans
  took over.' 'You used the home of the high priest? That's clearly forbidden!'
  'Did I not hear that Jesus was also transported to Herod before He was
  sent to Pilate?' 'Yes, but . . .'
- **Who were the witnesses?** Muttered names were offered with the
  chairman shaking his head in disgust. 'Jesus condemned Himself,'
  someone repelled. 'We didn't need any witnesses!'
- **What was the final charge that condemned this man to death?**
  'Blasphemy!' shouted one. 'Treason!' yelled another. 'Seems you still can't
  make up your minds,' the chairman replied. 'What a farce. A legal mess
  if ever I saw one!'
- **Where is Jesus now?** Heads dropped around the room. That was for
  another day.

Lord, despite the injustice, I am grateful that You willingly gave up Your life for me. Amen.

7 April

THINK ON THIS

'No one takes it [my life] from me,
but I lay it down of my own accord.
I have authority to lay it down, and I have
authority to take it up again. This charge
I have received from my Father.'

John 10:18

- Read through this verse a number of times – including out loud.
- Write it out, stick it on the fridge, have it on your phone.
- Meditate on the words, then respond in praise.
- Be a doer . . . Serve someone with an act of kindness today.

8 April

The Lamb slain from the foundation of the world.

Revelation 13:8, NKJV

Reading: 1 Peter 1:18–20

Only once did we consider buying property off-plan. It was so exciting, especially when we realized we could adapt the ink designs to produce a bungalow that would suit the needs of our disabled daughters. At the site, the foundations were already in place. But it's a foolish builder who doesn't have the architect's plans in front of him.

As they left the place of crucifixion, were the Pharisees pleased that their plan had been accomplished? When they heard the Roman centurion declare Jesus dead, did they breathe a sigh of relief? Did they believe that, finally, the self-professed Messiah would never again ridicule them? Now they could get back to their meticulous law-keeping. Surely they had done God a favour?

Somehow, they had missed God's clear plan. The plan that came together in eternity *before* 'God created the heavens and the earth', *before* 'the Spirit of God was hovering over the face of the waters', *before* God spoke light and life and everything wonderful into being (Genesis 1:1–4). *Before* God 'created man in his own image' and 'blessed them' (1:27–28), *before* God's perfect creation was spoilt by the disobedience of Adam and Eve (3:1–7). *Before* sin separated God from the jewel of His creation (Isaiah 59:2). *Before.*

Before the foundation of the world, and in cooperation with the Son and the Holy Spirit, the Father made a plan. Too holy to look on sin (Habakkuk 1:13), there was only one way for sin to be covered and fellowship recovered, for 'without the shedding of blood there is no forgiveness of sins' (Hebrews 9:22).

Imagining as I can, with only a human mind, I hear the Father's heart speak through the words of the Son: *I'll go, Father . . . It's the only way.* So, 'for our sake he made him to be sin who knew no sin, so that in him we might become the righteousness of God' (2 Corinthians 5:21).

From the beginning, the cross was always God's plan.

Thank you, Jesus, that although You knew 'before', You still became that Lamb for me. Amen.

9 April

'Let not your hearts be troubled,
neither let them be afraid.'

John 14:27

Reading: John 11:21–27

It was an Irish wake. Custom dictated the room be filled with family, friends and acquaintances to ensure that those grieving are not left alone. Wakes can be noisy affairs as everybody shares their memories of the deceased, while drinking tea and enjoying the food provided by the kindness of others. There's something lovely about others entering into your grief, except that it doesn't take it away. That night, as the door closed behind the last visitor, grief was all that remained, and in the silence sadness roared. This wake was ours. Our beautiful, blue-eyed, ten-year-old daughter was the deceased. Our hearts were the ones broken. Our lives forever changed.

Losing someone you love does that to you.

In another room, many years ago, there was another wake. Jesus was dead. But those gathered couldn't believe what had happened. It didn't make sense. Hadn't they watched Jesus raise people from the dead? There was Jairus's daughter (Mark 5:35–43), the widow from Nain's son (Luke 7:11–16) and their friend Lazarus (John 11:43–44). He was Master over death. How could He be dead? Why didn't He save Himself? And the questions kept coming . . . especially the ones about the Jews pursuing them. The bolt may have kept the door locked, but it was fear that locked their hearts from remembering what Jesus had said.

Hadn't the Master told them this would happen? Hadn't He also told them not to be afraid (John 14:27)? Best of all, hadn't He told them that He wouldn't stay dead (Matthew 16:21)? Why did they not remember?

Because grief clouds the mind. Sorrow blurs the memory. Mourning is all-consuming. And the enemy of our souls likes to add anger and regret to already breaking hearts – emotions the disciples had in abundance. They had run away. Abandoned Jesus when He needed them. Renounced Him. Rejected Him.

Yet, on the Third Day, when Jesus appeared, He didn't rebuke or criticize. He simply entered their place of fear and sorrow, stood with them and offered His peace (John 20:19).

Thank you, Lord, for understanding our sorrow and entering our grief. But most of all, thank you for Your peace. Amen.

10 April

Weeping may last through the night,
but joy comes with the morning.

Psalm 30:5, NLT

Reading: Psalm 13

She thought her tears would never cease. That her cheeks would never dry, nor her heart ever mend. Sitting opposite the tomb (Matthew 27:61), Mary Magdalene listened to the muffled whispers as Joseph and Nicodemus tenderly shrouded the broken, lifeless body of her beloved Jesus. She pictured the stone shelf where they had laid Him. Saw the lamp flicker as they stepped out into the encroaching darkness. It was almost Sabbath. She knew they had to leave.

Now, staring at the cold grey granite of a closed tomb, the finality of life's greatest enemy gripped her soul. Jesus was dead. Buried. And Mary didn't know how she could face a day without the One who had delivered, healed and changed her completely. If sobbing could wake the dead, Jesus would have left the garden with her.

I know all about weeping. There are few who don't. Grief is the cruellest of all emotions; sorrow the band that squeezes joy from our hearts. Too often the night of weeping spoken of in Psalm 30 stretches on, as if forever. Yet Solomon speaks of the important work of grief in our lives. 'It is better to go to the house of mourning,' he says, 'than to go to the house of feasting' (Ecclesiastes 7:2). It took me a long time to agree with him. Give me a party any day!

In time I discovered that grief brings perspective to life; a sense of what is truly of value and, more importantly, that God feels deeply for us in our pain. No tear goes uncaught, no sorrow unrecorded in the Father's journal (Psalm 56:8). But He doesn't only come around for the wake ... He's with us for the long haul. '"My steadfast love shall not depart from you, and my covenant of peace shall not be removed," says the LORD, who has compassion on you' (Isaiah 54:10).

The night of weeping will finally end. Rarely as quickly as Mary Magdalene's did, but morning will come. And as its dawn pushes back the darkness, joy returns ... 'inexpressible and filled with glory' (1 Peter 1:8).

Your promises always stand, Lord. I'm looking forward to the morning. Amen.

11 April

'But we had hoped that he was the one to redeem Israel.'
Luke 24:21

Reading: Luke 24:13–35

This is the second most beautiful story of the resurrection day. I can just picture the scene ... and yes, I can see myself right there in it. I've made the same mistakes as the two men trudging those long seven miles home from Jerusalem to Emmaus. I, too, have been discouraged with the injustices of life. I've even been disappointed with the One I thought could sort out the difficulties of our world, including mine. Unfortunately, these disciples couldn't see what God was doing right then. Sad to say, I've often done the same.

They had left the grieving, frightened company of Jesus' closest followers, even though they had heard from the women and Peter that Jesus was risen! The grave was empty! But they didn't believe it. The philosophical approach of accepting the obvious – Jesus had been crucified and was dead – was much easier than believing that He was alive. Although not among the twelve, these two men had also followed Jesus closely, to the point that they were discussing 'all these things that had happened' (Luke 24:14) as they walked. Yet, their disappointment in what they *thought* Jesus should have done prevented them from recognizing that, 'Jesus himself drew near and went with them' (24:15). The risen Saviour was the very person walking beside them on the busy pilgrim road. He was more than they hoped ... they had been looking for the wrong thing all the time.

When it seems our prayers are not answered; that Jesus couldn't possibly mean for this to happen to us; that He could have stopped that tragedy; that He should have turned up when we needed Him ... watch out. He is likely standing right beside us; we've just not recognized Him. We've allowed our disappointment, our discouragement, our pain – even our anger – to cloud Him from view. But Jesus is there, ready to walk with us and reveal Himself in more ways than we could ever have hoped.

Lord Jesus, break through the cloud of discouragement and disappointment that too often obscures Your presence. May I choose trust over doubt and fear every time. Amen.

12 April

And their eyes were opened, and they recognized him.
And he vanished from their sight.

Luke 24:31

Reading: Luke 18:31–34

'I can't find my glasses!'

I wish I had a pound for every time I've heard that. And for each reply of, 'You're wearing them!' to hear the retort, 'They're the wrong ones ... it's my reading glasses I'm looking for.' My husband's preference for two pairs of glasses instead of varifocals has resulted in many searches, and not a little frustration at times. You see, when you look through the wrong lens your vision is blurred, even distorted. It's difficult to see things as they really are without the correct glasses.

The two disciples walking to Emmaus were clearly dejected and sorrowful, but there was more than sorrow distorting their vision of the events of that momentous weekend. They were wearing the wrong glasses! They were still looking for a liberating, conquering, up-to-date version of a King-David-like messiah. 'We had *hoped* that he [Jesus] was the one to redeem Israel' (Luke 24:21, emphasis mine) they told Him. Is it any wonder that their messianic hopes perished on Golgotha?

Jesus hadn't lived up to their expectations. Their dreams had died on that cross. Their agenda was buried in a tomb. Worse still, they had ignored Jesus' personal predictions of His death (Matthew 16:21) and didn't believe the testimony of the women that Jesus had risen from the dead (Luke 24:22–24).

God's agenda – clearly spoken of by the prophets – was very different from what this pair had imagined; something Jesus pointed out when He said, 'O foolish ones ... Was it not necessary that the Christ should suffer these things and enter into his glory?' (24:25–26).

Obviously, they needed to change their glasses! Perhaps we do too. Could it be that our perception of the difficult thing God is doing in our lives is distorted because we *expected* Him to do things differently? Or perhaps because we haven't taken the time to look at God's agenda for us and His world through His word? Could it be that we are missing God's masterplan and walking away from where the action really is?

Lord, I want to catch a glimpse of what You are doing in my life. Help me to change my glasses! Amen.

13 April

The teaching of your word gives light,
so even the simple can understand.

Psalm 119:130, NLT

And beginning with Moses and all the Prophets,
he interpreted to them in all the Scriptures the things
concerning himself.

Luke 24:27

Cleopas and his friend had fallen into the trap of allowing circumstance to define their present and dictate their future. Jesus' death had changed everything. Then, despite their inability to identify God's agenda in the very thing that was distressing them, Jesus drew alongside, flipped their perspective and cleared the fog. 'And their eyes were opened' (Luke 24:31).

'Did not our hearts burn within us while he talked to us on the road, while he opened to us the Scriptures?' they said to each other after Jesus had vanished from their sight (24:32).

Jesus is always with us on the road of life; always willing to talk to us; always opening the Scriptures to us. Because it is in His word and through His word that we see things as they really are. Here we catch a glimpse of God's big picture and where we fit into it. And best of all ... it's in these very pages that we see the authentic Jesus. In doing so, we realize the importance of releasing our expectations and trusting the Saviour with all that's happening right now, and all He has for us in the days ahead. It's only empty hands that God can fill; uncluttered life pages upon which He can write. Giving up is not the same as giving in. It's life-changing!

> Lord, I am willing
> To receive what You give,
> To lack what You withhold,
> To relinquish what You take,
> To suffer what You inflict,
> To be what You require.[18]
> Amen.

14 April

THINK ON THIS

Having the eyes of your hearts enlightened,
that you may know what is the hope to which he has
called you, what are the riches of his glory in the
inheritance of the saints.

Ephesians 1:18

- Read through this verse a number of times – including out loud.
- Write it out, stick it on the fridge, have it on your phone.
- Meditate on the words, then respond in praise.
- Take steps to allow God's word to change you: perhaps . . . repent, forgive, love.

15 April

'Don't be faithless any longer. Believe!'
John 20:27, NLT

Reading: John 20:19–29

Miracles do happen! People do rise from the dead!

These things are not easy to get one's head around, even for those present when it happens. The disciples had witnessed Jesus heal many people (Matthew 15:30). They had even stepped back to give Lazarus space to emerge from his grave ... alive (John 11:44)! By the time Jesus appeared inside their locked hideaway (20:19) He had already sent word via angels that He was alive (Luke 24:4–5) and met with at least six of their company (24:1–35), yet still they were not convinced.

Books have been written on the evidence for the resurrection, yet still millions do not believe. In the main, science stands in ridicule over the very One who inspired it in the first place.

When it comes down to it, for the sceptics among Christ's followers – then and now – Jesus is the only One who can make any sense of it all. It was only when He spoke to Mary in the garden (John 20:16); to the women returning from the sepulchre (Matthew 28:8–9) and to the two on the road to Emmaus (Luke 24:31) that they discovered it was indeed true. Jesus was alive! But seeing alone was not what convinced them. They recognized Jesus by what He did.

Death hadn't changed Him.

The risen Saviour still spoke into their need as He had always done. Brought understanding into their bewilderment. Peace into their sorrow. Calm into their fears. And He showed them His hands. Hands that had multiplied bread for 5,000 people. Hands that had touched the destitute. Hands that had given sight to the blind. Hands that had wiped away the tears of the broken. Hands that had been willingly nailed to a Roman cross.

There was no doubt. This really was Jesus. He had returned to them – and for us – just as He had said (Mark 9:31). The difference happens when we decide not to 'be faithless any longer', but 'believe!'

Lord Jesus, thank you for those hands that soothe our sorrows and calm our fears, and for Your love that never fails. Amen.

16 April

'The Lord has risen indeed, and has appeared to Simon!'

Luke 24:34

Reading: Luke 22:54–62

'If only I hadn't gone home that night. If only I hadn't left her. Things might have been different.'

I had been asked to address a room full of professionals at a paediatric palliative care conference. My remit was to speak about whether there was such a thing as a good death for children and their families. It was all going so well until someone asked the wrong question of this still-grieving mother. 'Is there anything that could have been done better?' That's when the list of 'if onlys' poured from my mouth . . . when my regrets became a not-too-pretty public spectacle.

'If only' – the devil's torment of the soul.

We cannot go back to undo what we've done. We cannot take back that thoughtless word or remake the broken promise. Neither can we excuse distancing ourselves from those we should be supporting, nor denying we ever knew them in the first place.

'And Peter remembered the saying of the Lord, how he had said to him, "Before the rooster crows today, you will deny me three times." And he went out and wept bitterly' (Luke 22:61–62). I'm sure the 'if onlys' flowed faster than Peter's tears, regret shredding his already broken heart.

But Jesus wasn't prepared to let the devil torment Peter's soul. Soon after His miraculous exit from the garden tomb, Jesus tenderly met with the man who had been His fiercest defender – the man whose heart was bigger still than his mouth. The meeting was a private one. All we are told is that Jesus 'has appeared to Simon' (24:34). We don't know what the Master said to him. Neither can we tell how many more tears the Galilean shed when he saw the risen Lord. We only know that Jesus met with Peter – and that there was repenting and forgiving to do.

While we hide in the shadows of our mistakes and torture ourselves with the 'if onlys' of life, Jesus wonderfully and affectionately seeks us out. There's nothing He cannot mend.

Lord, thank you for those private meetings where together we can mend any rifts between us. Amen.

17 April

Peter asked Jesus, 'What about him, Lord?'
Jesus replied . . . 'What is that to you?
As for you, follow me.'

John 21:21–22, NLT

Reading: John 21:15–23

They had been away from fishing for a long time. After Jesus' death they returned to the water for a long night with nothing to show for it, and muscles aching where they'd forgotten they had muscles. Then, as if someone had pressed replay, they heard His voice: 'Cast the net on the right side of the boat, and you will find some' (John 21:6). And in dawn's early light, they laughed together over the breakfast Jesus had made. It was like old times for Peter and the others, yet it was altogether different.

The last time Peter looked at Jesus over a charcoal fire he had been denying he ever knew Him (18:25). The memory still hurt.

Why do I mess things up? Perhaps I'd be better back fishing.

After breakfast, on the walk across the stony beach, Jesus answered those very questions. He reminded Peter of the call he had responded to the last time He told them how to catch fish (Luke 5:4–6). As they walked, they talked. This time Jesus was asking the questions. Peter answered – honestly, yet fearfully. Gone were the self-confident, passionate outbursts. The impulsive Peter had learned around that other charcoal fire that he was, in fact, weak. Now, declaring his love for Jesus in less exuberant style, Peter responded a second time to the Master's call on his life: 'Feed my sheep' (John 21:17). From here on in he would depend on the Lord. However, it would take Peter a while to get the hang of it.

Suddenly, Peter caught a glimpse of John following them. John – the very opposite of Peter. John – the one who always got things right. He hadn't denied Jesus. He had stayed . . . at the trial and at the cross (18:15, 19:26), when Peter hadn't. But comparison is neither helpful nor productive.

'Lord, what about this man?' Peter foolishly asked (21:21), following one of the most serious conversations of his life. How cringeworthy is that? But Jesus was having none of it. *John is none of your business, Peter! I have asked YOU to follow me!* (my paraphrase of John 21:22).

Lord Jesus, keep me from comparing myself with others and help me to follow only You! Amen.

18 April

Concerning this salvation, the prophets who prophesied about the grace that was to be yours searched and inquired carefully.

1 Peter 1:10

Reading: 1 Peter 1:10–12

The Bible is a book about God, you and me.

Yes, it contains the amazing record of creation and the history of the Jews. Prophecy also features prominently between its covers; not only in announcement, but remarkably in fulfilment. Then there's poetry – beautiful in construction, awakening all our senses. But we dare not forget the more sober note of the law passages – everything from its moral code right through to the specifics of absolute right and wrong. And stories ... thought-provoking collections of illustrative allegory of the good to emulate, the bad to avoid, and the downright ugly to reject. I particularly love delving into the lives recorded in the narrative passages, while undoubtedly needing the wisdom sections as well. And who doesn't love a bit of future-gazing? It's all there.

But the Bible is much more than one of those omnibus tomes where you get a collection of books bound together as a great offer. It's also more than a library where you can scan the shelves and pick out what you want to read, while ignoring the rest. The complete book is one of plan and promise ... both fulfilled in Jesus.

As God's message to humanity, the Bible has a crimson cord running through it, from beginning to end. Wherever you start reading it's there – redemption – the promise that one day He would buy back what was originally His. But it would come at a great cost. Sin had stolen the gem of His creation and the love of His heart, yet God promised that the thief would one day be defeated, and we would once more be His – cleansed, liberated and fit for His kingdom ... redeemed.

And the promised finale is yet to come, for the Redeemer in the story will one day return to take His people home forever (1 Thessalonians 4:17). He's made good on every promise so far. I believe this one will be no different!

Father, thank you for that crimson cord running through the Bible straight to my heart. Thank you for buying me back. Amen.

19 April

If you hide your sins, you will not succeed.
If you confess and reject them, you will receive mercy.

Proverbs 28:13, NCV

Reading: Genesis 3:6–13

Our engagement party had been a great occasion. The following day I headed back to work, and to the nurses' accommodation. Almost another week had passed before I literally crawled back home, tired and ready for a good night's sleep. Unexpectedly, a foul smell almost knocked me over when I pushed open the bedroom door!

After a shout for help, Mum and Dad helped me search for the source of the stomach-churning odour. And there, secreted under my bed lurked the culprit – a plate piled high with fresh cream pastries from the party – hidden there by my brother's friend, who had intended to retrieve them for a midnight feast when he got home! Too embarrassed to admit his misdemeanour, he thought he'd get the goodies next time he visited. But the putrefying fresh cream gave him away. There was no hiding from it!

It is foolish to try to brush our sin under the carpet (or the bed!). We can't hide behind fig leaves either – or trees – as Adam and Eve discovered (Genesis 3:7–8). Even when we think we've covered our tracks, God knows. And when He calls our name there's no point trying to put the blame on others (3:12–19). Yes, Eve had taken what was forbidden in blatant disobedience to God's command (3:3). Yes, she had believed Satan's lies, but in the end she took the fruit because she wanted what she thought it could give her (3:6). But Adam didn't have to take what Eve had offered him! His compliance made him equally guilty.

How sad that God had to go looking for them (3:9). Worse still, they chose bickering and blame over repentance. So, God took the initiative . . . as He always does. Sadly, judgement was pronounced (3:14–24). But in His mercy, God set in motion the strategy He had conceived with His Son and the Holy Spirit before the foundation of the world (3:15).

When that first innocent animal's blood was shed to provide cover for sinful Adam and Eve, redemption's plan began. The crimson cord was let loose. One day it would arrive at Calvary.

Forgive me, Lord, for the times I have tried to hide my sin from You. Amen.

20 April

By faith Noah . . . in reverent fear constructed an ark
for the saving of his household . . . and became
an heir of the righteousness that comes by faith.

Hebrews 11:7

Reading: Matthew 24:36–39

On toy shop shelves it's likely you will find a reminder of redemption. However, the appearance of this particular toy has been adjusted to change it from
the remarkable to the cute . . . to transform it into a plaything in order to avoid the
horror that had required its original construction . . . or the mercy of God in
achieving its foreordained purpose: rescue.

You've guessed it. I am of course speaking about Noah's ark – the adorable toy with
detachable roof and animals . . . two of each kind, naturally. Yet, few children playing
with the animal boat on their nursery floor have any idea of the horror that took
place when the rain fell and the earth broke open, until the waters covered the
surface of the earth, allowing the real, not-so-tiny boat to float (Genesis 7:17–20).

Noah's ark has proved a perpetual money-spinner for toymakers, but today's
obsession with saving animals (not bad in itself) appears to be all that is left of this
Old Testament story of redemption. This huge vessel, whose very dimensions were
God-given (6:14–16, NLT), was prepared primarily as a place of safety and survival
for Noah and his family during the great flood of God's judgement (7:4).

How heartbreaking those words in Genesis 6:6–7 are: 'And the LORD regretted
that he had made man on the earth,' and said, '"I will blot out man whom I have
created from the face of the land."' Then immediately we read that wonderful
word – *but* – 'But Noah found favor [grace] in the eyes of the LORD' (6:8).

God's plan of redemption remained on course. Satan could not thwart it in the
garden of Eden. Man's depravity in Noah's day could not change God's mind. The
crimson cord continued to unwind, wrapping itself around that vessel of salvation
and beyond to its completion.

I can't help but wonder: is God filled with regret when He looks at us, or have we
found grace in His eyes? Is the crimson cord – now fulfilled in Jesus – wrapped
around your soul?

Lord, help us not to trivialize great biblical truths, but to apply them to our hearts. Amen.

21 April

THINK ON THIS

'With your unfailing love you lead
the people you have redeemed. In your might,
you guide them to your sacred home.'

Exodus 15:13, NLT

- Read through this verse a number of times – including out loud.
- Write it out, stick it on the fridge, have it on your phone.
- Meditate on the words, then respond in praise.
- Encourage someone by sharing this verse with them today.

22 April

Abraham said, 'God will provide for himself
the lamb for a burnt offering, my son.'
So they went both of them together.

Genesis 22:8

Reading: Genesis 22:4–14

Many Christians believe the Old Testament holds little relevance to their lives today. Yet, 300 Old Testament prophecies point to Jesus Christ, who directly quoted Old Testament passages seventeen times in His ministry. I'd say that if Jesus saw the Old Testament writings as important, we'd be pretty foolish not to.

The crimson cord – that redemption plan and promise of God – stretches right from the fall (Genesis 3) through the Old Testament to the cross of Calvary, where Christ's sacrifice finally fulfilled God's redemption. Each detail and story confirms God's love and patience to a wayward humanity. Remarkable parallels with Christ often catch my breath, for in them I see Jesus. None more so than the story of Abraham and Isaac.

- The story is set in the land of Moriah. Referred to in Jewish tradition as 'the place', Mount Moriah was the place where Solomon built the first temple over 'the place' where Abraham placed his son on the altar of sacrifice . . . 'The place' where Jesus would later be crucified.
- Abraham was willing to give up his cherished son for God's purposes (Genesis 22:12). And 'God so loved the world, that he gave his only Son, that whoever believes in him should not perish but have eternal life' (John 3:16).
- Both young men were innocents, but only Jesus was sinless (1 Peter 2:22).
- 'And Abraham took the wood of the burnt offering and laid it on Isaac his son' (Genesis 22:6). 'And he [Jesus] went out, bearing his own cross, to the place called The Place of a Skull, which in Aramaic is called Golgotha' (John 19:17).
- Isaac questioned his father about the sacrifice (Genesis 22:7). Jesus asks the Father, 'If it be possible, let this cup pass from me' (Matthew 26:39).
- Both sons willingly went to the place of sacrifice.
- Isaac was spared (22:12). But there was no ram in the thicket for Jesus (22:13). Only in the death of His Son could God fulfil His promise of redemption for a lost humanity (2 Corinthians 5:21).

Father, thank you for keeping Your promises. We would literally be lost without them. Amen.

23 April

Then the women said to Naomi,
'Blessed be the Lord, who has not left you this day
without a redeemer, and may his name
be renowned in Israel!'

Ruth 4:14

Reading: Ruth 4:13–17

The lives of Naomi and Ruth had been devastated by disaster, leaving them both widows. Naomi, who had left Israel during a famine, had no one in Moab to provide for her, so decided to make the long journey home to Bethlehem.

However, it appears that Ruth had learned much in Naomi's home, and declared more than a commitment to care for her mother-in-law. 'For where you go I will go,' she told Naomi, 'and where you lodge I will lodge. Your people shall be my people, and your God my God' (Ruth 1:16). Little did she know how her life would be impacted by Naomi's God.

For widows, starvation was always a risk, and a future without a man held few possibilities. But God, in His kindness, had made provision in the Law of Moses for the widow and the destitute. It took many forms. The kinsman-redeemer was especially helpful to the widow (Psalm 68:5–6). The nearest male relative could 'buy' the property of the widow's husband, and with it take on the responsibility to care for the female relatives – a form of redemption. Adding to his own family responsibilities made it costly for the redeemer, yet liberating for those redeemed.

Boaz became kinsman-redeemer for Naomi and Ruth, becoming Ruth's husband and father to their son Obed (Ruth 4:9–13). A very special child, Obed was great-grandfather to King David and a direct ancestor of the greatest of all kinsman-redeemers . . . the Lord Jesus Himself (Matthew 1:5–16).

The world would have to wait for more than a thousand years before Bethlehem would provide the birthplace of another special child. One who would carry the crimson cord for the final thirty-three years before the promise was fulfilled. As darkness fell on Golgotha's hill that day, you can almost hear the Father say to a lost world, 'Blessed be the Lord, who has not left you this day without a redeemer.' You can certainly hear our Kinsman-Redeemer shout, 'It is finished' (John 19:30)!

Father, thank you that You did not leave us destitute and without hope. Thank you, Jesus, for bearing the cost of my redemption. Amen.

24 April

'Truly this was the Son of God!'
Matthew 27:54

Reading: Matthew 27:50–54

Stand with me. It is a place where we would never choose to be. Yet, He was there. For us. Surely we can stand by His bloodied feet for these brief moments.

But it's hard to lift our eyes. To see the very worst that man can do. If only we could cover our ears. Not have to listen to the thud of hammer blows ... the anguished cries ... or sense the fear that clags the air like fog, yet does not shroud the sight of dying men. Men stripped of decency – manhood mocked. The One pinned to the central cross beaten beyond recognition. Eyes closed shut by the fists of wicked men. Blood coursing down His face in rivulets from holes pierced by a thorn-matted crown. He is the reason we must watch ... for He is taking our place.

How could they laugh? Is this some sport that draws amusement from Rome's legionnaires? Does gambling over a dying man's clothing really bring pleasure? Why does the proud centurion on the noble steed allow his men to behave like this?

Had he become so hardened? Can he sleep at night? Likely, he can. He's seen it all ... taken part in most ... received his country's honour in the position he holds. Yet, death duty is hardly battle. Does that steely gaze hide a sinking heart? His posture is not proud today. Crucifying an innocent man doesn't sit well with him. He had heard Pilate declare innocent the man called Jesus. He had seen the governor physically wash his hands of the matter. Yet, here he was overseeing His crucifixion. *Did his hands just tremble?*

From cross to soldiers to sky our eyes flit. There's a storm coming. Not like anything we've seen before. Nothing this day seems like anything we've seen before. Darkness falls at noon, blanketing the cruel scene – the Father giving privacy to His only Son from human gaze. And creation bows before its Creator.

Laughter ceases. Horses whinny. And the strangest sound of all in the bloodied muck of Golgotha are the words of a Roman centurion: 'Truly this was the Son of God!' (Matthew 27:54). Oh, how right he is!

Lord, may we never become familiar with Your sacrifice. May it always cause us to bow in worship. Amen.

25 April

And for fear of him the guards trembled and became like dead men.

Matthew 28:4

Reading: Matthew 28:11–15

The term 'graveyard shift' took on new meaning the night Flavius and the others arrived to guard Jesus' tomb. Who would want to steal *this* body? The man had nothing – neither home nor money.

Yet, after the day they'd had in Jerusalem – crucifixions, earthquakes, black skies the like he'd never seen before, vandalism at the temple – he could believe almost anything. The talk in the barracks was that He had been some sort of miracle-working rabbi; a do-gooding preacher. *Why are the top Jews so worried? Jesus is dead! Surely He can't do them any harm now.* Yet, standing in the dark garden, every innocent rustle sent shivers up his spine. Four hours until relief . . . Surely he could manage that.

Returning for a second guard duty, Flavius was more relaxed. For a whole day all was quiet. Soon the three-day stint would be over, and he could get back to more ordinary duty. There wasn't a body snatcher in sight. Mind you, the pre-dawn shift had never been his favourite.

The shuffling of feet and quiet voices drew closer. The guards stiffened, then relaxed at the sight of a few women approaching. 'They're probably wanting to anoint the body,' someone whispered. Flavius shrugged his shoulders.

'Suddenly there was a great earthquake!' The shaking ground beneath his feet threw Flavius sideways! 'For an angel of the Lord came down from heaven, rolled aside the stone, and sat on it. His face shone like lightning, and his clothing was as white as snow' (Matthew 28:2–4, NLT). The sound of rolling stone was the last thing Flavius heard as the light faded and his body hit the ground.

Lie! They want us to lie about what happened! But we saw it! The angel! The empty tomb! Don't they realize? Jesus is alive! As Flavius and his colleagues reached out their hands to take the bribe money, he heard himself croak, 'No one would believe us . . . it's lie or die!' (Adapted from Matthew 28:1–15.)

Lord Jesus, may I gladly display the evidence of Your resurrection in my life, and never lie to save my reputation or my life. Amen.

26 April

We were buried therefore with him by baptism into death,
in order that, just as Christ was raised from the dead
by the glory of the Father, we too might
walk in newness of life.

Romans 6:4

Reading: Romans 6:1–11

We had a baptism service in church last night. Oh, I do love a baptism! There's something wonderful about watching people profess publicly their faith in Jesus Christ. Seven folk – including one teenager – clearly, if nervously, told a full church how they had been born again and what that has meant to them since. Each one then bravely stepped into the tank, where they were fully immersed and quickly brought to the surface again. Such smiles spread across their faces as the congregation applauded the joyous event. Dare I say it? I sensed heaven's pleasure mix with ours.

God is always pleased with our obedience.

Obedience took Jesus from the courts of heaven to the confines of a tiny body nestled in the arms of a teenage mother. It then propelled Him from the safe family home of Nazareth into the public eye, drawing adulation from the needy and criticism from the religious. But His ultimate obedience to the Father led the sinless Son of God to a cruel death on the cross to pay for our sin (Philippians 2:8). He was obedient so that we could be released from the judgement we deserve. Then He rose from the dead to show us that death is not the end, but that 'we too might walk in newness of life' (Romans 6:4).

Of course, baptism is not essential for salvation. Rather, it is all about obedience to Jesus. The Saviour included it in His final and great commission to the disciples before His ascension. Go ... make disciples ... baptize them ... teach them ... (Matthew 28:19–20).

Is the Lord asking you to do something for Him? It may not be baptism, but whatever it is, imagine the thrill of knowing that you have been obedient ... and have brought delight to His heart. Go on – you know it's worth it!

Lord, open my ears to hear You speak; my heart to obey; my life to follow You completely. Amen.

27 April

And which of you by being anxious
can add a single hour to his span of life?

Matthew 6:27

Reading: John 20:19–21

It was Monday 23 March 2020. People across the UK were gathered around their televisions for a prime-ministerial broadcast that only survivors of the Second World War had previously experienced.

Boris Johnson sat behind the desk at 10 Downing Street, a Union Jack standing proudly behind him, as he announced to the nation, 'You must stay at home . . . you may only leave your home for the following reasons . . .' Fear surfaced as the prime minister went on to list the restrictions that would dominate our lives for a long time to come. Visiting with family and friends was forbidden; shopping was for essentials only; outdoor exercise was permitted for twenty minutes daily. And suddenly, people were fearful of those they met in the street – stepping aside to ensure personal safety.

Stay at Home   Protect the NHS   Save Lives

This became our mantra. Our nation was at war . . . with a virus! We were in lockdown! Shut behind the doors of our homes by something we couldn't see. Never had I sensed such widespread anxiety.

The disciples went into lockdown after Jesus' death. They also shut themselves behind closed doors, but their decision was not caused by the unseen, nor enforced by the government, but 'for fear of the Jewish leaders' (John 20:19, NIVUK). Having seen what hatred could do, and the power their religious leaders had, they were petrified of what might happen to them. And Jesus was dead! He wasn't there to tell them what to do. Every knock on the door filled them with terror.

Thankfully, Jesus didn't have to knock! Suddenly, He stood among them and said, 'Peace be with you!' and showed them His hands and side (John 20:19–20). What a change in atmosphere followed! There is no lockdown where Jesus is. His presence brings peace; His heart love; His words freedom from what troubles us. Anxiety need not be the door that shuts us away from His blessing.

Lord, free me from the anxiety that disturbs the peace You have for me. Amen.

28 April

THINK ON THIS

For from his fullness we have all received,
grace upon grace.

John 1:16

- Read through this verse a number of times – including out loud.
- Write it out, stick it on the fridge, have it on your phone.
- Meditate on the words, then respond in praise.
- Be a doer . . . Serve someone with an act of kindness today.

29 April

And Jesus said, 'Father, forgive them,
for they know not what they do.'
Luke 23:34

Reading: Romans 3:20–24

How could He? How could Jesus ask the Father to forgive when the first searing pains of metal were ripping through His flesh ... when He couldn't hold His head up because if He did the crossbeam would push the thorns deeper into His head ... when His lungs were beginning to burn in their struggle for air? And why, when every second should have been filled with the battle to survive, did Jesus bother to give a thought to those around Him? The soldiers gambling with His clothes? The proud centurion supervising His execution? The scoffer on the adjacent cross? The audience of mockers? The spit hurlers?

How was it that Jesus didn't hate them? That he didn't call down judgement from heaven on them all ... especially the Pharisees slinking nearby? Surely the forgiveness He sought did not include them?

And while the Saviour's eyes could still take in the scene, did His heart hurt to see His friends linger at a distance? Was His prayer for them? The ones He had lived with for more than three years? The men who had hung on His every word? Who had watched Him heal the sick, raise the dead, feed the hungry? The very people He had told the secrets of His heart, to whom He had spoken of the eternal place He was going to – to prepare a place for them? The ones who then ran away, fell asleep and disowned Him when He needed them most?

But wait ...

Could Jesus have been pleading with the Father for you and me? Was His grace stretching forward, through the centuries, to all of us who have sinned? Did His loving thoughts reach to the violent rejecters, the determined sceptics, the mockers, the repugnant persecutors, the fence-sitters, the backsliders?

How could He have prayed that prayer?

Because He is ... Jesus, the One who '... became flesh and dwelt among us ... full of grace and truth' (John 1:14). Grace runs through His veins, both spoken and spilled in abundance from that cross.

Words aren't enough, Lord, to say what my heart feels in the presence of such grace. Accept my humble thanks. Amen.

30 April

'In this world you will have trouble.
But take heart! I have overcome the world.'

John 16:33, NIVUK

Reading: Psalm 34

Have you ever visited Rock Bottom Canyon? It's not somewhere you would deliberately key into your satnav. But you're sure to know the place. You might even be there at this very moment. It feels like you can't sink any lower. That the sun never reaches this far down. Smiling is a distant memory, yet tears have no problem wetting your cheeks in this dark place. You feel completely alone. Pain is your only companion. And strewn all around your feet are broken pieces – shattered shards of a once-good life. *Your* life. Those of us who have visited Rock Bottom Canyon report that you can't see the way ahead. This place of brokenness has no way out – no illuminated sign pointing to the escape route. The only way you can look is up.

And that's good. Because that's exactly where we find rescue, healing and restoration. It's when we look up that we realize we've never been alone. That Jesus has been with us all the time. That He is reaching down to pull us out of this place of despair. And the moment we redirect our gaze, we begin to hear words of hope and healing. He simply asks that we bring the broken pieces with us. After all, repair and restoration are His speciality.

Surely the Japanese method of repairing precious items with gold – Kintsugi – illustrates what Jesus does with His broken people. We prefer to see what's broken returned from an expert with the damage undetectable, as if the breakage never happened. But the Japanese believe that the cracks are part of the item's story and should not be hidden, but made more beautiful.

When Jesus pulls us out of Rock Bottom Canyon, He takes the broken pieces of our lives and glues us back together with His healing and peace. Some cracks may require forgiveness, but not one broken piece is wasted. Each repair is used to show His glory to a hurting world. Each life is cemented together with His love, more beautiful than before.

Lord, I hate the breaking, but I am grateful that You add gold to every repair You make to my broken life. Amen.

May

1 May

'He will quiet *you* with His love,
He will rejoice over you with singing.'

Zephaniah 3:17, NKJV

Reading: Psalm 146:5–9

My mother had a song for every occasion. Where there was something to celebrate or merely the ordinary to-dos of every day, it would be accompanied by a song. Songs for fun and songs for sorrow. We were blessed indeed with a loving family and a house filled with song.

While I don't have the same memory for lyrics as my mother, I have found peace and joy in songs, especially those that minister God's word to my heart. Perhaps more singing was done in my home in the dark recesses of the night than in the daylight hours. When one of the girls was distressed, in pain or recovering from a seizure, I would hold her close, gently stroking her temple and singing to her of Jesus. I doubt it was the quality of my singing that quietened her, but rather the closeness of my presence and the depth of my love as we rocked together in the shadows.

Often, in the darkest of circumstances, I experienced the reality of God's love. When I didn't know where to turn, He was there. When my grief seemed inconsolable, He would whisper His peace in my ear (Isaiah 41:10). Undoubtedly, it was the closeness of His presence and the depth of His love that quietened my soul as He and I rocked together in similar shadows.

Zephaniah broke fifty years of prophetic silence to bring God's message. Distress and despair were the daily companions of the exiled Israelites. With judgement past, God sent them a message of hope and a declaration of His love. He would quiet them with His love, and one day he would rejoice over them with singing.

What a joy to know that the promise still stands. If we stay close enough for His embrace, He will quiet us with His love. And one day, as part of His redeemed bride, He will rejoice over us with singing!

Lord Jesus, I look forward to the day when You return for Your bride. Then we can sing together! Amen.

2 May

He was despised and rejected by men,
a man of sorrows and acquainted with grief,
and as one from whom men hide their faces
he was despised, and we esteemed him not.

Isaiah 53:3

Reading: Psalm 22:6–8

The old children's rhyme, 'Sticks and stones may break my bones, but names can never hurt me', is a nonsense. Name-calling inflicts wounds that humiliate and can cause irreparable damage. It's also the first form of unkindness we learn as children – perhaps even from those who should know better. Comedians habitually use certain place names to produce laughs, reinforcing an unfortunate, and often inaccurate, reputation.

Nazareth had a dubious status. The large number of Gentiles and Zealots living there definitely put it on the wrong side of the tracks, in today's parlance. No strict Jew would want to live there (John 1:46). Jesus' dowdy hometown drew scorn from many quarters – it was indeed a despised and rejected place; an address you wouldn't want to shout about, with a poor and needy population. Adding such a placename to your own name would be folly. Yet that's exactly what Jesus did.

He happily embraced the name 'Jesus of Nazareth'. The Saviour hadn't come to impress. His home address wasn't important. His employment didn't need to be rated by the educated, neither did He dress to impress. He didn't change His name to avoid the embarrassing rumours surrounding His birth. He chose not to hang with the 'right' people or to gain influence with lawmakers, whether religious or civic. Neither money nor fame drew Him, and the opinions of others didn't change what He knew was right.

In fact, all of these things clearly identified Jesus of Nazareth with the despised, the outcasts, the rejected, the poor and the needy. They had only to hear His name, and they knew He would never turn them away. Like them, He had experienced poverty, pain and rejection, just as the prophet Isaiah said He would. Jesus of Nazareth was one of them ... yet, as they came to discover, He was nothing like them – a perfect combination for a Saviour!

Jesus, thank you for becoming like us in our humanity, yet never losing the deity that allowed You to become our Saviour. Amen.

3 May

'Is not this the carpenter, the son of Mary and brother of James and Joses and Judas and Simon?'

Mark 6:3

Reading: Philippians 2:3–7

Jesus the carpenter? Wait a minute. Wasn't the Messiah meant to come from the kingly line of David (Jeremiah 23:5)? Then why was He not born a prince? Why did he not live in a palace? Had it not been prophesied that He would deliver His people (Isaiah 59:20)? Should He not have been a general? The sword His weapon of choice?

It's remarkable, and yet not so unexpected, that Jesus became a labourer. Someone who learned a trade from His earthly father in the same way most sons did in His day. To work with your hands was seen as good, honest work. Creating, building or repairing – a special talent indeed. In many ways this was not new to the One who had created the very wood with which He was working (Colossians 1:16). Or to Him who would one day leave Nazareth's workshop to build God's church (Matthew 16:18). To say nothing of how He repairs the broken of body, heart and soul, making them new again (John 10:10).

Jesus the Carpenter sees the potential in our lives, just as He did with a piece of wood at Joseph's bench. Cutting, chipping, shaping, sanding and polishing our lives to make us into the people He wants us to be. Like wood in the Master Craftsman's hand, we yield to His tools of rebuke, judgement, forgiveness, design and mending. Each instrument carefully applied where needed. Always used with love and patience, Jesus the Carpenter never leaves a piece of work incomplete. He always finishes what He starts (Philippians 1:6). And His plan for each of us is only ever for our good (Jeremiah 29:11).

If we could examine the hands of this artisan, we would see the marks and callouses of a workman. Yet, the same Carpenter who shapes and repairs our lives also bears the scars of His greatest work: our redemption.

Dearest Saviour, I give my life and heart into Your skilful hands. Do what is needed for me to be shaped into Your likeness, that I might glorify Your name. Amen.

4 May

'The Son of Man has come eating and drinking,
and you say, "Look at him! A glutton and a drunkard,
a friend of tax collectors and sinners!"'

Luke 7:34

Reading: Luke 15:1–7

'How many of your friends or acquaintances are not Christians?'

The preacher's question disturbed me. I was so busy with family and church that I had surrounded myself with people who thought like me. Friends who could encourage and pray with me. People I could share my heart with. Safe people. But in that moment I couldn't think of one person in answer to the preacher's question.

What would you do if you were invited to the home of someone with a dubious reputation? Or what about having coffee with that person from the office with questionable business dealings? Do you fear the gossips? Are you concerned that association with certain people might damage your reputation or, worse still, your Christian testimony? Would you rather keep your distance than deal with the critics?

Jesus fell foul of those same accusations. The wagging finger of the religious elite dared to question whose company He kept. What they didn't take time to notice was that Jesus neither condoned nor endorsed the sin of His hosts. In fact, His presence resulted in changed lives. Take Matthew. When Jesus called the former tax collector to be his disciple, Matthew couldn't wait to introduce his friends to Jesus (Mark 2:14–17). Then there was Zacchaeus. When Jesus invited Himself to this hated man's house for dinner, Zacchaeus' modus operandi changed from theft to generosity, from fraud to honesty (Luke 19:1–9).

When you think about it, where would any of us be if Jesus were not the friend of sinners? How could my heart have been cleansed, or my sins forgiven, if He had not shown me the awfulness of my sin in His sacrifice for me? For 'while we were still sinners, Christ died for us' (Romans 5:8).

At a meeting, missionary doctor Helen Roseveare spoke of a college student who had built a bridge of friendship to her heart, and then Jesus walked over that bridge. Maybe it's time we started building!

Lord Jesus, make me the kind of friend who makes a difference in the lives of others. Amen.

5 May

THINK ON THIS

'And there is salvation in no one else,
for there is no other name under heaven given
among men by which we must be saved.'

Acts 4:12

- Read through this verse a number of times – including out loud.
- Write it out, stick it on the fridge, have it on your phone.
- Meditate on the words, then respond in praise.
- Take steps to allow God's word to change you: perhaps . . . repent, forgive, love.

6 May

My little children, I am writing these things to you
so that you may not sin. But if anyone does sin,
we have an advocate with the Father,
Jesus Christ the righteous.

1 John 2:1

Reading: Romans 8:1–6

Injustice strikes at the heart of who we are. We are outraged when we read of those who have languished in prison for years for something they did not do. Even ill-founded accusations can cause devastation in health, reputation, relationships and business. For Christians they can damage our testimony, split churches and destroy ministry. We need to be careful what we say about others. Accusatory words should never be used without the evidence to back them up.

Guilty!

I can't imagine what that verdict sounds like when pronounced in a court of law. True, there are some who always blame circumstances or poor advocacy for their fate, but there are those who accept – deep down – that they have committed a wrong worthy of that verdict.

Guilty!

We may never stand in an earthly court before a bewigged judge or do 'time' at His Majesty's pleasure. But all of us who breathe God's good air will one day hear the Supreme Judge of eternity pronounce us guilty and worthy of the most horrendous punishment imaginable: separation from Him. And it won't be because of false accusation or an incompetent lawyer. The accusation is correct, 'for all have sinned and fall short of the glory of God' (Romans 3:23), and the verdict will not be unjust because 'the wages of sin is death' (6:23).

We have nothing with which to plead our case. We cannot earn, buy or achieve forgiveness from our sin. There is no way to redeem our souls from the judgement of a holy God. Except, that is, for our Saviour, as 'the blood of Jesus his Son cleanses us from all sin' (1 John 1:7). Therefore, when I stand before God the Judge, I have a righteous Advocate – a lawyer, a representative – who presents His own death as a substitute for what I deserve . . . and I am forgiven, pardoned, set free! Praise to heaven's Advocate!

Lord Jesus, even now You stand before Your Father in heaven when I sin. Thankfully, He sees You and not me. Amen.

7 May

He who is the blessed and only Potentate,
the King of kings and Lord of lords,
who alone has immortality, dwelling in unapproachable
light, whom no man has seen or can see,
to whom *be* honor and everlasting power.

1 Timothy 6:15–16, NKJV

Reading: Hebrews 2:5–9

At times, Paul could be really wordy. But in this case I'm glad he was, for the description of Jesus in this first letter to his mentee, Timothy, takes my breath away. 'Jesus of Nazareth', 'carpenter', 'Son of Man' and the many other titles given to Jesus are undoubtedly amazing, and make us stop and think, but the images conjured up by Paul's words leave us in no doubt as to who Jesus was to the early church, and who He is for eternity.

The NKJV's use of the word 'Potentate' has the effect of wrapping up in three syllables what volumes could never achieve. Potentate. The One who possesses power. In this case not a self-obsessed dictator, but a loving, giving God. In a world of emperor worship, Paul wanted his readers to discover Who had the real power: the One who was above all kings and lords. The One Who will never die; whose magnificence is bathed in supernatural glory; who cannot be seen by the natural eye, but whose power is everlasting and deserving of all honour and praise.

As the inhabitants of Ephesus daily passed the massive statues of muscular Roman gods and emperors, Paul's words rendered these fakes insignificant. They stood in cold, lifeless stone. Dead or dying. While nothing and no one could ever match Jesus – the I AM of Scripture – the resurrected, living Saviour, and no sculpture could ever do justice to the one true Potentate, neither did God permit the worship of idols (Leviticus 26:1). This King of kings was looking for a different kind of worship (John 4:24). Neither would this Lord topple at the whim of a nation, nor this God crumble when the earth shook.

For the only Potentate will one day return for His church, and on that day He will award a crown of righteousness to those who have crowned Him King (2 Timothy 4:8). Do I hear a hallelujah?

I bow before Your Majesty with reverence and delight. Amen.

8 May

'Behold, my servant whom I have chosen,
my beloved with whom my soul is well pleased.'
Matthew 12:18
(echoing Isaiah 42:1)

Reading: Mark 10:41–45

Many biblical teachings are paradoxical. They quite literally turn the accepted upside down, and in doing so reveal great truth. 'A servant is not greater than his master,' Jesus said (John 13:16). And this after humbling Himself to the servant's role of washing the disciples' feet. Jesus the Master became the servant (13:4–10), elevating the lowest of service into the spiritual (Mark 9:41).

In the Old Testament, the most honourable title given to anyone was that of 'servant of God'. Those we would easily identify as the heroes in Israel's story were called servants – a name as far away from greatness and accomplishment as you could imagine: Abraham (Psalm 105:42); Moses (Exodus 14:31); Joshua (Joshua 1:1); Caleb (Numbers 14:24); Elijah (2 Kings 10:10); David (1 Kings 8:66). Their role was not to become great leaders or prophets, but to do as God asked them.

Obedience is the quintessential of good servanthood. Is it any wonder that this title was applied to Jesus – the One whose very existence was to do 'the will of him who sent me' (John 6:38)? Moses was the servant who liberated the enslaved Israelites out of Egypt and took them into the old covenant with God. Jesus became the greater servant, tasked with rescuing the whole world from sin. He 'emptied himself, by taking the form of a servant ... becoming obedient to the point of death, even death on a cross' (Philippians 2:7–8), and in doing so brought about the new covenant.

There was no job He did not do; no place He would not go; no 'untouchable' on whom He refused to lay His hands; no sinner He ever turned away; no demon He dared not face; no sickness He would not cure; no company He thought beneath Him; no dwelling unsuitable for this Servant of God – this King of kings.

Surely, if we are to leave an indelible mark on this world that will count for eternity it will be through service ... nothing more.

Lord Jesus, forgive me when I chase after recognition. Help me instead to choose obedient service. Amen.

9 May

'Nevertheless, I tell you the truth:
it is to your advantage that I go away, for if I do not
go away, the Helper will not come to you.
But if I go, I will send him to you.'

John 16:7

Reading: Acts 1:6–11

At I write this, I'm sitting in a holiday apartment in Germany listening to church bells ringing in celebration of Ascension Day. The sound echoes across brilliant blue skies with such a sense of joy that it makes the hairs rise on the back of my neck and fills my heart with praise.

Jesus has been reunited with the Father!

Thirty-three years before His ascension, the skies above Bethlehem were filled with music as the angels announced His birth – something we attempt to emulate each Christmas. How wonderful that God gave us the gift of music and singing for the purpose of praise, and also for the good of our own hearts.

But there was no singing at the cross. The only worship came from the lips of a Roman centurion declaring Jesus' deity (Matthew 27:54), proving that praise can happen even in the darkest of days.

For the early disciples, fear and confusion followed Jesus' resurrection, praise coming eventually. Yet, for us, Easter Sunday is probably the greatest opportunity for celebration in Christendom, declaring as the angels did: 'He is not here, for he has risen' (28:6).

Yet, as I listen to the bells ringing across the land here in Germany, I can't help but wonder what sound filled heaven when Jesus returned to the Father. What a reunion that must have been! What delight in the Father's heart. What joy for the Son in knowing He had finished the work He had been given to do (John 17:4). It is one of those times I wish I'd been a fly on heaven's walls, so to speak.

Ascension Day allowed Pentecost to happen, for the Spirit could not have been sent unless Jesus had left (16:7). And Jesus could not have prepared a place for us if He had remained (14:2). So, as the bells ring out, I choose to praise God for this glorious day.

Lord Jesus, I await Your return, when the trumpets will sound and all earth will bow before You. Amen.

10 May

The Author of life.
Acts 3:15

Reading: Acts 3:12–16

Sometimes just a single name or title hooks you and reels you in. Why? Why was that particular name given to that person? Was it to carry on a family tradition or is it a term of endearment, a nickname?

The names and titles of Jesus are as heavy with meaning as flowers weighed down by rain after a storm. No ancestral label or parental preference for Jesus. His names carry profound implications for us all; to meet every need and circumstance of life.

The title 'author' is one that particularly interests me, for unsurprising reasons. I think I was on my sixth book before I dared to call myself an author. The description of 'I write books' seemed less weighty for me to carry. I mean, authors are famous and make plenty of money! When I realized that neither was true – apart from for the very few – I reluctantly agreed to the tag. After all, an author is simply someone who sits in front of a blank screen and fills it with words, hoping a reader will be enticed into the story. We are creatives, making something from nothing.

The Greek word for author – *archegos* – has other meanings attributed to it. Prince. Captain. Pioneer. Whichever word you use, the meaning is the same: 'Someone who starts something up, opens the way, and then leads that others may follow.' The translation 'Pioneer' is the one favoured by many because it suits Jesus so well. He is the Pioneer of life (Acts 3:15) – opening up new life for us through salvation. The Pioneer of faith – teaching us not to look back but to forge ahead as He leads (Philippians 3:13). The Pioneer of eternity – taking us into the forever when we leave the here and now (3:20).

But I have to finish by using the word 'author', because we read in Hebrews 12:2 that Jesus is 'the author and finisher of our faith' (NKJV). What Jesus starts, He finishes. He will never abandon us. We can safely follow Him, knowing that when we break through the finishing tape, He'll be just a few steps ahead.

Trailblazing Saviour, where You lead me, I will follow. Amen.

11 May

'Those who are well have no need of a physician,
but those who are sick. I have not come to call the
righteous but sinners to repentance.'

Luke 5:31–32

Reading: Matthew 9:9–13

To be both a good Jew and a good doctor was a contradiction in terms. A Jewish student of medicine was not allowed to touch the dead (Numbers 19:11), making studying anatomy extremely difficult. His knowledge and expertise came from examining only the living. The rabbis did allow the 'healing' of the sick, but not the touching of the dead.

Jesus never claimed to be a physician, although He healed many (Matthew 4:23). In fact, He endorsed the work of doctors in today's verse by confirming that the sick needed them. Jesus' skill, however, lay in the healing of the soul, hence His turning of the conversation to people's spiritual sickness. Though the healing of the soul did require a similar approach to that of the doctor.

- While the doctor seeks to diagnose and cure a person's ailments, the Great Physician immediately identifies the soul's sickness of sin and is the only One who can provide a cure.
- The doctor usually sees the patient at their worst, some conditions rendering the sufferer deformed and rejected by others. The Great Physician is repulsed by sin but never turns His back on the sinner – never sends away those seeking the cure.
- Once the diagnosis is made, the doctor does everything in his power to make the person well again. But the Great Physician always has the perfect, permanent cure for what ails the soul . . . salvation through faith, made possible by Christ's death on the cross. No other doctor has a remedy for what afflicts the soul, but we can rest easy, for Jesus – the Great Physician – has the remedy ready at hand. And it is never in short supply.

While diagnosis and treatment are needed for both body and soul, neither can be helped or healed if the sufferer doesn't seek help. Neglecting either could end in death. But death of the soul is totally avoidable – the Great Physician awaits the patient's call for help.

Thank you, Jesus, that You continue to heal the sin-sick soul. Amen.

12 May

THINK ON THIS

'For this people's heart has grown dull,
and with their ears they can barely hear,
and their eyes they have closed,
lest they should see with their eyes and
hear with their ears and understand
with their heart, and turn,
and I would heal them.'

Matthew 13:15

- Read through this verse a number of times – including out loud.
- Write it out, stick it on the fridge, have it on your phone.
- Meditate on the words, then respond in praise.
- Encourage someone by sharing this verse with them today.

13 May

Now may the God of peace himself sanctify you
completely, and may your whole spirit
and soul and body be kept blameless
at the coming of our Lord Jesus Christ.

1 Thessalonians 5:23

Reading: Hebrews 4:14–16

After a career in nursing that spanned more than thirty years and covered several disciplines, I am still fascinated by the medicine that facilitates the body's ability to heal and recover.

The Great Physician undoubtedly specializes in sin-sickness, and His cure is complete. But there are other soul diseases that He addresses – situations that disturb our peace and restrict the healthy growth He wants to see in our lives. There are no spiritual ailments that we cannot take to Him. The Physician's office is always open to deal with:

- **Short-sightedness.** Too often we see no further than ourselves, our needs, our desires. Jesus wants to expand our sight and to develop our spiritual vision. 'Look, I tell you,' Jesus says, 'lift up your eyes, and see that the fields are white for harvest' (John 4:35).
- **Deafness.** Our world is filled with the kind of noise that distracts us and deafens us to God's voice. Jesus fine-tunes our ears to recognize His voice, enabling us to follow Him (John 10:27) and to hear Him speak through His word (Luke 11:28).
- **Worry.** Jesus frequently rebuked the disciples for worrying rather than trusting (Matthew 14:31). This is not how Jesus wants us to live. Instead, He counsels us to 'seek first the kingdom of God' (6:31–33).
- **Lameness.** Jesus provides the light that ensures we do not stumble (John 8:12), and that's where we should walk. It is darkness that causes us to stumble.
- **Bitterness.** Nothing spoils like bitterness. It is destructive and chokes the life out of what is good. The writer to the Hebrews instructs us not to let it take root, but also that we need to obtain grace to deal with it (Hebrews 12:15). And isn't grace the most prescribed medicine on the Great Physician's prescription pad?

Lord, may I deal quickly with what ails my soul, that I might be spiritually fit for Your service. Amen.

14 May

Christ Jesus himself being the cornerstone.

Ephesians 2:20

Reading: Ephesians 2:17–22

It is likely that Paul would have heard from others about the first time Jesus was described as the cornerstone prophesied by Isaiah (28:16). Jesus Himself had declared it to the Jewish establishment, which caused ridicule and accusations of blasphemy. In the context of Matthew 21:42–44, Jesus was affirming that, because of Israel's rejection of Him as the Messiah (cornerstone), judgement was coming. And it did. In August AD 70, Jerusalem fell to the Romans and the temple was destroyed, fulfilling Jesus' prophecy that not one stone would be left standing – including the cornerstone.

In biblical times, a cornerstone was used in building projects to guide the workers and to determine the rest of the construction. The cornerstone had to be the largest and strongest, for if it was removed or damaged the rest of the structure would also fall.

When Paul wrote to the early church about Jesus as the Cornerstone, he was speaking about a completely different kind of building. This was a 'living' structure made up of believers and followers of Jesus Christ. The church – the household of God – was the new temple within which God would dwell. As the cornerstone, Jesus is the standard by which we live. Our guide. Our strength. The One who not only holds the church together but holds each individual stone in place. Peter writes, 'You yourselves like living stones are being built up as a spiritual house, to be a holy priesthood, to offer spiritual sacrifices acceptable to God through Jesus Christ' (1 Peter 2:5). In this holy building, God 'will make justice the line, and righteousness the plumb line' (Isaiah 28:17).

Attempting to build differently from God is foolish in the extreme. Self-righteousness – the ultimate rejection of the Cornerstone – led to the destruction of the temple and will also lead to our fall. Without the stability of the true Cornerstone, all other life structures will crumble. Let's choose to build on Christ today.

Just like the man who built on the rock, Lord, I choose to build on You, the immoveable One. Amen.

15 May

This makes Jesus the guarantor of a better covenant.

Hebrews 7:22

Reading: Philemon 1:8–19

Onesimus had vowed he would never sail this stretch of water again after he had crossed it as a runaway slave. His master had been good to him; he had trusted him. But the young man had wanted freedom, and left Colossae with haste. Rome was his destination. Surely he would never be found there.

But dreams have a habit of being only that: dreams. Rome didn't deliver on freedom – only poverty and hopelessness. Until, that is, Onesimus met up with a prisoner called Paul. He taught the young runaway about true freedom – forgiveness from sin – including his own. And about liberty that was found in a different kind of service – that of following Messiah Jesus. Now only one thing kept him awake at night: Philemon. Onesimus knew he would never experience true freedom until he returned to face Philemon and ask for forgiveness.

As the sea breeze cooled Onesimus's cheeks, he patted the leather pouch attached to his belt. It contained a letter from Paul to his old friend. (Onesimus couldn't believe it when he heard that Paul actually knew his master, Philemon!) But this was more than a letter. It was a document of guarantee. Paul was offering to be Onesimus's guarantor. Whatever debt the runaway owed Philemon, Paul pledged to pay in full. Onesimus' debt was cancelled by the surety from Paul, and for the first time in his life his future looked bright.

Yet this amazing story of grace is as nothing compared with our divine Guarantor, Jesus:

> He paid a debt He did not owe,
> I owed a debt I could not pay.
> I needed someone to wash my sins away.
> And now I sing a brand-new song –
> Amazing Grace!
> Christ Jesus paid a debt that I could never pay.
> (Author unknown)

Thank you, Jesus! My debt is paid. My future is secure. What more can I say? You are simply the best! Amen.

16 May

For I can do everything through Christ,
who gives me strength.

Philippians 4:13, NLT

Reading: Psalm 84:5–7

The image of Jesus created by artists, historians, writers and film-makers is often so far from the truth as to be ridiculous. Their desire to portray a gentle other-worldliness, acceptable to the masses, has produced a false picture of a weak Christ. The reality is very different.

It took supernatural strength to:

- willingly give up heaven and be confined to human flesh (John 1:14);
- be subject to human parents when He knew where He had come from (Luke 2:51);
- live in homeless poverty even though he owns 'the cattle on a thousand hills' (Psalm 50:10);
- endure ridicule, abuse and rejection from those He had come to save (Luke 17:25);
- face injustice, even though He will one day judge all people (Acts 17:31);
- suffer, bleed and die for a thankless humanity, who He came to give eternal life (Romans 5:8).

This is not a picture of weakness, but of strength. And it doesn't even begin to demonstrate Christ's creative, healing, transformative and resurrection power. Neither does it explain the authority He wields against the powers of darkness in our world. We cannot conjure up this kind of strength on our own. Daily workouts at the gym won't do it for us!

Thankfully, our mandate is not to rule the world but to live godly lives in it (Titus 2:12). This life is only achievable with the kind of strength Jesus willingly gives to those who gladly trust in His power alone, who lay down meagre attempts at self-sufficiency. Once we own up to our inability to live the Christian life by ourselves, we receive all we need to empower us to live as we should. Yes, even in the face of difficulty, distress or despair.

When faced with his own human weakness, the Lord told Paul: 'My grace is sufficient for you, for my power is made *perfect* in weakness' (2 Corinthians 12:9, emphasis mine). Perfect. Complete. Nothing else required. Absolutely everything we need for all situations. Jesus has it covered, so we don't have to!

Lord, I need Your strength today. Thank you that Your grace is sufficient and Your power is perfect. Amen.

17 May

Jesus Christ is the same yesterday
and today and forever.

Hebrews 13:8

Reading: Hebrews 1:8–13

'I have a bank card now, Granny.'

I could hardly believe my ears. Surely our granddaughter was too young to have a bank card. Yet, here she was telling us how her pocket money is transferred on to the card, along with money she earns from doing chores, etc. Her mum has it connected to a phone app, meaning she can see when and where the money is spent. While I was taking it all in, this eleven-year-old concluded, 'It teaches me about managing my money.'

Oh, how things have changed!

Sometimes we're not good with change, are we? Probably because we take comfort from knowing exactly what to expect in certain situations and with certain people. Confidence in another grows with trust. Trust happens with consistency. It's difficult to rely on someone who is always changing their mind.

So it is with Jesus. He remains the same . . . in every way . . . every day. The word 'same' in today's verse means 'unchanging' – not in a boring or stubborn sense, but in the 'I-don't-move-the-goalposts' kind of way. Jesus is consistent in His immovability towards His plan for humanity, and for us individually. What He has said in the past, is doing in us today and has prepared for our future, can be relied on completely. No ifs, no buts, no maybes. He remains unchanging (James 1:17).

Yesterday proves it. The history. The fulfilled prophecy. The determination to complete the plan, even within the fragility of human flesh. Right from creation (Genesis 1:3) through to the cross (John 19:30) He refused to waver, for His eyes were fixed on 'the joy that was set before him' (Hebrews 12:2).

Today verifies it. Yesterday brought it to us, but it is in today that we who follow Christ experience His forgiveness and all that is involved in walking with Him. The 'same' of all that had been promised is our experience today.

Forever is where our hope lies and will be realized. Because He is the 'same', we can have complete confidence. The evidence is irrefutable!

Unchanging One, whose love never fails and promises never falter, I stand in awe, looking forward to the 'forever' You have planned. Amen.

18 May

And he is before all things,
and in him all things hold together

Colossians 1:17

Reading: 2 Corinthians 4:7–10, 16–18

Even the strongest among us is breakable.

Wealth, influence, power and status provide no protection against what shatters lives. When everything lies in pieces at our feet, the realization hits that we can't hold it all together by ourselves. We need a Sustainer. One who gives the protection and encouragement necessary for us to get up again. One who puts us, and holds us, together when we are at the end of ourselves. One who wraps His blanket of comfort and love around our brokenness and assures us that we are not alone (Isaiah 43:2). This battle is not unwinnable – not with Jesus by our side.

When I buy something, particularly something electrical or technical, I always check out the manufacturer's guarantee. What happens if something goes wrong? How can I get it fixed if it breaks? What should I do if it doesn't work as promised? I should take it back to the manufacturer. The one who put it together in the first place is best qualified to repair the damage.

We can stick all the Band Aids we like on to our broken lives and hearts, but they will eventually come undone. Human resilience only goes so far. Only the Creator can mend His creation. And the same God who aligns the planets holds us in the palms of His hands. He sustains all things by the word of His power (Hebrews 1:3), using grace as His healing balm.

Grace is there 'on the side of the road, in the darkness, amid all the trouble and pain – to sustain us,' says John Piper:

> Not grace to bar what is not bliss,
>   Nor flight from all distress,
> But this, the grace that orders our trouble and pain,
>   And then in the darkness is there to sustain.[19]

Jesus, Saviour, I may not understand the darkness of the night, but I sense Your presence and grace in it. And I know that Your sovereign plan is always, only, best for my life. Amen.

19 May

THINK ON THIS

'But you will receive power
when the Holy Spirit has come upon you,
and you will be my witnesses in Jerusalem
and in all Judea and Samaria, and
to the end of the earth.'

Acts 1:8

- Read through this verse a number of times – including out loud.
- Write it out, stick it on the fridge, have it on your phone.
- Meditate on the words, then respond in praise.
- Be a doer . . . Serve someone with an act of kindness today.

20 May

They were completely amazed. 'How can this be?'
they exclaimed. 'These people are all from Galilee,
and yet we hear them speaking in our
own native languages!'

Acts 2:7–8, NLT

Reading: Acts 2:1–12

'You nailed Jesus to the cross! With the help of the Romans, you killed Him!'

The lad almost fainted as Peter's words hit the listening crowd. *What are you doing, Peter?* He had been thrilled the day Peter and the other disciples returned from Galilee. He had thought he would never see his hero again. Big Peter. Strong Peter. Outspoken Peter. Well . . . outspoken until they dragged Jesus away.

'Death couldn't keep hold of the One you crucified!' Peter's words momentarily broke through the lad's fear. The thoughts of that weekend still tormented him. He couldn't point an accusing finger at Peter for running away - hadn't he run away when the guards arrested Jesus in the garden that night? Even now the memory flushed his teenage cheeks.

'God raised Jesus from the dead!' Peter's words dragged him back from his thoughts. 'We saw Him for ourselves!' Lifting his head, the boy, not quite a man, still couldn't believe what he was witnessing. *We all hid away in my family's upper room. The door was securely bolted because we were so afraid! What's happening, Peter? Why aren't you afraid any more?* On the edge of the crowd, he saw the very men who had spent weeks searching for the body of Jesus. *Ha!* He wanted to shout. He wanted to tell them Peter was right. *Jesus is alive! I saw Him too! In my own house!*

And the strength that had drained from him when he saw Jesus die began to rise again in the young lad's heart. Peter had returned from Galilee, even though the lad thought he never would, and told him that Jesus had ascended to His Father, but had instructed them to wait. To wait for the promised gift – the Holy Spirit – who would fill them with the power they needed for the mission Jesus was giving them.

Is this it? Is this why Peter is no longer afraid? Is this why he's preaching like . . . like Jesus?
(Adapted from Acts 2.)

Come, Holy Spirit, fill my life with the power it lacks that I too might powerfully speak of Jesus. Amen.

21 May

Peter's words pierced their hearts,
and they said to him and to the other apostles,
'Brothers, what should we do?'

Acts 2:37, NLT

Reading: Acts 2:36–41

I clearly remember the night my own heart was pierced by what happened at Calvary.

I, too, was like those gathered around Peter on the day of Pentecost. Religious. Regularly at a place of worship. Lived as best I could. Not outwardly rebellious. Liked to be seen with the 'right' crowd. Compliant with the law.

Then one particular evening, while hiding in a crowd, I was challenged by someone who had also been with Jesus. Not in the same way Peter had, but every bit as real. After the young man told his captive audience how Jesus had changed his life, he went on to talk about Jesus dying on the cross. Blunter and more descriptive than I'd been used to in my quiet, inoffensive church, I, like Peter's audience, was taken aback by what I heard.

The 'this Jesus, whom you crucified' (Acts 2:36, NLT) is brought right up to date for us as, 'He himself bore our sins in his body on the tree' (1 Peter 2:24).

I was shocked! I'd never dreamt that Jesus' death on the cross was so personal. That He *had to* die so I could be forgiven. I thought I was all right. That going to church was enough of a nod to God to show Him I was a pretty good teenager. That to be called a sinner was for those bad folk my parents had warned me to stay away from.

My heart was pierced – just like those in Peter's crowd. My question was exactly theirs: 'What shall we do?' (Acts 2:37).

Later that night – broken by the vision of the cross – I did in response what the apostle instructed (2:38). I repented of my sins and received forgiveness from the One who had been wounded for me (Isaiah 53:3).

Has your heart ever been pierced by Christ's sacrifice for you? Why not look to Calvary today?

Lord Jesus, may I never become familiar with Your sacrifice. Thank you for the cross. Amen.

22 May

'So if the Son sets you free,
you will be free indeed.'

John 8:36

Reading: John 8:31–36

The journey home was like so many before: guilt, remorse and longing that he could be free: free from the inability to control his life; free from his sin. Stinking with drink and dope, Ricky sat on his sofa, weeping over the life he had lived. Shame and misery had brought him so low that he didn't know where to turn. It all spilled out in a verbal torrent of genuine repentance and a pleading with God that found its way to the courts of heaven.

'God help me! You've got to help me!' And that night, Ricky's cry was heard.

After so many anguished tears, Ricky was surprised that he had slept. As he lay in the silence, he had no idea what had happened to him. He only knew that he felt different. The constant turmoil in his heart had stilled . . . a comforting presence filled every space. And he no longer felt guilty. Instead, he felt forgiven, and free!

Jumping out of bed, he ran to the kitchen. Down the plughole went the drink. Then he surprised himself by destroying the dope and dumping it in the bin. He had never done that before! And as the day passed into another night's restful sleep, his comfort didn't have to come from a bottle.

He couldn't wait to tell his mates that he was now a new person; a follower of Jesus. Unfortunately, the men at work took bets on how long it would last – especially as the weekend approached. But Ricky didn't care. He was experiencing first-hand what Jesus promised in John's Gospel: '[When] the Son sets you free, you will be free indeed.'

Friday night arrived, and while the men in his local talked all night about Ricky 'getting religion', his seat remained empty. And hell groaned. The victory had been won and another prisoner had been released![20]

Thank you, Jesus, that while every story is different, You are still changing lives. Only Your Spirit can give us the power we need to live as we should. Amen.

23 May

Jesus said to him, 'I am the way,
and the truth, and the life.
No one comes to the Father except through me.'

John 14:6

Reading: Romans 8:18, 24–28

I think it's fair to say that we can bear most things if we know that the outcome will be worth it. When Jesus announced Himself as the only way to God, and to an eternity with Himself, He was speaking to a bunch of confused men who had problems accepting that He would soon leave them.

What will happen to us when He's gone? How will we reach the place Jesus said He was going to make ready for us? How will we know what's right?

Trust was key. But wait, hadn't Jesus said 'I am the truth' right in the middle of this trio of truths? After three years with Jesus, the disciples had already proved that He spoke and lived truth. Surely, with all that He was telling them now, they had a solid foundation to work on? The empty tomb built on that. Time with the resurrected Jesus cemented their belief, while His ascension took them up another level. But it was the coming of the Holy Spirit that ultimately propelled the building of personal faith heavenward. Pentecost changed them. The Holy Spirit's arrival confirmed Jesus as the only way to God, the truth to clear their confusion, and the only One who could give them a new, abundant life.

Ricky's story in yesterday's entry told of the catastrophe alcohol and drugs had caused in his life. Sadly, it's a story that could be multiplied many times. So much heartache. So much addiction. Lives destroyed, with little hope for the future, were it not for Jesus.

Ricky found new life in Jesus when he thought his own was pointless. He found a strength to deal with his addiction that he had never experienced before. And he discovered that what lay ahead was worth the difficult road he had yet to travel. But this was one road he wouldn't have to walk alone ... Jesus had promised.

Jesus, thank you that I can always trust Your words and walk Your way with confidence. Amen.

24 May

Again Jesus spoke to them, saying,
'I am the light of the world.
Whoever follows me will not walk in darkness,
but will have the light of life.'

John 8:12

Reading: Matthew 5:14–16

I am a townie, so I had never experienced proper darkness until I visited the jungle area on the Burma–Thailand (now Myanmar–Thailand) border. Neither did I realize how noisy and frightening night could be.

In our remote guesthouse the electricity was switched off at 9 p.m., and the term 'plunged into darkness' took on a whole new meaning. That posed more than the usual problems. The night supervisor laughed when I reported that a chameleon had attached itself to the wall of my room, saying how lucky I was: 'No mosquitoes!' I couldn't sleep a wink, what with the monster with the rolling eyes and the incredible noise from the surrounding forest!

Imagine, a grown woman afraid of the dark! Well, more afraid of what lurked in the shadows – perhaps something that might harm me. After a very expensive call home to my rather surprised husband, and a conversation that helped me to 'see' in the dark, he prayed with me, and eventually I fell asleep. The sun rose just before I did, and in the light, life took on a more comfortable glow. My room-mate lizard had gone, and peace reigned once more.

Yet, there is a darkness to fear more than the blackness of any night, which no candle of self-righteousness or torch of good works can dispel. For 'Satan, who is the god of this world, has blinded the minds of those who don't believe. They are unable to see the glorious light of the Good News' (2 Corinthians 4:4, NLT). How awful that darkness is!

Only Jesus – the Light of the world – can show us the way out of sin's darkness. Only He can bring us into the light that gives both eternal life and light for the life we have now. We don't need to stumble on in the darkness. Instead, we can walk in the light . . . and *with* the Light! What a difference that makes to life's journey.

Lord, it's now my time to shine. Help me reflect Your grace, love and truth to others. Amen.

25 May

'I am the door. If anyone enters by me,
he will be saved and will go in and out
and find pasture.'

John 10:9

Reading: John 10:1–10

Jesus knew about doors. He was a carpenter, after all. Doors have three main purposes: to provide an entrance, an exit and a means of protection to a building and its occupants. I'm sure Jesus constructed or repaired many when He worked alongside Joseph.

While visiting the larger houses in Palestine, Jesus would have seen the high wall around the courtyard, which became the night-time fold where the household sheep were brought for protection. There was only one door, managed by a gatekeeper. Family, visitors and sheep all had to enter the same way. Only thieves would dare scale the wall. Interestingly, Jesus didn't call Himself the gatekeeper. He said, 'I am the door' – the very access to home and security.

The ancients believed there was a dome-like structure covering the earth, behind which was heaven, where there was a door that allowed God to send things to earth, like the manna from heaven during the desert wanderings (Psalm 78:23–25). They believed the door was also the way to reach God, perhaps by something like the ladder in Jacob's dream (Genesis 28:12). Therefore, when Jesus spoke of Himself as 'the door' in John 10:9, it was an analogy they understood. Only this time He was not speaking of vivid imaginings, but of reality.

He declared Himself to be:

- the place of entry into God's kingdom;
- the provider of all we need for salvation, and for satisfaction in life;
- the security against the enemy of our soul, who seeks only to kill and destroy.

What a remarkable statement! Jesus – the Door – is not only the means through which salvation comes to us, but through this Door we get to glimpse heaven until the day we arrive through the Only Entrance there is.

Thank you, Lord Jesus, that You are the Door – the only way through which we find salvation and all that means. Your word is clear. Help me to spread it to those who attempt to climb up another way. Amen.

26 May

THINK ON THIS

Therefore God has highly exalted him
and bestowed on him the name that is above every name,
so that at the name of Jesus every knee should bow,
in heaven and on earth and under the earth.

Philippians 2:9–10

- Read through these verses a number of times – including out loud.
- Write them out, stick them on the fridge, have them on your phone.
- Meditate on the words, then respond in praise.
- Take steps to allow God's word to change you: perhaps . . . repent, forgive, love.

27 May

Jesus said to her, 'I am the resurrection and the life.
Whoever believes in me, though he die,
yet shall he live, and everyone who lives and
believes in me shall never die. Do you believe this?'

John 11:25–26

Reading: 1 John 5:11–13

I was a young teenager when I first encountered death – that of my grandmother. I also remember my first death in nursing. Of course, I cannot forget the death of our first child, followed ten years later by that of our third, and the impact that had on my life and in our family. You will have your own stories. But one thing is sure, each of us will experience death and its accompanying sorrow. And one day each of us will face death personally.

The doctrine of the final resurrection, so fundamental to Christian faith, seems like a distant event for those looking for comfort now. Yet, when Jesus met Martha after Lazarus' death (John 11:17–44), He makes a statement concerning Himself that is life-altering for all of us. When He said, 'I am the resurrection and the life' (11:25), Jesus was changing the event into a person – Himself. He was announcing Himself as not merely the life-giver, but the Life itself. Therefore, death has no power over Him or those who follow His call to believe: 'Whoever believes in me, though he die, yet shall he live, and everyone who lives and believes in me shall never die' (11:26).

Jesus declares that heaven is not for the dying . . . it is for the living! Those living in Him. Jesus is the only reality that brings hope and comfort now, but more so for each of us who wait to enter heaven through Jesus, our Resurrection. Life will not have ended, but will continue in its fullest sense – beyond what we could ever imagine (1 Corinthians 2:9).

'Weep not. I shall not die but live; and, as I leave the land of the dying, I trust to see the blessings of the Lord in the land of the living' (Edward the Confessor's last words).

Lord of life, thank you that death is swallowed up in victory! I eagerly await what lies beyond the Door. Amen.

28 May

Jesus said to them, 'I am the bread of life;
whoever comes to me shall not hunger,
and whoever believes in me shall never thirst.'

John 6:35

Reading: John 6:25–34

Bread. We know it as a staple. You will see it at the top of most shopping lists. Yet, in our culture, with so much available food, bread is not as essential for life as it is in Majority World countries.

However, when Jesus made this statement, bread was essential for living. So, at first glance it seems easy to catch what He was saying: *Just as bread keeps your bodies alive and satisfies your physical hunger, so you need Me for your spiritual life. Only, once you receive of the life I give, you'll never be hungry again. I completely satisfy.* Simple, isn't it? Well, no. This particular 'I am' said much more to those in that crowd.

Not since the days of Moses had a prophet provided miracle bread (Exodus 16:15), and Jewish tradition held that there would come another prophet who would again miraculously give them bread. But they even got that wrong, as Jesus had to remind them that it was God who had provided the manna, not Moses (John 6:32). Manna had met the physical hunger of their ancestors during the long desert wanderings. But they still died! And manna was so perishable that it couldn't be kept overnight. Even the miracle bread Jesus provided to the 5,000 eventually became inedible.

Jesus had to explain that: 'The bread of God is he [not *what*] who comes down from heaven and gives life to the world' (John 6:33). He was neither a baker nor a prophet. He was the Saviour!

They came to Jesus for a loaf. He was offering *life* . . . eternal life!

We are not so different. We also run after what ultimately will perish – things that can never fill the eternity that God has put into our hearts (Ecclesiastes 3:11). But Jesus, the Bread of life, can. He calls us believers to shift our focus from the physical to the eternal . . . from the trivial to the vital.

Lord Jesus, I choose today to feed spiritually on You. To seek satisfaction in You alone. Amen.

29 May

'I am the good shepherd.
The good shepherd lays down his life for the sheep.'
John 10:11

Reading: Hebrews 13:20–21

God had always been committed to Israel's welfare. The Old Testament in its entirety is evidence to that. He gave them leaders to guide, direct and protect the nation He called His people. It was the ultimate shepherd-and-flock situation. God appointed shepherds – priests and prophets – and if the sheep were to stay safe and satisfied they had to follow them. Yet, in Ezekiel 34, Yahweh challenges the shepherds, denouncing them for their poor care and lack of protection, which allowed the sheep to be scattered, destitute and lost (34:3–6), and pronouncing His determination to rescue them Himself (34:11–12).

So, when Jesus declared Himself to be *the* Good Shepherd – not merely one of many – he disturbed those who regarded themselves the current shepherds of Israel. The religious establishment didn't like it one bit (John 10:19–20). Using this title, Jesus stretched beyond the reassuring stuff we read into His words, to announcing Himself as the fulfilment of prophecy. He was taking on God's role. Jesus was establishing Himself as Saviour and the new leader of Israel. The old guard of Pharisees and priests was being displaced. The years of lining their own pockets and adding burdens to those already oppressed (Matthew 23:23) were coming to an end.

Jesus, the Good Shepherd, would do whatever it took to get the sheep to their appointed destiny: reunion with the Father. He was even prepared to '[lay] down his life for the sheep' (John 10:11), which ultimately He did.

Humanity has always been sheep-like. We are needy, dependent creatures. We need a shepherd, but sometimes follow the wrong one. Salvation is in returning to the Good Shepherd, for in Jesus we find the care, provision, protection and guidance we need for life's difficult terrain. There are no other substitutes, no other shepherds; only Jesus. And listen ... the Good Shepherd is calling your name.

Great Shepherd of the sheep, thank you for Your compassion and care. May my ears listen for Your voice and my feet be swift to follow where You lead. Amen.

30 May

'I am the vine; you are the branches.
Whoever abides in me and I in him,
he it is that bears much fruit,
for apart from me you can do nothing.'

John 15:5

Reading: John 15:1–11

Many budding artists begin by painting the proverbial bowl of fruit depicting a bunch of grapes hanging over the side. There's something eye-catching about those little globes of juicy flesh clumped together at the end of tiny little twigs. Yet, cultivating the real thing is not for the faint-hearted. Vines need to be planted in the right place and conditions, and require daily care and attention to produce the very best crop. Nobody likes sour grapes!

When Jesus declared Himself the True Vine (John 15:1), He had just shared a final meal with those closest to Him. They were a confused and troubled bunch. Judas had already left, and the Saviour was attempting to bring encouragement before He was physically taken from them. Using the vine analogy, Jesus explained that He wasn't asking the disciples to do the impossible (15:4). Grapes are only produced when a vine is planted and cared for. Spiritually, God the Father chose His Son to be the True Vine, which would give life and productivity to the branches attached to Him.

Jesus doesn't call us to produce fruit. Rather, He calls us to bear 'much fruit, for apart from [Him we] can do nothing' (15:5). Producing fruit is the job of the Vine, so we shouldn't try to do it by ourselves. The branches merely have to stay attached to the Vine to receive all that is needed for fruit-bearing.

Abiding is the key. Trusting that what comes from the Vine is essential for spiritual growth. Giving up our self-sufficiency for His all-sufficiency. Accepting the Gardener's attention – even painful pruning (15:2) – as the only way to fruitfulness. The kind of fruitfulness that reflects Galatians 5:22–23: 'Love, joy, peace, patience, kindness, goodness, faithfulness, gentleness, self-control.' What more could you want your life to portray? We could never achieve those results by our own efforts . . . nor should we want to!

Lord, I happily admit that I can do nothing without You. Live through me, Saviour, and may I bear much fruit. Amen.

31 May

'Truly, truly, I say to you, before Abraham was, I am.'

John 8:58

Reading: John 8:52–59

When the Jews reached for those stones, they understood exactly what Jesus meant when He said, 'Before Abraham was, I am'. Those very words condemned Jesus as a blasphemer, having just declared Himself the 'I AM'. God come to man. There was only one problem with the Jews' verdict. They were wrong! Jesus' claims were far from spurious.

Centuries earlier, when Moses knelt in the dirt before the burning bush, he asked the Voice coming from it who he should tell the enslaved people of Israel had sent him (Exodus 3:14). It seemed that to use 'the God of your fathers' (3:15) as an answer wasn't enough for God's newly appointed rescuer. So, God told Moses to tell them that, 'I AM has sent me to you' (3:14). In Hebrew 'I AM' is the ultimate statement of self-existence. The 'I AM' doesn't need anyone else. He accomplishes whatever He wills. He is omnipresent, unchangeable, omnipotent. The name God chose identified that He alone could rescue them from Egypt's tyranny and set them free.

That day in the temple, Jesus dared not only to declare himself to have existed before Father Abraham, but to be the I AM of the great exodus from Egypt, and the I AM who was now the truth who had come to rescue them – this time from their sin (John 8:31–32).

In Moses' day, Pharaoh refused to accept there was anyone more powerful than him, and he perished (Psalm 136:15). In Jesus' day, the Jewish leaders refused to accept Jesus as the I AM, despite the evidence to the contrary. Sadly, we're not much better today, as we prefer to do life our own way and not yield to the great I AM. How sad are Henley's words in his poem 'Invictus':

> I am the master of my fate:
> I am the captain of my soul.[21]

It is not true. Only one can be Captain of our soul. Oh, how we need to fall on the mercy of the great I AM.

Great I AM, I bow before Your pre-eminence with a grateful heart. There is none like You. Amen.

June

1 June

Seeing the crowds, he went up on the mountain,
and when he sat down, his disciples came to him.
And he opened his mouth and taught them.

Matthew 5:1–2

Reading: Romans 10:14–17

As the speaker announced his Bible reading, I glanced along the long row where we were seated and observed an open Bible on every knee. It was a glorious sight! We had come to this tented conference to listen to a man, but we really wanted to hear from God. Wonderfully, God still speaks today. The way He does this is through His word – often through those He has gifted with the ability to preach and teach, but also in the quiet place directly from Scripture to our hearts.

Here we sit while the preacher stands, but I love how Jesus 'sat down' when He addressed the people – a common practice for rabbis, indicating that the teacher was about to spend time with those willing to listen. Jesus wasn't in a hurry that day, so He sat down. These days, hurry can be the bane of our lives. We're always doing something. Or going somewhere. Someone needs us. Work, family, church. We groan when we can't find time to meet a friend or have a day to ourselves. We squeeze in time with Jesus when we can, and even manage to feel good about it. But in reality, the clock on the wall keeps ticking and we move on to the next thing.

The crowd had it right that day on the hillside by the lake. They sat down. Took time. Listened to Jesus. They didn't realize that what He was about to say would become known as the greatest sermon ever preached. They simply wanted to hear what this new rabbi had to say. Each one was there for a different reason, yet all were curious to know what distinguished Jesus from the rest. Perhaps He might even say or do something life-changing.

So, when Jesus sat down . . . they did too. They didn't want to miss a word. Neither should we.

Teach me to recognize the importance of sitting down with You, Lord. Nothing is more essential than hearing Your voice. Amen.

2 June

THINK ON THIS

My son, be attentive to my words;
incline your ear to my sayings . . .
keep them within your heart.

Proverbs 4:20–21

- Read through these verses a number of times – including out loud.
- Write them out, stick them on the fridge, have them on your phone.
- Meditate on the words, then respond in praise.
- Encourage someone by sharing these verses with them today.

3 June

'Blessed are the poor in spirit,
for theirs is the kingdom of heaven.'

Matthew 5:3

Reading: Luke 18:9–14

Both men were in Jerusalem. Both men went to the temple to pray. It was expected of them. Both were Jews, but they were as different as night and day. You would have thought that since they were in a holy place the ground would have been level. But not so. One was a member of those thought elite in religious circles: a Pharisee. The other was about as far as possible from what most would call decent, never mind Jewish. He was a tax collector.

Their individual prayers were astonishing. Well, the Pharisee's was. The tax collector knew exactly who he was: a sinner (Luke 18:13). Pleading for God's mercy, he was afraid to lift his head in such a holy place before the God from whom he expected nothing but judgement.

Conversely, the Pharisee only thought he knew who he was, even going as far as to thank God for not making him like that tax collector . . . over there (18:11)! Little did he know that finger-pointing doesn't work with God. Neither does attempted self-justification. His numerous efforts at impressing God didn't bring him spiritual brownie points; they only exaggerated his folly.

God is never impressed when we think we can approach Him through our own merits. We have none! The tax collector got it right. He was in the right place, with the right attitude, praying the right prayer to the right Person. 'God, be merciful to me, a sinner!' (18:13).

When they left the temple, it was the tax collector who went away justified, and the Pharisee the unforgiven sinner (18:14).

I wonder if this story Jesus told resonated with those who had heard His Beatitudes on the hillside at Tabgha. 'Blessed are the poor in spirit, for theirs is the kingdom of heaven' (Matthew 5:3). It is only those who recognize their spiritual poverty, Jesus explained, who will be welcomed into God's kingdom. Not merely after death, but into the kingdom Jesus was setting up right in their midst. A kingdom of His followers – totally reliant on their King.

Lord, forgive me if I ever try to brag about myself. Rather, may I only ever give the glory to You. Amen.

4 June

'Blessed are those who mourn,
for they shall be comforted.'

Matthew 5:4

Reading: 2 Corinthians 7:8–13

Galilee glistened beneath us the day we stood on the ridge at Tabgha. The silence spoke to my heart as I surveyed the natural amphitheatre sloping down towards the lake. Even now, as pictures form in my mind, a sense of awe begins to surface. Jesus was here! And it wasn't quiet that day. The crowds had followed Him for miles. People had filled every patch of grass, settled themselves on each mound. What a mixed bunch they were: disciples, the religious, the curious and the sick. One thing was sure, silence fell when Jesus sat down to speak to His disciples, because everyone else wanted to listen in.

Perhaps they were surprised at how His message started. They had come for the exciting; the miraculous. But Jesus began by rattling off short, snappy couplets about the challenges and blessings of living in His kingdom. A bit like a preacher's introduction to what's coming up in his sermon. Those who recognize their spiritual poverty would be welcomed into the kingdom, swiftly followed by the promise of comfort given to those who mourn ... over their sin! Grief following the death of a loved one was one thing they all understood, but grieving over sin was a new thought entirely.

Jesus always cut to the chase. He didn't attempt to make us comfortable before introducing a difficult subject matter. By using the word 'mourn' in this second beatitude, the Saviour explains the seriousness of sin and the necessary response to it. Our sin should distress us. It's easy to become anesthetized to sins we encounter every day, yet complacency should never be an option. Sin devastates families, communities and churches. But more than that, it damages us and our personal relationships – not least with God. Look to the cross and see what sin cost Jesus!

Thankfully, the Beatitudes declare both responsibility and results. For Jesus rewards this specific grief with forgiveness and cleansing – the ultimate comfort for our soul. The greatest blessing.

Lord, forgive me when I don't take sin seriously. Rather, may it produce in me a godly grief that leads to repentance. Amen.

5 June

'You will be sorrowful,
but your sorrow will be turned into joy.'

John 16:20

Reading: Revelation 21:1–4

In a little cemetery set on the edge of a small country town there is a certain grave I visit regularly. Two names are etched in gold leaf on the grey granite stone. The ages recorded probably raise an eyebrow, perhaps even a sigh, in those who pass by. The dates of their deaths read ten years between. But few know the sorrow of the hands that clean the cold stone, or the comfort God gives while we wait for the joy that will come in the morning (Psalm 30:5).

I frequently stood by that grave and repeated the words of yesterday's verse: 'Blessed are those who mourn, for they shall be comforted' (Matthew 5:4). I never really understood how it could be a blessing to mourn, but I did cherish the reality of God's comfort. Then one day those precious thoughts were dashed by a sermon that explained the context of Matthew 5:4. Jesus was speaking about sorrow over sin, not grief over human loss. And my hurting heart sank a little deeper. Was He not concerned about my pain after all?

Perhaps yesterday's words disappointed you – even added to your pain. Context and correct interpretation are vital when studying Scripture, so we can't get away from the original intention of those words of Jesus. He was teaching kingdom principles. But remember . . . His loving character can never be separated from the words He says.

On that Mount of Beatitudes, I can't help but wonder who Jesus might have seen in the crowd. Did His eyes fall on Jairus and his daughter playing nearby? Was the widow of Nain talking with her son as the crowds gathered? Or could Lazarus' laugh have reached Him at the water's edge? Or did the Saviour pause momentarily at the sight of the women in black, forever grieving their loss? It is who He was. It is who He is today. He sees us in our grief, feels our pain and continues to comfort those who mourn.

Take heart . . . joy *will* come in the morning.

Thank you, Jesus, that one day You will wipe away every tear, for the former things will have passed away. Amen.

6 June

'Blessed are the meek,
for they shall inherit the earth.'
Matthew 5:5

Reading: 1 Peter 5:6–7

Recently I sat with my elderly mother looking through the hymn book to select her funeral hymns. Previously, she insisted I write down who would receive the few items of jewellery Dad had given her on occasions special to them both. Her will is made. Her wishes known. She is ready to go Home, and at ninety-two her impatience is starting to show. The recipients of what Mum will leave behind are those she loves. Inheritance is for family.

Jesus was speaking to 'family' on the hill that day when He spoke of inheritance. Except He wasn't speaking of a few trinkets or a fancy house. The inheritance kingdom children will obtain is staggering. Jesus was promising the earth – something only He can truly deliver. Was He speaking of the earth today? Or was it the new earth, in the age to come (2 Peter 3:13)? Well, both actually. Jesus makes it clear that kingdom life starts in the here and now, when we surrender to Him. Therefore, our inheritance has already begun because the old life has been buried with Him (John 5:24).

Therefore, He blesses us with things not available outside our relationship with Him – strength, peace and joy – on this earth. While the world shouts 'get', 'take', 'achieve' and still we are not satisfied, God's word tells us that 'godliness with contentment is great gain' (1 Timothy 6:6). To put our head on the pillow each night with contentment as our tranquillizer is surely the best kind of inheritance. Then to rise one day to the glories of the new earth as children of the King (Revelation 22:3–4) is beyond our wildest dreams (1 Corinthians 2:9, NKJV).

But there's a caveat. This inheritance is designated for the meek. Not the weak . . . the meek. Those who are not self-seeking but God-seeking – where surrender ranks higher than achievement, and God's greatness obliterates any pretending to be our own. And where meekness is to be gentle and lowly in heart, just like Jesus.

I deserve nothing from You, Lord, but my heart rejoices in Your abundant grace. Amen.

7 June

'Blessed are those who
hunger and thirst for righteousness,
for they shall be satisfied.'

Matthew 5:6

Reading: John 4:5–15

The woman stamped her feet firmly as she took those final steps towards the well, the jingling of her anklets confirming her approach. 'Give me a drink.' The words startled her. The sleeping stranger was now awake, His shawl draped across strong, broad shoulders. Catching her breath, the woman looked Him over, well used to sizing up men at the well. Avoiding the local women wasn't the only reason she visited Jacob's well at this time of day.

'How come you're asking *me* for a drink?' she asked as His eyes met hers. Sweeping the air, she pointed out the obvious: 'You're a Jew. I'm a woman . . . and a Samaritan one at that.' *Surely he can't be so thirsty that he'd render himself unclean by asking me for a drink?* 'If you knew the gift of God,' the Man interrupted her, mid-thought, 'and who it is that is saying to you, "Give me a drink," you would have asked Him, and He would have given you living water.'

Gift of God? Living water? Has he got some magical drink? He doesn't even have a bucket! She pried further: 'How are you going to draw water, never mind this *living water* you speak of? Where does it come from? Are you greater than our father Jacob?' The words had barely left her mouth when the Man sitting on the well replied, 'Everyone who drinks of this water will be thirsty again, but whoever drinks of the water I give him will never be thirsty again. The water I give will become in him a spring of water welling up in eternal life.'

Never to thirst again! Never to have to sneak to the well when others weren't around. What did she have to lose? 'Sir, give me this water,' she responded, 'so that I will not be thirsty or have to come here to draw water.'

But the woman didn't yet understand that the rabbi at the well wasn't merely speaking of a different kind of water, but of a different kind of thirst . . . one she was only beginning to recognize in her life.[22]

Lord, give me the satisfaction that is found only in You. Amen.

8 June

He satisfies the longing soul,
and the hungry soul he fills with good things.

Psalm 107:9

Reading: John 4:16–42

Just when she thought the Man, whose name she did not yet know, could actually give her something that would change her life, He threw a spanner in the works. 'Go, call your husband, and come here.'

Why does it always come down to this? Can I not have the living water without a husband? Is the stranger sitting on the well only interested in judging me, like all the other men in Sychar? 'I have no husband,' the woman answered, steeling herself for criticism.

'You are right in saying, "I have no husband."' *How does he know?* 'For you have had five husbands, and the one you have now is not your husband.' The woman stood speechless. All the bravado she had summoned now melted under the scorching sun, while the faces of the men she had blamed for spoiling her life flashed through her mind.

'What you have said is true.' Those final words of her life summary touched her. They were laced with kindness, softening His awareness of her sinful life by acknowledging her confession. *Confession?* She hadn't really thought of her words as confession, but they were. And the look on His face spoke compassion, not judgement.

The minutes passed by in conversation about worship, and as the Man spoke the woman longed for her heart to be changed. The law pronounced her guilty. But this man spoke of salvation, true worship and a Father who was seeking; perhaps even for her – a Samaritan, a woman spoiled by sin. How could that be? 'I know the Messiah is coming,' she blurted out, 'some call Him the Christ.'

And a smile crossed the stranger's face as He replied, 'I who speak to you am He.' She was dumbstruck . . . couldn't respond . . . *wouldn't* respond. Because deep in her heart she knew it was true. And as she dashed back along the road to Sychar, she knew her life would never be the same again. Her hunger and thirst for righteousness was being satisfied as she ran. The Man at the well was delivering what He had promised.[23]

Fill my cup, Lord, with living water from Your eternal supply. Amen.

9 June

THINK ON THIS

So flee youthful passions and pursue righteousness,
faith, love, and peace, along with those who
call on the Lord from a pure heart.

2 Timothy 2:22

- Read through this verse a number of times – including out loud.
- Write it out, stick it on the fridge, have it on your phone.
- Meditate on the words, then respond in praise.
- Be a doer . . . Serve someone with an act of kindness today.

10 June

'Blessed are the merciful,
for they shall receive mercy.'
Matthew 5:7

Reading: 1 Samuel 24

'Don't get mad, get even!' is a mantra about as far from Jesus' teaching as a bunny rabbit is from a fox. The advice, 'If someone hits you, hit them back harder', has the potential for creating yet another bully.

Jesus' teaching was undoubtedly countercultural. His kingdom-living principles went against everything natural, but it was not a new theme in Scripture. Even the 'eye for an eye' form of judgement (Deuteronomy 19:20–21) was not intended as a vendetta, but rather to prevent inappropriate punishment ... another form of mercy.

Jesus took things further in this age of grace that He was ushering in. He wanted His followers to display not the nature of their 'father the devil' (John 8:44), but that of their Father in heaven (Ephesians 2:4–5). Mercy coursed through the Saviour's veins – His blood the very agent that brought it to us as it flowed from the cross.

Mercy was David's response in the cave at En Gedi when King Saul brought an army to kill him. It is a strangely humorous yet touching story of both grace and mercy. Saul, with 6,000 soldiers outside giving their monarch some privacy for his bathroom break, had no idea that David and his warriors were hiding way back in that very same cave. David's men wanted him to finish off the king who had pursued him all over Israel, yet David could not. 'The LORD forbid that I should do this thing ... he is the LORD's anointed' (1 Samuel 24:6). Instead, he clipped the corner off Saul's cloak, later waving it at him as the king returned to his men. That little piece of cloth was the woven evidence of the mercy of God's anointed. Saul didn't deserve it ... but then that's what mercy is.

Grace gives what we don't deserve, while mercy holds back what we do.

Mercy and meekness go together like bread and butter. You can't have one without the other. That day on the mountain Jesus wasn't only telling his followers how they should live; He was showing them. Mercy is His middle name.

When everything shouts revenge, Lord, teach me mercy. Amen.

11 June

'Blessed are the pure in heart,
for they shall see God.'

Matthew 5:8

Reading: Psalm 24:3–6

Our little girl was one of only four very sick children in the small ward. I wanted to pick up her limp little body and run away with her. Instead, I held her hand, while our pastor sat opposite stroking the other one. All the while my husband was frantically returning from Scotland to be with us.

'I'm afraid,' I said to the pastor. 'I'm afraid,' I repeated, 'because she could never understand the gospel, never ask Jesus into her heart. She didn't know how to sin . . . couldn't ask to be forgiven.' As the tears flowed, I heard myself say, 'What if she dies?' His hand stretched across my most precious possession in the world and settled on mine. 'Oh, Catherine,' he whispered. 'Don't you know your God? "Blessed are the pure in heart," Jesus told us, "for they shall see God."' He sighed, recognizing that our profoundly disabled child might not make it to another day. Squeezing my hand tightly, he continued: 'Shall not the Judge of all the earth do right?' (Genesis 18:25, NKJV).

As I buried my head in the cot covers, God's peace settled my anxious heart. The promise-keeping God I had come to know would 'do right' by our precious child. Cheryl *would* see God, just as He promised. As it turned out, it wouldn't be for another four years.

When Jesus looked the disciples in the eye, He was promising them something they had previously never thought possible. 'No one may see me and live,' God had told Moses (Exodus 33:20, NIVUK). Yet, here was Jesus promising that they could. One day they would even see Him face to face – in all His glory – *if* they were pure in heart.

Jesus was of course speaking of the blameless, not the sinless. He judges our heart towards Him, even if our actions are not always right. He seeks transparency without hypocrisy or duplicity, measuring whether our focus is to please Him in all things and above everything else. With His help, these are the hearts that will see God.

Create in me a clean heart, O God, and renew a right spirit within me. Amen.

12 June

'Blessed are the peacemakers,
for they shall be called sons of God.'

Matthew 5:9

Reading: Colossians 1:18–23

Some colloquialisms require more thought than others. I love the one that says, 'His father will never be dead while he's alive!' Simply put, it says that the son is the image of his father in every way: looks, speech, mannerisms. You know what I mean. Here in Northern Ireland we often look at someone we meet for the first time, but from a family we already know, and invariably say, 'Who's he like?' There then follows a variety of opinions. It seems that the person's identity has to be proven by an observable family likeness or trait.

Just so with what Jesus was teaching through the Beatitudes. Evidence of belonging to God's family was to be seen in our likeness to the Father's Son, including the character traits Jesus identified in His discourse with the disciples on that hillside. God's family is unique. Kingdom living must include the characteristics the Father had passed on to the Son ... those of poverty in spirit; mourning over sin; meekness; hungering after righteousness; being merciful and pure in heart ... and now, peace-making.

From the beginning of time, God has been in the business of peace-making, specifically 'to reconcile to himself all things, whether on earth or in heaven, making peace by the blood of his cross' (Colossians 1:20). It is a costly business, but it's Christ's business. That makes it our business too. Like Father, like sons ... and daughters.

To be 'blessed' goes beyond the simple translation of 'happy'. It means 'to be made happy by God'. Rather than taking sides to get our own way, we will be made happy by God if we choose rather to reconcile the estranged by denying our own desires and practising these kingdom principles instead. A few of us may be charged with greater peace-making than the petty everyday, but all of us are commissioned to lead others to peace with God (Matthew 28:19).

Jesus is the 'Prince of Peace' (Isaiah 9:6). As members of His family, are people still asking, 'Who's she like'?

'Lord, make me an instrument of your peace ... Where there is despair, let me bring hope.'[24] Amen.

13 June

'Blessed are those who are persecuted for righteousness'
sake, for theirs is the kingdom of heaven.'

Matthew 5:10

Reading: John 15:18–21

'The world's ill-divid!' is another Northern Irish colloquialism, closely followed by its meaning, 'There's the haves and the have-nots.' I don't have the skill to write the Belfast intonation with which it's spoken, but it speaks truth even without the accent.

There are indeed the 'haves' ... fortunate to have money, education, homes, food, water, democracy, equality, employment, relative safety, healthcare, happy and healthy children, loving families, freedom of speech, and freedom to practise their religion.

While the 'have-nots' ... have not! For millions in our world, 'nothing' takes on its true meaning, and suffering – its bitter companion – delivers horrendous consequences.

Jesus, however, was speaking of one particular group of 'have-nots' – those without the freedom to live in open confession of their Christian faith, or those who are forbidden to share that faith with others, which is an essential component of following Him.

In the 'have' countries, we have long lived with a freedom others have never known, yet many of them would say it has made us soft; more willing to compromise on what the Bible says is immoveable. In the UK, the flood of poorly named 'equality' legislation, has brought about religious freedoms for others, rather than for those who hold to biblical truth. A subtle, and sometimes not so subtle, form of persecution is increasing.

Why are we surprised? Didn't Jesus say, 'If they persecuted me, they will also persecute you' (John 15:20). Note, in this beatitude Jesus is speaking of persecution 'for righteousness' sake'. Don't live like a graceless buffoon and then dare to shout 'Persecution!' when you're called out on it! It's time to step up to the mark now – to live as we ought, speak of Jesus often, and graciously explain the gospel while we can. Whether or not the day is coming when these freedoms will be lost to us matters not. This is how we ought to be living every day, for even in times of persecution we are made happy by God.

Lord Jesus, give peace and consolation to those of Your children who are suffering for Your name's sake. Amen.

14 June

'But woe to you who are rich,
for you have received your consolation.'

Luke 6:24

Reading: Luke 6:20–26

Jesus had set out the characteristics expected in those who followed Him. Characteristics others would see as unnatural, but which mirrored His own. Life would be tough in this kingdom He was building, but His followers would be blessed – made happy by God. It is paradoxical living. Contrary to life in the world around them. Yet, placed within each of us is the potential for joy – that remarkable feeling not dependent on circumstances. An emotion the psalmist identified as associated with God's presence: 'In your presence there is fullness of joy; at your right hand are pleasures forevermore' (Psalm 16:11).

When Luke wrote concerning this teaching, he included some additional material. It is quite possible that it was on a different occasion, with Jesus preaching a similar message but expanding on it somewhat. That's common for preachers. It is also possible that Luke and Matthew included different things from the same sermon. Also common for listeners. Whatever the case, Jesus didn't only speak about the blessings of kingdom living. He also spoke of the woes – the sorrow – of rejecting them, choosing instead to live as we see fit.

'What sorrow awaits you who are rich, for you have your only happiness now. What sorrow awaits you who are fat and prosperous now, for a time of awful hunger awaits you,' Jesus said (Luke 6:24–25, NLT).

Wealth and prosperity are not sinful in themselves, for God has undoubtedly blessed some with both. The problem lies in where we put our confidence. What is our priority in life, and in our walk with Christ? Do my material possessions obscure the real need to recognize that I am spiritually poor? Or that wealth does not impress God? Nor can I pay my way into heaven.

Or am I so full of self-righteousness that there is no room for hungering after His? Do I really believe that I am worthy of God's salvation? Jesus' answer to such folly is clear . . . only sorrow awaits.

Lord, thank you for material and spiritual blessings. Help me to get the perspective right and always choose to put You first. Amen.

15 June

'Woe to you who laugh now,
for you shall mourn and weep.'

Luke 6:25

Reading: Romans 12:9–10, 14–18

The Beatitudes were difficult teachings but were laced with the hope of promised blessing. The four woes of Luke's gospel (6:24–45) contrast with that gift of being made happy by God, and speak instead of a sorrow that is not cancelled by wealth or position.

Laughter is often an outward expression of a joyful heart, which Solomon likens to good medicine (Proverbs 17:22), so if it is so good for us, why is Jesus condemning those who laugh? This passage on the behaviour of the 'haves' is not merely addressing their false spiritual superiority, but also how they treat others. The laughter spoken of by Jesus here concerns those who laugh at others, especially at the misfortunes in their lives. The Saviour is clarifying that finger-pointing and ridicule of people because of their social standing or poverty is not only unacceptable but will be turned on its head and produce a sorrow of its own. As my dad would have said, 'What goes around comes around!' And it won't be pretty.

Luke's final 'woe' follows a similar pattern: 'What sorrow awaits you who are praised by the crowds, for their ancestors also praised false prophets' (Luke 6:26, NLT).

The craze of our age is to be noticed. To make a name for ourselves. And helped along by the reality shows and social media, it seems everyone wants to be famous, even if it means stooping to the outrageous or immoral to do so. How sad. Even in Jesus' day fame was seen as something to be sought after. Yet, Jesus' response to such self-seeking adulation was crystal clear. The praise of the crowd is fleeting and doesn't bring lasting happiness. They'll run after others when your crown has lost its shine. Fame is false when pursued for personal gain, and pride is the rope that trips many . . . causing even those in Christ to fall.

Is it any wonder that Jesus praised the meek, whose mantra is always: 'Others before self – and Christ first of all'?

Fame and fortune are the devil's trinkets. Lord, may I always, only, seek Your approval, and the kind of blessing that never fades. Amen.

16 June

THINK ON THIS

For the eyes of the Lord are on the righteous,
and his ears are open to their prayer.
But the face of the Lord is against those who do evil.

1 Peter 3:12

- Read through this verse a number of times – including out loud.
- Write it out, stick it on the fridge, have it on your phone.
- Meditate on the words, then respond in praise.
- Take steps to allow God's word to change you: perhaps . . . repent, forgive, love.

17 June

'You are the light of the world . . .
let your light shine before others,
so that they may see your good works and
give glory to your Father who is in heaven.'

Matthew 5:14–16

Reading: Matthew 5:13–16

In the same way that the disciples were an unlikely band of potential future leaders, so the characteristics Jesus desired in His followers hardly look world-changing. The mourners, meek, merciful and peacemakers don't exactly fit the picture of earth-shakers, or of attracting others to join them. Surely it's the wealthy and the well-known who would be the influencers for a powerful new movement? Not according to Jesus. The status quo is not the way to go in the kingdom that is to be like no other.

In the United Kingdom, a flurry of activity ensues as soon as a prime minister has been discarded by once-adoring followers. In Westminster, candidates frantically plan how to make themselves look impressive enough to fill the role, and to garner the necessary votes from their party colleagues. Those who hold such power will no doubt look for the best personal return for giving their much-needed vote. Cynical? Perhaps. Sad? Definitely. For none of those hoping to move into Number 10 are displaying even a hint of the qualities Jesus deemed necessary for kingdom building.

Different kind of kingdom, you say. And you'd be right, but oh what change we would see in our nation if our leaders would allow even a smidgen of God's kingdom principles to influence the one they are trying to build.

Salt-and-light living is what Jesus is looking for. We are to impact our communities with a cleansing influence, brightly shining the light of the gospel message to push back the spiritual darkness shrouding our streets. The transformation Christ makes in our hearts is not solely for our benefit. We are to share it widely with those around us. Jesus isn't looking for votes that could change with the wind. He's looking for permanent, decisive commitment to a kingdom that cannot be brought down. Let's shine the light for Jesus!

Lord, may I take the light You have given me and shine it far and wide for Your glory. Amen.

18 June

'For I tell you, unless your righteousness
exceeds that of the scribes and Pharisees,
you will never enter the kingdom of heaven.'

Matthew 5:20

Reading: Matthew 5:17–20

Now there's a sentence to cause a sharp intake of breath! It certainly blows a hole in the trying to 'tip the imaginary scales of heavenly justice with our good works' theory. Jesus announced that even the super-righteousness of the Pharisees isn't enough to let us glimpse God's heaven. What is required must *exceed* even that.

Jesus' summary of the law in Matthew 22:37–40 also seems an impossibility. Which of us has ever loved the Lord our God with all our heart, soul, mind and strength, or loved our neighbours in the same way as we love ourselves? And when Jesus adds the perfection clause of Matthew 5:48 – 'You therefore must be perfect, as your heavenly Father is perfect' – we can't help but wonder what hope there is for us.

We are sinners by nature – morally and spiritually incapable of standing before a holy God (Romans 3:23). We have no righteousness of our own. Once our sinful nature is exposed before God we are 'condemned already' (John 3:18). What Jesus expects is impossible! Right! And that's exactly the conclusion He wants us to reach, in order that we might be in the place where He can assign His righteousness to us.

Jesus is different. He is righteous by nature; He knew no sin. He is already accepted by the Father – the Son who pleased the Father (Matthew 3:17). Since God, the Three-in-One, is holy, what we need is for the Father to see His Son's righteousness when He looks at us. That is possible through justification. Jesus' sacrificial death on the cross renders us just as if we've never sinned. Once we have accepted our sinful position, repented and trusted in Christ for forgiveness, His righteousness is imputed, assigned, credited to us.

'For our sake he made him to be sin who knew no sin, so that in him we might become the righteousness of God' (2 Corinthians 5:21). Now the Father sees us as sinless, because of Jesus. That's amazing grace!

Lord, I cannot meet the Father without the covering of Your grace. Thank you. Amen.

19 June

'Beware of practicing your righteousness before
other people in order to be seen by them,
for then you will have no reward from your Father
who is in heaven.'

Matthew 6:1

Reading: Matthew 6:1–4

Has anyone ever said to you, 'The Bible is full of contradictions'? It's usually an attempt to throw you off your guard – to make the Bible appear untrustworthy. A good response is to turn the tables by asking them to show you one, which usually stops that particular ruse. However, if you compare Matthew 6:1 (Jesus' command not to display your righteousness for others to see) with Matthew 5:16 (Jesus' command to let your light be seen clearly by others), you yourself might feel you are on the shaky ground of contradiction.

What is Jesus asking? Show and tell? Or hide when tempted to show? Both, actually. But Christ's focus was on the motivation behind our actions. It isn't what we do that produces either godliness or worldliness in us, but *why* we do what we do. What drives what we might see as good in our lives? And ultimately, who are we trying to please? Perhaps it is time for some self-examination.

Would we do what is being asked of us if no one else knew or saw? Do we need the approval or applause of others in our Christian service, or for it to happen at all? If 'we have been approved by God to be entrusted with the gospel' (1 Thessalonians 2:4), why do we worry about what others say? We have the message a lost world needs to hear, and they need to see it lived out humbly through us.

Rather, let's learn 'not to please man, but to please God who tests our hearts' (2:4). What He thinks of us is more important than the commendation of any other. Publicly shining His light while resisting the need to draw attention to ourselves is not ambivalent. It is all about bringing glory to God. There is no contradiction here! But it does confirm our need to show and tell with humility and passion.

Tester of my heart, I pray that Your gaze is the only one I submit to, and Your glory all I seek to promote. Amen.

20 June

'But when you fast, comb your hair
and wash your face.'

Matthew 6:17, NLT

Reading: Matthew 6:16–18

I love this sentence. I'm sure Jesus' original audience did too. This Sermon on the Mount was no quick thought to tickle their ears and send them on their way happy. It was a lengthy discourse, full of spiritual challenge not previously heard. But remember there were families in the crowd, as well as a mix of the well-educated and the illiterate. Jesus was aiming His teaching at the disciples – also a mixed bunch – yet fully aware of the large crowd beyond the men seated at His feet.

What an orator and master illustrator He was. Jesus knew which pictures to paint in the listeners' minds; pictures that would not only grab their attention and pull them back when minds began to wander, but also evoke laughter at the everyday images He used.

Jesus had moved on from teaching about the character He expected in His followers to its practical outworking. How should we live as children of His kingdom while still in this world? He begins with three staples, well known to a Jewish audience: giving to the needy, prayer and fasting. Each point was pressed firmly home with a touch of humour. The hillside crowd had witnessed the hypocritical habit of publicly calling the poor to oneself to fulfil the command of giving to the needy (Deuteronomy 15:11). Jesus' illustration of trumpet-blowing for that practice would certainly have caused a ripple of laughter (Matthew 6:2). Our giving is to be kept between ourselves and God alone. It's not something to display along the bottom of the television screen on Children in Need day or the like!

Fasting for spiritual focus and benefit was understood by the Jews – the Pharisees practised it twice weekly (Luke 18:12). Jesus humorously painted a picture of the normally well-dressed hypocrites going to the bother of taking on the dishevelled, miserable look they kept exclusively for Tuesdays and Thursdays! Let's beware though ... attending a lunch function on a day we've chosen to fast, with the words, 'I'm not eating today,' has a ring of the Pharisaic about it!

Lord, may my motivation in all I do be always directed towards You. Amen.

21 June

'Therefore I tell you, do not be anxious about your life,
what you will eat or what you will drink,
nor about your body, what you will put on.'

Matthew 6:25

Reading: Matthew 6:25–34

The first time I stood on a steep down-escalator in the London Underground I felt slightly anxious, so I distracted myself by looking at the multiplicity of colourful advertisements pasted on to the walls as we descended. Theatre posters shouting: 'Come and experience!' Exotic perfumes, seductive clothing, exquisite food and the 'must-see' attractions of that great city. Poster reading became a must-do while negotiating the underground, providing me with a false impression of what I needed to feed, clothe, relax and entertain myself.

Our thoughts are focused on our bodies – food, drink, clothing – and whatever else we think we need. Things haven't changed much from that moment when Jesus brought up the big three questions – What shall we eat? What shall we drink? What shall we wear? – two millennia ago. Considering the socio-economic climate of His day, these questions appear fairly reasonable. The command not to worry, however, came because of the word that begins the sentence – 'Therefore' – causing us to ask, 'What is it there for?'

Jesus' command for us not to worry about these material things comes directly after His teaching on prayer, specifically the Lord's Prayer (Matthew 6:9–13). Having asked for God's will to be done, and for Him to supply our daily bread – in essence, all we need for this life – Jesus tells us not to worry about what God has already promised to supply. We are not to be like unbelievers, 'for your Father knows what you need before you ask him' (6:8).

Worry reveals distrust, while faith is the very opposite – trusting the One who is our Creator. Just look around, Jesus says, at the natural world, and you will see all the evidence you need of a Father who loves and cares for His creation. 'Are you not of more value than they?' (6:26). So, let's do as Jesus says and stop worrying!

I believe Your promise to meet my need, Father. When worry knocks on my door I'll send Jesus to answer! Amen.

22 June

> 'No one can serve two masters . . .
> You cannot serve God and money.'
>
> Matthew 6:24

Reading: 1 Timothy 6:17–19

Money. It had to be somewhere in Jesus' teaching about kingdom living. Money has caused division from the beginning of time. There are those with an abundance of everything, while the rest of us fall into the category of getting by, wishing we had more or struggling daily to make ends meet. One thing is sure: the word 'enough' is a rare concept for either group to grasp, and contentment is often lost in the race to accumulate.

Yet, we need to be clear that nowhere does Jesus condemn having money. In fact, Paul confirms to the young church that it is God 'who richly provides us with everything to enjoy' (1 Timothy 6:17). There's a false religiosity that conflates wealth with ungodliness and poverty with righteousness. That thought is more akin to jealousy, and is certainly not what Jesus is getting at here.

The Saviour is not speaking about having either God or money, but rather about which of the two is our master. Where does our allegiance lie? One word is key in Jesus' teaching on the money issue. He says, 'Do not lay up for *yourselves* treasures on earth . . . but lay up for *yourselves* treasures in heaven' (Matthew 6:19–20, emphasis mine). Right living, Jesus says, isn't about the amount of money we have in the bank or in things, but how we respond to it. Those who have been entrusted with much are required to choose whether their lives are consumed by building their own temporary 'kingdom' on earth or to serve God in building His kingdom here, accumulating the kind of spiritual wealth that will meet us in heaven one day. God can only be served with our entire devotion, as His glory cannot be given to another (Isaiah 42:8).

We are to be different from the materialistic culture around us, living instead a life of contrast, where our allegiance is to the Father and what He is building through the Spirit living in us.

While grateful for Your good gifts, Lord, may I only hold them lightly that You might receive the glory You are due. Amen.

23 June

THINK ON THIS

'For where your treasure is,
there your heart will be also.'
Matthew 6:21

- Read through this verse a number of times – including out loud.
- Write it out, stick it on the fridge, have it on your phone.
- Meditate on the words, then respond in praise.
- Encourage someone by sharing this verse with them today.

24 June

'For with the judgment you pronounce
you will be judged, and with the measure you use
it will be measured to you.'

Matthew 7:2

Reading: Matthew 7:1–6, NLT

Jesus is about to conclude His revolutionary sermon. In true style, His words hit the mark yet again. From start to finish, the message He preached was laced with lessons on humility. His followers were to be different from others – showing mercy, and promoting peace and blessing to those who persecute them. This lesson on the hypocrisy of judging others naturally follows.

Unfortunately, there is a misconception that it is not our place to judge anyone – ever! Not so. Rather, Jesus is saying that we shouldn't identify the sin in others to make ourselves feel good – the 'I'm not as bad as him' attitude. Discerning sin in a fellow Christian's life should lead us to guide them towards repentance and restoration (Galatians 6:1), something we cannot do if we haven't first scrutinized our own lives. 'The standard [we] use in judging is the standard by which [we] will be judged' (Matthew 7:2, NLT). Faithful followers will always examine their own hearts before the hearts of others.

Jesus, ever our supreme example, could have spent His whole ministry finger-pointing. He was surrounded by sinners ... some notoriously so. But when faced with the accusations of others about these sinners' lives, Jesus' response was to lace His own words with grace and mercy. He never excused their sin, but instead lovingly reprimanded them, telling them to 'go, and from now on sin no more' (John 8:11). Those who know they are sinners are ripe for forgiveness.

Tongue-lashing judgement – 'whitewashed tombs', 'serpents', 'vipers' (Matthew 23:27, 33) – was kept specifically for those who were so full of self-righteous pride that they only ever saw 'specks' in the eyes of everyone else, while totally ignoring the 'logs' that blinded them (7:3). Jesus' words were scathing, but truth needs to be heard if it is to be acted upon.

We who think we would never be guilty of such behaviour should beware lest we also fall (1 Corinthians 10:12).

Lord, may keeping my own heart right be a daily discipline. Amen.

25 June

'For everyone who asks receives,
and the one who seeks finds,
and to the one who knocks it will be opened.'

Matthew 7:8

Reading: Matthew 7:7–11

The 'ask, seek, knock' formula introduced here by Jesus sounds a bit like hitting the jackpot when you put your coin into a fairground machine, especially one that says: 'Everyone a winner!' Yet, perhaps like me you have struggled with this passage because it did not result in getting what you prayed for.

Do we really believe prayer to be a magic wand? Is Jesus actually pledging to give us what we ask with no strings attached? Or is the Father our servant, there to grant our every request? Could prayer be wasted breath?

Before doubt overwhelms us, let's set the picture of answered prayer firmly within the frame of context and relationship. These verses are not a digression from Jesus' theme of humility of heart. Prayer shows the humility that declares our need of God's wisdom, guidance and help. It's the cry that says, 'I can't do this without You.'

Jesus has already told us that our Father always knows what we need (Matthew 6:8) – even providing it before we ask. Here He surprises the Jews by addressing God as 'Abba'. It's a comforting family name for 'Father', and by using it Jesus reminds us that we are part of God's family. He loves us. He cares for us. He wants to give us good gifts. What we sometimes forget is that our Abba Father can only give *good* gifts.

It is irresponsible parenting to grant every child's wish, and God doesn't spoil His children by pandering to our every request. Sometimes He says 'No' or 'Wait'. We may never know why. But as we keep on asking, our hearts begin to change in response to seeking Him through His Word. Before long, the knocking seeks His presence above all else, the humility of which allows the Father to give us what we *need* ... in whatever form he feels best. That's when the formula produces the treasure we sought all along: His good and perfect will for our lives.

Lord, teach me to ask according to Your will, recognizing Your love and care in each response. Amen.

26 June

'Beware of false prophets,
who come to you in sheep's clothing
but inwardly are ravenous wolves.'

Matthew 7:15

Reading: Matthew 7:12–20

As I was studying Jesus' teaching in what is known as the Sermon on the Mount, a lot was happening beyond my laptop and books. The Omicron variant stormed across our little province, felling even those who had previously managed to avoid the dangerous Delta variant. It became easier to name the friends who hadn't fallen like pins in the proverbial bowling alley by the slightest glancing blow from the spiky sphere.

You've guessed it. Both lines of my lateral flow test popped up boldly across the test window. Coronavirus stuck its tongue out at me like a naughty child, shouting: 'I've got you at last!' I couldn't believe it – despite my gravelly throat. I felt cheated. I had carefully followed all the rules and guidelines; behaved impeccably; taken no risks and ignored foolish advice (even that given by some in high places), and yet a piece of plastic, in harmony with my bodily aches, was evidence of my predicament.

This is a common mistake, even in our spiritual lives. We think we're on the right track, even believe we're listening to the right people, only to discover the opposite is true. Too much time is spent on the plausible, especially if the way others interpret the Bible makes us feel good. Meanwhile, personal time with Jesus and His word shrinks because we don't like that 'the gate is narrow and the way is hard that leads to life' (Matthew 7:14). Centuries earlier, Solomon warned: 'There is a way that seems right to a man, but its end is the way to death' (Proverbs 14:12).

Let's take care where we're walking, and who is talking to us while we walk. It might look and sound good, but there is trouble ahead if we choose the Easy Way, where all the signs point to Destruction Valley – and where isolation doesn't end in five days!

Lord, it's life I want. Please help me to recognize those peddling a softer way and choose only to walk with You. Amen.

27 June

But God's firm foundation stands, bearing this seal:
'The Lord knows those who are his.'

2 Timothy 2:19

Reading: Matthew 7:21–27

When my husband was leaving for Bible College, he was gifted a number of books. Some of them were huge, such as *Hard Sayings of the Bible* (IVP USA, 2013). Back then I hadn't realized how many hard sayings there were in the Bible to warrant the thickness of this book!

The Bible is not an easy book, and I'm not talking highbrow – it is accessible to all – but rather that it is deeply impactful, and at times disturbing. None more so than the words Jesus predicts he will use with some who, on the Last Day, will call Him 'Lord, Lord', seeking entrance to heaven. 'I never knew you,' will be the Saviour's reply. 'Depart from me, you workers of lawlessness' (Matthew 7:21–23). It seems quite shocking, especially since those engaged in this conversation all identify not only as Jesus' followers, but as those who have carried out the supernatural in His name. These words certainly caused my heart to race!

Jesus isn't trying to frighten us, or to make us doubt our salvation, but He is in warning mode. Having cautioned us of the danger of false teachers, He now turns to the disaster caused by false profession. Jesus sees right through those who are depending on talking up their relationship with Him, as opposed to those acting out their faith in response to what He has done for them.

Reciting a creed amounts to mere words if our hearts don't follow them with obedience. Signing a baptismal or confirmation roll might seem to be all we need, but Jesus wants us to do what we say . . . every day, in private as well as in public. 'Whoever says he abides in him ought to walk in the same way in which he walked' (1 John 2:6).

And remember, 'The Lord knows those who are his' (2 Timothy 2:19). He keeps those dreadful words, 'depart from me', only for those who are 'workers of lawlessness' (Matthew 7:23).

Lord Jesus, impressing You isn't what You look for. Help me to walk in the reality of true faith. Amen.

28 June

'Everyone then who hears these words of mine
and does them will be like a wise man
who built his house on the rock.'

Matthew 7:24

Reading: Matthew 7:24–27

Every year, swollen rivers and surging tides flood the delta that makes up the greater part of the low-lying country of Bangladesh. Many people die each year, yet its citizens refuse to move to the safety of higher ground, choosing instead to rebuild their rickety shacks on stilts on the flood plain once again. They prefer to risk losing everything, including life and family, to stay close to where they can fish and plant rice. But as surely as the seasons change, they dice with death. What they build has no chance against the storm.

So it is with us, as we consider the spiritual choices we make. Jesus tells us that doing what we say makes the difference between false profession and true faith (Matthew 7:21). The same goes for hearing and doing, as Jesus defines wisdom as obedience to what He says (7:24). To whom are we listening in this world of noise? Are we sure they are speaking truth?

Jesus wants us to listen to His words – to be influenced by them – then to do as *He* says. True spiritual wisdom is translated into godly living by action. We are not merely called to listen ... but to hear ... and to do! The time we spend with Christ – in study, prayer and worship – may be unseen by others, but it undergirds who we are becoming in Him. That's how foundations are built. It is the very thing that provides strength for when life's storms batter us – as they surely will. But survival or devastation will be determined by the base upon which we build: the Rock called Christ, or the sand of self.

It is the storm that reveals the truth – every time! Proof, as if we needed it, that no matter how strong we appear, it is God's strength that is essential both in life and in death.

Solid Rock, there is no place I'd rather be when the storm strikes or when the sun is shining. I love You, Lord. Amen.

29 June

You are my hiding place and my shield;
I hope in your word.

Psalm 119:114

Reading: Matthew 7:28–29

The sermon had come to an end. The crowd covering the hillside had never heard anything like it before. They were 'astonished at his teaching' (Matthew 7:28), even though they were no strangers to preaching. Their ancestors had heard God speak directly through the prophets, much of which had been written down and was used by their religious teachers in the synagogues and in the temple. But God had been silent for 400 years – until now.

What Jesus had to say was unlike all the others. As they listened to Him that day, He didn't add greater burden to their lives. He wasn't increasing taxes or telling them they needed to work harder to earn God's favour. Jesus' message was about living in His kingdom – both now, and while preparing for His heavenly kingdom in the future. Yes, He instructed them to display His character, to deny themselves and to live differently from those around them. It was tough teaching, but it was laced with something the teachers of the law never displayed: hope; the promise of God's care for His children (6:25).

Jesus, in this instruction manual for His followers, doesn't sugarcoat the Christian life, but He does set the example by blazing the trail before us. He doesn't tell us to get out there and 'just do it', without having first shown us how (Mark 10:45). Neither does He leave us to live as He expects without the strength needed ... 'with power through his Spirit in your inner being' (Ephesians 3:16). And when the storms attempt to destroy us, Jesus Himself is our Rock of stability and safety (Matthew 7:25).

Following Jesus will always feel like we're swimming against life's natural flow, but remember there are others with us, heading in the same direction. Best of all, the 'river' has already been crossed by Jesus, and He has promised, 'I am with you always, to the end of the age' (28:20). The journey will be worth it – Jesus is waiting for us on the other shore!

Lord Jesus, one day You will descend from heaven with a shout ... and perhaps I will be among the dead in Christ who will rise first! Hallelujah!

30 June

THINK ON THIS

Turn my eyes from looking at worthless things;
and give me life in your ways.
Psalm 119:37

- Read through this verse a number of times – including out loud.
- Write it out, stick it on the fridge, have it on your phone.
- Meditate on the words, then respond in praise.
- Be a doer . . . Serve someone with an act of kindness today.

July

1 July

The old has gone, the new is here!

2 Corinthians 5:17, NIVUK

Reading: Ephesians 4:21–24

Jesus was a change-broker. Living at a time and in a culture that was dominated by men, the Saviour elevated the status of women in a revolutionary way. His teaching in the Sermon on the Mount had focused on countercultural living. His followers were – then and now – not only to be different on the inside, but to live as salt and light in their communities (Matthew 5:13–16).

Jesus didn't just preach it … He embodied it. He didn't merely show us how to become a light to shine in this dark world, but how to embrace His light to expose and push back that darkness. No one shook things up more than Jesus. No one became an instigator of change as He did. He was neither a policymaker nor a placard waver, yet He was the greatest change-maker who ever lived. Ignoring the taboos of centuries, He lived His life in righteousness before God and humanity. Jesus never preached a sermon on the position of women in His kingdom – He simply included them everywhere He went. It was a practice that often brought rebuke and criticism.

Women had always been treated respectfully in Old Testament Scripture, even when societal traditions did not live up to God's word. Heroines such as Ruth, Esther, Deborah and Rahab were given their place in Israel's history alongside male heroes such as Abraham, Noah, Moses, Joshua and David. But by the time Jesus was born, the rabbinical era was teaching that women were responsible for sin coming into the world, and therefore should not be trusted. But Jesus was having none of it, teaching the men around Him by example.

Men and women are different by design; their individuality a rich blessing both for each other and society; their roles complementary in displaying the image of God (Genesis 1:27). This was the equality Jesus taught – the change He brought. Women were also made in the image of God, and should therefore never be deemed inferior!

Thank you, Jesus, that my identity is found solely in who You created me to be. Make me an instrument of change today. Amen.

2 July

There is neither Jew nor Greek,
there is neither slave nor free,
there is no male and female,
for you are all one in Christ Jesus.

Galatians 3:28

Reading: Galatians 3:25–29

Can you remember a time when you had an epiphany, when you were instantly struck by something that was life-changing? As Christians, the best example of epiphany is when we unexpectedly recognized our sinful condition and our need of a Saviour, which resulted in a transformed new life (2 Corinthians 5:17). Epiphanies happen in the ordinary and the everyday – a word is spoken, an incident occurs, a meeting takes place that suddenly changes your life. It's that 'Aha!' moment that opens the gate of change and opportunity for you to walk through.

Imagine such moments flashing across the minds of the women listening to the Sermon on the Mount. Or the epiphanies that occurred when He spoke in His hometown synagogue of Nazareth, where families had gathered for worship. Never before had any rabbi included women in their teaching – it was only ever directed towards the men. Yet, Jesus mentioned both a woman (the widow of Zarephath) and a man (Naaman) in His sermon to illustrate what He was teaching (Luke 4:26–27), and both were Gentiles!

Using parables with illustrations that included both genders became a regular habit for Jesus as He travelled widely. In one such story He likened the kingdom of God to a mustard seed – sown by a man at work – and also to a woman kneading bread at home (13:18–21). That may not seem unusual to us, but it was revolutionary back then. Is it any wonder that women began following Jesus? They mattered to Him.

Discrimination is always unbiblical – something Peter affirmed in Acts 10:34–35 (NLT): 'God shows no favoritism. In every nation he accepts those who fear him and do what is right.'

Feeling undervalued today? Remember there is no race, status or gender upon which God does not pour His grace ... no individual Jesus does not love ... no soul to whom His word is not freely available.

Thank you, Jesus, that in You we are equal. The only hierarchy we need is You as our King to follow and adore. Amen.

3 July

'I love those who love me,
and those who seek me diligently find me.'

Proverbs 8:17

Reading: Luke 2:36–38

'Peace! All is peaceful!' broadcast the temple's dawn patrol, briefly interrupting the old woman's repetition of the ancient song of pilgrimage.

My soul is at peace, Lord, but it continually yearns for your coming One. Will the Messiah come soon? The affliction of Your people is great. Anna breathed deeply, as though the weight of these burdens required the deepest intake of air to meet her body's need. But she would not allow the external to stop her from completing her early morning psalm of praise:

'O Lord of hosts, blessed is the one who trusts in you.'

At eighty-four, Anna's bones felt the cold more keenly now. As she wrapped a blanket tightly around her, she thought of the beautiful teenager who had gifted it. Anna had not been blessed with children – the sad blemish on a perfect marriage that had lasted a mere seven years. Anna's mind often visited the day of her husband's death. She had learned that grief cannot be erased; it is merely managed. Yet, after losing the love of her life, Anna only ever sought the presence of one other, and discovered the truth in Isaiah's words: 'The reproach of your widowhood you will remember no more. For your Maker is your husband, the LORD of hosts is his name . . . For the LORD has called you like a wife deserted and grieved in spirit' (Isaiah 54:4–6).

Pushing through the sorrow once more, a smile crossed her face, thankful for this new Husband who filled her days with purpose and the assurance of His eternal love.

'The time has arrived!' echoing through the temple drew Anna back from her reverie, the call announcing that soon the gates of the sanctuary would be open to the public. She must ready herself for the day. As she reached for the jug and basin in the corner of the small room, an unusual sense of excitement came from deep within.

'What is it, my Lord?' she asked. 'Do you have someone special for me to meet today?'[25]

Thank you, Lord, that You reveal Yourself to those who love and seek You . . . even today. Amen.

4 July

'Whoever is of God hears the words of God.'

John 8:47

Reading: 1 Peter 3:10–12

Many of the religious leaders regarded housing a woman on temple grounds as sacrilege at worst and disrespectful at best ... even a woman of Anna's age. Yet none of them could get past the obvious spirituality of the daughter of Phanuel, from the tribe of Asher. Some even dared to call her a prophetess, a title Anna disliked.

Listening, however, was a skill she had developed over the years as daily she watched the broken, widowed and desolate walk these courts she called home. And in the mix of the multitude, she prayed for God to guide her to those who needed a listening ear and a compassionate heart. But it was God's voice Anna listened for in the stillness of her room after the temple gates had slammed shut for the night.

'Speak, Lord, I am Your devoted servant,' she whispered, as the sound of passing traders broke into her prayers. The air around her moved as though another were in the room. 'What is it, Master?' Anna questioned. 'Is He near?' The question was not new, but this time she extended it. 'Is He *here?*' Rising to her feet, Anna thought she heard her name. There it was again. 'Anna, it's time.'

As she rushed into the crowded courtyard, Anna's eyes quickly fell on the sight. Clutching her chest, she gasped, the air thick with delight and expectation, desire propelling her feet towards her friend Simeon, and a young couple holding a newborn infant. *He is here, Adonai, just as you said!*

Anna arrived just as Simeon was finishing, not daring to interrupt as her dear friend prophesied over the child – with words that sounded disturbing to the new parents. But Simeon's grim pronouncement was quickly turned upside down as Anna started jumping up and down for joy, praising God for their son. She could hardly contain herself as she and Simeon rejoiced in the fulfilment of God's promise. The Messiah was still a baby, but one day He would rise and rescue Israel. Of that the old woman of the temple was sure.[26]

Lord, give me faith like Anna, who listened for Your speaking voice and waited for its fulfilment. Amen.

5 July

Mary . . . sat at the Lord's feet and listened to his teaching.

Luke 10:39

Reading: Luke 10:38–42

While arranging for a group of women to attend a convention across the Atlantic, my friend phoned the centre. Her call was answered by a lady with a wonderful Southern US drawl. 'Good morning, Mary speaking. How may I help you?' My friend, who has a keen sense of humour, smiled as each struggled with the other's distinct accent. 'Hold the line,' Mary eventually said, 'I'll transfer your call to Martha.' *Of course*, you *will*, my friend thought, stifling laughter at the thought. *I'd expect nothing less.*

The story of Mary and Martha is a staple at ladies' meetings. Speakers often seem to take the simplistic approach that women need to determine whether they are a spiritual Mary or a practical Martha. Yet, both were remarkable women. Both, at different times, showed their spirituality in distinctive ways. Both loved and served Jesus. But there is much more to their story than is seen at first glance.

When the apostle Paul was giving his spiritual CV, he mentioned that he had been 'educated at the feet of Gamaliel', the famous rabbi (Acts 22:3). The term 'to sit at someone's feet' indicated that you were his disciple, something to which the twelve were called by Jesus. A rabbi would teach and engage in spiritual discussion with his disciples, which they then passed on to others. Only men sat at the feet of a religious teacher – only men could be disciples.

When Jesus entered her home that day, Mary broke with tradition and sat at the rabbi's feet – with the men! More remarkably, Jesus welcomed her keenness to learn from Him, describing her choice as necessary, good and lasting (Luke 10:42). Mary was, perhaps, Jesus' first female disciple in the truest sense of the word. We are not told what the men present thought of this woman's behaviour. That didn't matter. Jesus was the rabbi, and just then He was teaching them something important. No one is excluded from following Jesus. His teaching is for everyone – something the brave Mary claimed for herself . . . and opened up for us.

I love to sit at Your feet, Jesus. My heart is open to what You say. Amen.

6 July

Martha was distracted with much serving . . .
But the Lord answered her, 'Martha, Martha,
you are anxious and troubled about many things.'

Luke 10:40–41

Reading: Proverbs 2:1–5

Sometimes the questions we ask hide what is really on our minds. Thankfully, Jesus sees beyond what we are saying to the things that really bother us.

Martha was undoubtedly distracted by preparing food for her large group of unexpected guests, but I have a feeling she was cross with her younger sister, Mary, for more than neglecting the kitchen duties. Jesus saw the problem right away, gently chiding Martha about the 'many things' that were troubling her.

Imagine this older sister seeing Mary sit down with the men . . . *What will people think? She's been brought up better than to behave like this! It's not proper for her to sit at Jesus' feet . . . as if she's one of His disciples!* Shame was one of those 'many things' Jesus had identified. Certainly, Martha needed help to cook for all these men, and perhaps also for the women who travelled with them, but there would be plenty of time for cooking and probably more than enough help when the time was right.

Martha wanted to be seen to do the right thing. She wanted to impress Jesus with the very best she could give Him. Nothing wrong with that, we might think, but Jesus gave her a brief lesson in priorities. Mary's goal that day was about what she could receive from Jesus, and for that she needed to sit at His feet. Something that Jesus commended – much to Martha's surprise. Change was happening before her eyes, and it disturbed her.

Change often brings anxiety with it, and if we are not careful we can be distracted from seeing the good it is bringing because we tie ourselves to the way things used to be. I believe Martha learned the lesson and accepted the change – women could be disciples, and that included her as well as her sister. How do I know? Because later when we read of these siblings it is Martha who first runs out to meet Jesus.

Lord, help me not to panic when change happens, but to accept it when it comes from You, and for Your kingdom. Amen.

7 July

THINK ON THIS

'Behold, I am doing a new thing;
now it springs forth, do you not perceive it?
I will make a way in the wilderness
and rivers in the desert.'

Isaiah 43:19

- Read through this verse a number of times – including out loud.
- Write it out, stick it on the fridge, have it on your phone.
- Meditate on the words, then respond in praise.
- Take steps to allow God's word to change you: perhaps . . . repent, forgive, love.

8 July

She said to him, 'Yes, Lord;
I believe that you are the Christ,
the Son of God, who is coming into the world.'

John 11:27

Reading: John 11:17–44

Disappointment can be heart-rending. Not the deflation you feel when a night out is cancelled or when the restaurant recommended was less than expected. I'm speaking of the devastation felt when someone you really trusted has let you down – when all you had previously believed about them crashed when they hurt you deeply over something important. To be betrayed by a friend is heartbreaking.

The three siblings – Martha, Mary and Lazarus – had become close friends of Jesus. They were devoted followers, acutely aware of His miraculous healings and life-changing teaching. John even records that Jesus loved this trio (John 11:5). Yet, in their time of greatest need, Jesus disappointed them. He let them down. Didn't come when they sent for Him. Appeared not to care that Lazarus was dying. Even though they believed Jesus could heal their brother, the Saviour stayed away (11:6), and they were distraught.

Lazarus was dead by the time Jesus arrived. But Martha, who previously preferred the kitchen to listening to Jesus, ran out to meet Him (11:20). 'Lord, if you had been here.' she cried, 'my brother would not have died' (11:21), but deep down her disappointed heart was screaming, *Why didn't You come? I thought You loved us!* Yet, despite her disappointment, Martha declares her faith in Jesus as never before. 'But even now,' the broken sister says, 'I know that whatever you ask from God, God will give you' (11:22).

It is in the 'even now' situations of our lives that God does His greatest work; in those times when we dare to trust that the rubble in which we stand can be rebuilt – even become the miraculous – at Jesus' command. When Lazarus stepped out of the tomb, Martha got more than she had ever dreamed possible (11:43–44). She also learned that the situation was about more than them, as Jesus said to the Father: 'That they may believe that you sent me' (11:42).

Even now, Lord, I know You will do what's best, even if I have to wait. Amen.

9 July

Mary therefore took a pound of expensive ointment
made from pure nard, and anointed the feet of Jesus
and wiped his feet with her hair.

John 12:3

Reading: John 12:1–8

It is another dinner in Bethany. Martha is in her happy place, serving. Only this time, reclining at the table with Jesus and His disciples is a man who has been raised from the dead. Yes, Lazarus is the reason for the celebration. Jesus is the focus of their thanks. Both of Lazarus's sisters are trying in their own way to thank Jesus for returning their brother to the family. It is quite a night!

As they eat, faces crowd the windows, attempting to catch a glimpse of the man who has been dead for four days. They have never seen a corpse eat before! Yet, little do those inside and outside that home know of the murderous plans afoot (John 12:10–11), apart from Jesus. He knew exactly how the next week would proceed.

And where was Mary in all of this? She was also in her happy place, at the feet of Jesus. Only this time was different. For in her hands was a jar; a special jar. A flask that probably could have financed Mary's future – perhaps the very dowry she would need for a good marriage. For whatever reason the very expensive perfume had been kept, Mary knew what she wanted to do with it right there and then. So, she knelt low on the floor while the others were eating and laughing, and poured the oil over Jesus' feet, where it trickled across His ankles and ran down the creases on the soles of the Master's feet. If King David had been anointed, why shouldn't King Jesus? Soon the aroma filled the room, turning heads. But Mary, so engrossed in her sacrificial act of worship, didn't notice the commotion her actions had provoked (12:5).

Jesus deserved the best she could give ... and Mary didn't hold back. For the spilling of her treasured perfume symbolized her willingness to be poured out in service for the Saviour she loved.

May I be willing to spill out all that I hold dear at Your feet in worship, my precious Lord. Amen.

10 July

For she said, 'If I touch even his garments,
I will be made well.'

Mark 5:28

Reading: Mark 5:25–29

Jesus loves to respond to those who come to Him in faith. The Gospels are full of physical encounters of the Saviour with people in great need. With barely a smidgen of faith, Jesus rewarded their belief in His power to heal by doing just that ... healing them. The diseased, the broken, the smelly, the destitute, the possessed and the mentally unstable all felt His touch. He never kept his distance from those who, according to the law and the religious, rendered Him ceremonially unclean. His compassion had no boundaries.

His love was never rationed ... even towards women – including this woman who was in a permanent state of *niddah* (menstruation/female bleeding). A man – even a husband – rendered himself unclean for religious worship or service by touching a bleeding woman. Imagine the loneliness this woman had experienced after twelve long years of not having as much as a hug from the man she loved, never mind the sheer physical weakness that accompanied the condition.

Then she heard about Jesus.

From the virtual prison of her home, she was told about the miracle-working rabbi from Galilee, and this sparked a childhood memory. It was believed that the tassels hanging from the outer mantle of a holy man's clothing had special powers to heal. Instantly, she knew she had to get to Jesus. She could take no more. Doctors couldn't help her, and the Talmud 'cures' had been no better. She had tried it all – from foul-tasting tonics, skin-burning astringents and dishes of Persian onions boiled in red wine, to carrying the ashes of an ostrich egg in a linen cloth all summer. None of these had delivered anything except poverty, destroying every vestige of hope for health and a normal life.

Pushing through a crowd was a risk worth taking, even if she was recognized or punished for making others unclean. Jesus was her last and only hope. And so, she nervously stretched out her fingers ...

Lord Jesus, thank you that no one is excluded from Your touch or far from Your love ...
including me. May I always rush to You, whatever the risk. Amen.

11 July

And he said to her,
'Daughter, your faith has made you well;
go in peace, and be healed of your disease.'

Mark 5:34

Reading: Mark 5:30–34

Jesus specializes in identifying those who are seeking Him. The minute the woman touched the tassels hanging from Jesus' prayer shawl she was outed. Even with the large crowd all around, bumping and jostling Him in the narrow street of Capernaum, Jesus knew the very moment the woman had touched Him. He felt power leave Him – at the very same time the woman felt the trickle dry up and strength rise within her weary frame (Mark 5:29).

It was true! The tassels have special power!

She tried to disappear as quickly as she'd come, knowing that her body had been healed and her life restored . . . until she heard the rabbi's voice asking who had touched Him (5:30). Fear glued her to the spot. She had touched a holy man while she was unclean. *Is He angry? Should I run?* In the seconds that followed, she could hear His disciples laugh at the question. Everyone was touching Jesus. There were people everywhere! But the woman knew she had to own up. She owed Him that much.

Now on the ground, at His feet, her life story gushed from her in fear and trembling. She held nothing back (5:33). The crowd may have gasped at her indiscretion, but the only words the woman heard were the gentle words of Jesus. No condemnation. No wagging finger. No stepping back from her. Her heart missed a beat when the rabbi tenderly called her 'Daughter' – declaring that it was her faith that had made her well, while pronouncing peace and healing upon her (5:34).

Turning to leave, the woman grasped what Jesus had said . . . it was her faith, not some magical tassels that had healed her. Faith plus Jesus was all she needed.

There's no hiding in the crowd with Jesus. He always sees. He always knows. He simply waits for us to come closer and reach out to Him in faith . . . whatever we may be bringing with us.

Lord Jesus, thank you that no one is unacceptable in Your eyes. You are always listening for our heart's cry. Amen.

12 July

This they said to test him,
that they might have some charge to bring against him.

John 8:6

Reading: John 8:1–11

You can't fool Jesus. The scribes and the Pharisees couldn't do it when He walked among them, neither can we today. Such was their hatred of Jesus for publicly challenging their hypocrisy and making them a laughing stock before the people they controlled (Matthew 23:27) that they tried every means to catch Him out as a lawbreaker.

Remarkably, the Pharisees weren't particularly interested in the adulterous woman they brought to the temple that day, despite their love for pointing out the sins of others. It was Jesus they were after. Jesus who they wanted to see committing a sin by refusing to condemn the woman to death. After all, they taunted: 'In the Law, Moses commanded us to stone such women' (John 8:5). Actually, Moses said that both adulterers were to be put to death (Leviticus 20:10). Funny how they didn't bring the man with them!

In their smugness, they used this woman as bait to find fault with the Son of God. The woman was not innocent of wrongdoing, having been 'caught in adultery' (John 8:3). God always treats sin seriously, but she was now in the presence of the One who gave the law in the first place – and whose own substitutionary death would soon be undertaken for her sin . . . and for us all. Jesus was bringing in a new covenant based on forgiveness for the repentant.

His response to the situation was legendary. Facing the sniping Pharisees, Jesus said, 'Let him who is without sin among you be the first to throw a stone at her' (8:7). And those old snakes slithered away in silence, their own sin condemning them, leaving Jesus to act in mercy towards the woman. 'From now on sin no more,' He told her (8:11).

The Pharisees should have known better: 'You shall not put the Lord your God to the test' (Deuteronomy 6:16; Luke 4:12). We can never pull the wool over Jesus' eyes. He sees the thoughts and intentions of every heart (Hebrews 4:12).

Lord, forgive me when doubt and questioning replace faith and trust. May I be willingly transparent. Amen.

13 July

'For the Son of Man came to seek and to save the lost.'

Luke 19:10

Reading: Luke 15:1–7

Suddenly, a poster picture of a scrawny dog filled the screen behind the conference speaker. Soon everything became clear.

The speaker had been cycling along a very busy road in central London when he noticed that every lamppost – a few hundred, at least – had a poster attached, so he stopped to take a look. In large, bold letters was written, 'LOST: Disco.' A large picture of a small dog stared back at him with this description: 'Scrawny, Thin, Elderly 17-year-old-dog. Also, deaf. Very friendly. If found, please contact . . .'

Instantly, everyone under the roof was thinking the same thing. I mean, the dog wasn't just old – it was *very* old! What's seventeen in doggy years? It wasn't even healthy . . . scrawny, thin . . . and it was also deaf! What hope did it have of being found alive on that busy London road? 'It's probably dead already!' the speaker shouted into the microphone.

This lost dog didn't have much going for it, except that someone obviously loved it enough to have hundreds of posters printed and pasted on to every lamp-post on the road. However pathetic it looked – however lost it was – its owner was doing everything in his power to save this old, sick, deaf, friendly dog from harm, and to bring him home.

The speaker turned towards the screen: 'I mean, who would go to these lengths for the likes of this?' Then came the epiphany: 'Jesus! That's exactly what He did when He was here on earth . . . what He continues to do even to this day.'

It's true. Jesus has always sought out the marginalized; the ones we see as lost causes. Those living in the dangerous places of life and experiencing every problem it throws their way. Whether young or old, healthy or sick, hearing or deaf, friendly or unfriendly, male or female, we are all lost. The Father is still doing all He can to rescue us from disaster and bring us home. We see it every time we look at Jesus.

Thank you, Jesus, that we come to You just as we are. You are still seeking and saving the lost. Amen.

14 July

'Why does he eat with tax collectors and sinners?'

Mark 2:16

Reading: Mark 2:15–17

I think, if we're honest, we would rather sit beside the sweet-smelling washed of our society at church than those with whom Jesus chose to spend most of His time. A short mission trip to the world's unfortunates is often preferrable to engaging with the needy living in our own cities. We might feel justified at leaving such 'ministry' to those we see as gifted in that area, while secretly concerned that such individuals demand too much time and might perhaps be a detrimental influence on our children.

God sometimes brings us up short by the reality checks He sends our way. It has happened to me, and I blush as I share. When our son befriended a boy from his class and started to bring him home after school, I became anxious. He was unkempt, with a habit of using bad language. And with a complicated home life, he wasn't the kind of friend I wanted my child to have. Despite the good relationship our son was developing with him, I never made this boy feel welcome in our home. It wasn't long before he stopped coming. And much to my shame, I was glad.

A few years later, I heard singing coming from the garden, and recognizing that it was a Christian song – and not our son singing – I went to investigate. There he was . . . all changed . . . clean and smiling . . . and singing about Jesus. His story tore at my heart. A young Christian couple had moved into a house near his, taken him into their hearts and loved him for Jesus.

I sent him to you, Catherine, I heard God whisper, *and you didn't think him good enough to love, so I gave him to someone else to nurture for me.* I'd missed the opportunity because I hadn't thought like Jesus, and my guilty sorrow took a long time to overcome.

There's no such thing as a 'clean side' to the Broad Road. All who have ever travelled it are sinners, saved by One who didn't turn away from them.

Lord, teach me to think like You, love like You and give of myself the way You did. Amen.

15 July

THINK ON THIS

'For if you love those who love you,
what reward do you have?'

Matthew 5:46

- Read through this verse a number of times – including out loud.
- Write it out, stick it on the fridge, have it on your phone.
- Meditate on the words, then respond in praise.
- Encourage someone by sharing this verse with them today.

16 July

'Do not fear, only believe.'

Mark 5:36

Reading: Mark 5:21–24, 35–43

Don't you hate it when you are interrupted? You finally managed to get the attention of someone you've sought for a while, and then their phone rings or another person steps in . . . and you've lost them. It can be infuriating. Imagine what it was like for Jairus. He had been anxiously waiting in the crowd by the lakeside for Jesus to return to Capernaum, urgently needing to tell Him about his daughter. You see, she wasn't only sick, she was near death (Mark 5:23). The little girl's last chance was Jesus. Jairus had to get His attention before anyone else snatched the rabbi away.

And that's exactly what he did. Jairus's heart must have leapt when Jesus agreed, and they walked as hastily as anyone could through the crowd. But then Jesus stopped dead in His tracks, and the ensuing interruption surely made the father despair. He heard Jesus talk to a woman from the town. He knew her. She'd been ill for a long time – since shortly after his little girl was born. He felt sorry for her, but he needed Jesus to hurry . . . there was no time for delay. Didn't Jesus understand that?

What Jairus didn't comprehend was that time isn't important to Jesus. Interruptions were merely other appointments. Nothing would stop Him from doing what He needed to do. Even when messengers arrived to tell Jairus it was too late for the Teacher to come – the little girl had died – it didn't matter. Jesus still had time. It is never too late for Him. He had ordered the days before one of them began. What was important to Jesus was the father's faith. 'Do not fear, only believe,' Jesus said to Jairus when He had finished with what others might have seen as an interruption.

Jairus did believe . . . and his little girl was raised from death (5:41–42)!

Think what Jesus could do if our faith were greater than our fear!

Forgive me, Lord, for ever thinking I could miss Your blessing because of circumstances. I believe; help my unbelief! Amen.

17 July

But she came and knelt before him,
saying, 'Lord, help me.'

Matthew 15:25

Reading: Matthew 15:21–28

Talisha (my name for the unnamed woman in the text) had reached the end of her tether. Life literally lay in pieces around her. Devastation was her daily companion. With each passing day she became more fearful that the demons oppressing her daughter would take her life. Something she couldn't bear.

Sleep overtook the exhausted child just as the door creaked open. 'Shhh,' Talisha whispered to the young man entering. Shocked by the fresh bruises on his mother's face, he gasped. 'She's getting worse, Mother. What are you going to do?' Before she had time to answer, the troubled son caressed her swollen cheek, saying, 'Why don't we take her to the temple at Sidon?'

'It's twenty-two miles away, Son! We'd never make it – and I have no faith in these gods of stone any more!' Shocked by his mother's blasphemy, the young man tried to coax her into letting him pay for a sacrifice to Eshmun, the god of healing.

'No,' she replied. 'I've made up my mind. I'm going to seek out the rabbi, Jesus. I've heard he's close by.' 'A rabbi, Mother? You know these Jews. He'll never speak to a Gentile … especially not a woman!' Talisha pulled a shawl around her shoulders and looked her sad son in the eye. 'I've heard He's not like the others, and I won't return until He hears me.'

Sitting in the darkness, the young man watched his little sister's chest gently rise and fall. He longed for her to be freed from the demons that tormented her, but seriously doubted that some Jewish rabbi would want, or be able, to help them. But as he swiped at the tears, his mind went back to a story he had heard as a child, of a prophet from Israel who had raised a child to life, not fifteen miles from where he sat. Zarephath! That's where it was! Maybe this Jesus could help a Syrophoenician woman after all. With all his heart, he hoped so.[27]

Lord, seeking You is the best thing to do in life. Only You are truth. Only You are able to meet my need. Amen.

18 July

Then Jesus answered her,
'O woman, great is your faith!
Be it done for you as you desire.'
And her daughter was healed instantly.

Matthew 15:28

Reading: Mark 7:24–30

Matthew and the others packed a little bread in their pouches. They were going for a rest, Jesus had said, but he couldn't imagine where they could go and not be found by the needy poor . . . until the hills of Phoenicia came into view. Away from Israel, they settled quietly in a little house, with Tyre silhouetted beyond.

Suddenly, loud wailing shattered the silence. 'Have mercy on me, O Lord, Son of David' (Matthew 15:22). Matthew and the others sprang up, startled from slumber, but Jesus didn't react. 'My daughter is severely demon-possessed,' the woman called out, louder than before. The disciples feared the noise would attract a crowd, and any hope of rest would be gone.

Talisha had been searching for hours, so she wasn't about to give up now that she knew Jesus was only feet away. Bursting through the door she fell at His feet, pleading, 'Lord, help me.' The rabbi's reply stung: 'I was sent only to the lost sheep of the house of Israel' (15:24). The unspoken 'yes' of Jesus' companions cut through the air, but the woman continued to beg. She'd heard Jesus had cast demons out of a man at Gadara – and he wasn't a Jew!

Talisha listened carefully as Jesus continued: 'It is not right to take the children's bread and throw it to the dogs' (15:26). She knew the Jews regarded foreigners as vicious dogs, but she recognized that Jesus was showing her a different picture – one that reminded her of her childhood home – of the pets around the family table. 'Yes, Lord,' she countered, 'yet even the dogs eat the crumbs that fall from their masters' table' (15:27). Silence fell with the wisdom of her words. Only Jesus spoke.

'O woman, great is your faith! Be it done for you as you desire' (15:28). And Matthew watched as this 'little dog' wept her thanks to Jesus, his own heart forever softened by the love and devotion of this mother's pleading faith, and by the action of the Father heart of God (Jesus) come to earth.

Jesus, I'm grateful that the crumbs from Your table are greater than any banquet elsewhere. Amen.

19 July

Jesus said, 'Let the little children come to me
and do not hinder them, for to such
belongs the kingdom of heaven.'

Matthew 19:14

Reading: Matthew 19:13–15

Jesus had acted miraculously in the lives of the two little girls. The heart of parents towards their sick children was the same then as it is now. What's interesting to note is that in one case the parent who approached Jesus was a Jewish male, while the other was a Gentile woman. Their gender, race and life experiences were very different from each other's, but that mattered not to Jesus. He healed both children.

It's easy to forget that children were regarded then in the same way as women and slaves – as inferior. Boys, however, were treated much better than girls, given an education and taught a trade, while girls learned to be good homemakers until a marriage could be arranged for them, usually in their teens. Girls were expensive to keep in a society where poverty broke many a man. But there was also love in the mix of family life, as we have already seen.

In this world where children were shown no respect, Jesus did the opposite. He treated them with dignity, love and concern. When those big men we know as His disciples had the audacity to argue over who among them was the greatest, Jesus used a living object lesson to set them straight. 'He took a child and put him in the midst of them, and taking him in his arms, he said to them, "Whoever receives one such child in my name receives me, and whoever receives me, receives not me but him who sent me"' (Mark 9:36–37).

Greatness in God's kingdom is all about how we treat others, especially those who can give us nothing in return – either in status or wealth. Jesus used a little boy to show those who should have known better their own pride-filled hearts. True greatness always begins and ends with humility ... and a willingness to confer value to those others overlook. I guess the little boy slept peacefully that night.

Lord, teach me to respect even the youngest among us. Amen.

20 July

'Whoever causes one of these little ones
who believe in me to sin, it would be better for him
if a great millstone were hung around his neck
and he were thrown into the sea.'

Mark 9:42

Reading: 2 Timothy 3:14–17

In my family home, Wednesday's evening meal was an off-the-knee affair, the kitchen table having been replaced by three long, low benches. Shortly after 6 p.m., the Good News Club was in full swing, filling the house with the noise and laughter of children participating in songs, quiz, memory verses and Bible stories. This was my mother's happy place – ministering God's love for, and to, those boys and girls ... for years! Throughout the week, after a full working day, she prepared for the club and prayed for each of those precious children by name. She even had the added joy of leading some to new life in Christ.

Years after the club finally closed, a young man called on her, introducing himself as having attended her Good News Club. As they talked, he told her he had recently trusted in the Saviour, and his first thought was, 'I must tell Mrs Fraser, she'd be pleased.' That was an understatement! There have been a number of those who once graced Daddy's wooden benches who have returned as adults to tell my mum how the Good News Club influenced their lives and was an important link in bringing them to Christ.

Tears were sometimes shed when children were prevented by their parents from returning to the club because of what they called 'the nonsense' they heard there. But Mum never stopped praying for them.

Jesus had something to say about this – of which we should take note (Mark 9:42).

When we visited Capernaum in Israel, I was amazed by the number of millstones strewn among the ruins. Even the smallest of these bygone harvesting tools weighed heavily. Staring at them, the words of Jesus mixed with the memories of Mum's little forbidden ones, causing my heart to sink. Jesus said that torturous judgement involving these stone giants would be *better* than what was planned for those who prevented a child's walk with Him.

Lord, may all I do and say only ever encourage little ones to come to You. Amen.

21 July

THINK ON THIS

'Whoever humbles himself like this child
is the greatest in the kingdom of heaven.'
Matthew 18:4

- Read through this verse a number of times – including out loud.
- Write it out, stick it on the fridge, have it on your phone.
- Meditate on the words, then respond in praise.
- Be a doer . . . Serve someone with an act of kindness today.

22 July

'Truly, I say to you, unless you turn and become like
children, you will never enter the kingdom of heaven.'

Matthew 18:3

Reading: Matthew 18:1–4

While parenting isn't all cute smiles and baby powder, I wouldn't have missed it for
the world. And it frequently brings an added bonus only revealed in later years:
grandchildren. My husband often jokes: 'If I'd known having grandchildren was
such fun, I'd have had them first!'

Crowds followed Jesus everywhere He went, and where there were women there
were children. Little shy ones hanging on to their mothers' skirts; boisterous ones
playing at the edge of the gathering; big sisters keeping toddler siblings enter-
tained. Jesus invariably used what was visible around Him to illustrate His
preaching, including the children around His feet, and He cared deeply for them.

In children, Jesus identified what we adults require to display genuine faith:

- **Helplessness**. They needed to be brought to Jesus – they couldn't find
  their way by themselves. 'No one can come to me unless the Father who
  sent me draws him' (John 6:44);
- **An immediate cry for help**. Too often pride gets in our way and slows the
  help God has available. 'God opposes the proud but gives grace to the
  humble' (James 4:6);
- **Complete trust**. There is no one bigger in a child's eyes than Mummy
  or Daddy. 'Trust in the LORD with all your heart . . .' (Proverbs 3:5);
- **Teachability**. Like little sponges they drink it all in, constantly
  questioning with an insatiable desire to learn more. 'If any of you lacks
  wisdom, let him ask God . . .' (James 1:5);
- **Focus on the now**. The young are only interested in what's happening
  today. Personal ambition comes later, and is often a distraction from
  seeking what is truly important. 'But seek first the kingdom of God and
  his righteousness' (Matthew 6:33);
- **Joy**. Is there anything more wonderful than the uninhibited joy exhibited
  in the belly laugh of a child? It's infectious! Jesus is our joy-giver. 'These
  things I have spoken to you, that my joy may be in you, and that your joy
  may be full' (John 15:11). Let's infect the world with it!

*Lord Jesus, give me these childlike attributes, that You might see my heart is always and
only Yours. Amen.*

23 July

'You don't know what you are asking!'

Matthew 20:22, NLT

Reading: Matthew 20:20–23

Sometimes the pendulum swings too far in one direction.

From a time when children were given no status at all, and there are places today where that is still the case, has come a swing in the West that has put children on a pedestal. Parental behaviour towards officials at sports events and lying for their offspring when they're in trouble with law enforcers – to say nothing of giving in to their every whim and fancy – is proving detrimental to our children. Some church leaders go as far as to describe it as child worship.

Mrs Zebedee was like many of us. She wanted the best for her two sons, James and John. She wanted them to succeed in life; to have positions of authority; to be looked up to. What could be better than having them honoured by sitting next to the Man who would overthrow the Romans and lead Israel's new kingdom? So, she decided to speak up for them . . . put in a good word. Unfortunately, she totally misunderstood what Jesus' kingdom was all about. He set her straight. In today's parlance, Jesus said: 'Woman, you have no idea what you're talking about. You haven't a clue what you're asking for your boys!'

This mother was thinking of her lads moving up the social ladder – from fishing to management. Jesus, however, was setting up a kingdom of servitude, humility and suffering, where 'the last will be first, and the first last' (Matthew 20:16). Yet, Mrs Zebedee and her husband had done something wonderful for her sons . . . released them from the family business to follow Jesus. As she herself followed the Saviour, even to the cross (Mark 15:40) and then to the tomb (16:1), she undoubtedly discovered the cost of discipleship. It's probable that she was still alive when James was martyred at the hands of Herod Agrippa (Acts 12:1–2), and while John was later enslaved in the mines of Patmos.

Her sons were right up there after all . . . and the 'Well done' would have come from the ascended Jesus (Matthew 25:21).

Lord, teach me to ask of You only what is right. Amen.

24 July

I have no greater joy than to hear
that my children are walking in the truth.

3 John 1:4

Reading: Deuteronomy 11:18–19

One day my father-in-law reached his car to find two young lads trying to syphon petrol from his tank. Giving them a little lecture, Sammy asked them what they wanted to do when they grew up. The reply was both sobering and sad. 'Go on the dole, like me da!' was the reply (that is, the unemployment register).

How sad when kids have nothing to aim for, and don't even dream dreams.

When our son was studying for his A levels, I set a tiny card on his desk with the words 'Don't let the weeds grow around your dreams' scrawled on it. Today we are proud of his many and varied accomplishments in music, but what causes my heart to swell most is that he is a committed follower of Jesus. While we join with the applause of others at his achievements, it's the Bible verses messaged to me just when I need encouragement that remind me of his love for God's word since childhood. Recently, when in a family crisis, he became the one to hold my hand and pray for me . . . our roles had been reversed.

Ambition is not wrong. However, we should be careful which wall of success we place our ladder beside. God has His people in every walk of life: politicians, financiers, businesspeople, medical staff, creative arts professionals, factory workers, Brussels sprouts pickers and cleaners – it matters not. What matters is that our children are 'walking in the truth' (3 John 1:4), and that our desire for them to succeed is always secondary to seeing them find and follow Christ.

So, let's hold that ladder they are trying to climb with continual prayer, and early in their lives teach them to look for God's guidance as to which wall they should lean their ladder against.

Lord Jesus, today we place the children in our lives once more into Your care. May those who are wayward find You, and those who know You stay with You. Amen.

25 July

'For this child I prayed . . .'
1 Samuel 1:27

Reading: 1 Samuel 1:27–28

Jesus had no physical children, but He had a multitude of spiritual children – those who were birthed by the Holy Spirit (John 3:6–7), and for whom He prayed. His powerful intercession for those the Father gave Him (17:6) sets a perfect example for us as parents and grandparents . . . and all the godly substitutes in-between.

In a world that seems determined to destroy biblical truths, and to blur the Scripture's very clear truths that we teach our children, our prayer for them needs to be as intense – if not more so – than the enemy's attack (2 Thessalonians 3:3).

Let's pray fervently for our children:
- for salvation early in life, and that no one will stand in their way (Romans 10:1);
- that they will love the Lord with all their heart, soul, mind and strength (Mark 12:30), because weak faith will falter under pressure;
- to be assured that God loves and accepts them exactly as they are – both in gender and in every little idiosyncrasy that makes them an individual (Psalm 139:13–16);
- to recognize they are a gift from God to our family . . . loved, accepted and precious (Psalm 127:3, NLT);
- to be healthy and safe from accident or danger. And for those children impacted by disability or chronic illness, that they might know God's protection and healing touch (Psalm 91:4);
- that God would protect their impressionable minds at school, and with their peers, teaching them discernment (1 John 4:1);
- to make good friendships, and also to be a good friend to others (Proverbs 18:24);
- to look beyond themselves, to see and act on behalf of those in need (Philippians 2:3).

Lord, give my children 'enough success to be certain of Your love for them, enough favour to be aware of Your kindness, but enough humility to know that they can do nothing worthwhile without You'.[28] Amen.

26 July

Be imitators of me, as I am of Christ.
1 Corinthians 11:1

Reading: 1 Corinthians 13:1–8

How often have you heard the words: 'He's so like his dad!' Do we really get like the people we live with? That's a scary thought.

Jesus had only three years in which to tell and show His disciples how to live in a godly way in this world (John 13:15). The apostle Paul emphasized the principle of being an example for others to follow with this very bold statement: *Do what I do, just as I do what Christ did!* (1 Corinthians 11:1, my paraphrase). Whether or not we're brave enough to repeat Paul's words publicly, our lives declare it to our children every day.

We are watched and imitated in more than our speech and mannerisms. It's not merely what we say that influences our children – although that is important – we are their daily living object lessons. They watch us . . . intently! What do they see?

One elderly gentleman we know often remarked that the greatest thing a man can do for his children is to love their mother. Love displayed in the home, where we can become careless when away from the scrutiny of others, speaks volumes. And love isn't merely the occasional hug, but all that 1 Corinthians 13 teaches: patience, kindness, humility, modesty and good humour. From our love for each other our children will learn 'not to rejoice about injustice but to rejoice whenever the truth wins out . . . never to give up or lose faith . . . to always be hopeful, and to endure through every circumstance' (adapted from 13:6–7, NLT).

This kind of love is not sickly sweet. It's tough, yet tender. And better than anything, it demonstrates the kind of love Christ had for His own spiritual children and for His church. Twelve men, in particular, watched closely how Jesus lived and how He prayed. They trusted His example and believed what He said. Then they went on to change the world . . . one loving encounter at a time.

Lord Jesus, may the love we have found in You be the benchmark in all our relationships. Amen.

27 July

That you, being rooted and grounded in love . . .
may be filled with all the fullness of God.

Ephesians 3:17–19

Reading: Ephesians 3:14–19

Parenting is all about establishing our children in love, acceptance and security, while teaching them what they need; not only to survive in what lies outside the home, but to flourish within it in confidence. Christian parenting always brings God into the equation, adding the richness of His love and grace . . . and especially the wisdom we so often lack when raising our children (James 1:5).

Jesus taught the disciples – His spiritual children – that He would not always be with them in person (John 16:7). They would have to face the world armed with what He had taught them, but also with the promise of the Holy Spirit's empowering and guidance (14:15–17). They would be without Jesus physically, but He promised His presence would be with them forever (Matthew 28:20).

We spend the early years of our children's lives giving them roots that enable them to grow and learn – teaching them biblical principles and godly habits, alongside everything else that makes up their busy lives. The years whizz past, and suddenly they're all grown up – making their own decisions and finding their own way. And then one day the inevitable happens . . . roots become wings and they fly from our homes, though never from our hearts. Suddenly their concerns are grown-up ones; their love is given to another; their decisions not necessarily ours . . . and one day, they will hopefully have children of their own to nurture.

As our hands come off, I think Paul's prayer for his spiritual children in Ephesians 3:16–19 is perfect for those adult children we love:

- that from His glorious, unlimited resources God will empower them with inner strength through His Spirit;
- for Christ to make His home in their hearts, His love and strength keeping them strong;
- that they might have the power to understand and experience all facets of the love of Christ;
- that they will be made complete with all the fullness of life and power that comes from God.

Lord Jesus, we release our adult children into Your hands. May the distractions of life never keep them from You. Amen.

28 July

THINK ON THIS

For the eyes of the Lord are on the righteous,
and his ears are open to their prayer.

1 Peter 3:12

- Read through this verse a number of times – including out loud.
- Write it out, stick it on the fridge, have it on your phone.
- Meditate on the words, then respond in praise.
- Take steps to allow God's word to change you: perhaps . . . repent, forgive, love.

29 July

'Then what shall I do with Jesus who is called Christ?'
Matthew 27:22

Reading: Matthew 27:15–19

This is a question we all must face. It matters not whether you're the king on the throne or the person sleeping on the streets; whether you have millions in the bank or owe more than you'll ever earn; whether you have a graduate-level education or left school as early as possible. One thing is sure: we cannot ignore Jesus and His claim on our lives (Romans 14:12).

Pilate had been sent to Israel to sort out the political insurgency. He showed no mercy to those who acted against Rome, while attempts at diplomacy with the religious leaders was fraught with difficulty. Pilate's wife – so disturbed by the arrest of Jesus – did the unthinkable, even for a woman in her position. She interrupted her husband while he was right in the middle of state business by sending him a note. 'Have nothing to do with that righteous man,' she pleaded, 'for I have suffered much because of him today in a dream' (Matthew 27:19).

We have no textual evidence that Pilate's wife was a follower of Jesus, but to her husband she declared Him a 'righteous man'. She was willing to speak up for Jesus in front of a mob baying for His blood, and cared little for the consequences of interrupting her husband at such a time. Mrs Pilate was one very brave lady, except for one thing ... her warning asked for the impossible. None of us can 'have nothing to do with' Jesus. Each of us must decide whether we are for Him – by placing our trust in Jesus through faith – or against Him, by rejecting His sacrifice for our salvation.

> What will you do with Jesus?
> Neutral you cannot be;
> Someday your heart will be asking,
> 'What will He do with me?'[29]

Lord Jesus, my heart is Yours in worship, love and commitment. May I bravely declare You Saviour, encouraging others to also make that choice. Amen.

30 July

'God bless your mother – the womb
from which you came, and the breasts that nursed you!'
Luke 11:27, NLT

Reading: Luke 11:27–28

Occasionally the Gospel writers include something that makes you wonder: *Why?* These few verses do that for me. Why, in the middle of serious, and at times frightening, teaching on demonic activity did Luke record the shouted words of a woman from the crowd? Heckling was nothing new to Jesus. There was always someone in the crush of the many who taunted Him – usually those of the religious elite – but this was an arrow of praise.

Some see it as an attempt to venerate Jesus' mother, Mary, and quickly condemn the heckler. Surely her praise should have been directed towards Jesus, not His mother? And didn't Jesus' reply put the woman in her place? But maybe there's another angle to consider.

We are not told the context of the woman's cry. What made her shout out those words is not clear. Why she was there is not explained, but her words indicate that Jesus had impacted her life. Whether by healing (could the man healed in Luke 11:14 have been her husband or her son?) or, since her interjection came right in the middle of Jesus speaking about demons (11:14–26), had she herself been delivered from a life of torment? Or had she suddenly realized the truth of the Saviour's words to those trying to trap Him that 'the Kingdom of God has arrived among you' (11:20)?

Whatever the reason, I believe her interruption of praise was indeed directed at Jesus, simply by saying how glad she was that He had been born. Today we might say of someone's exceptional achievements: 'Your mother must be so proud of you! God bless her for bringing you into the world!'

Jesus humbly replied to the praise directed towards Himself and His mother by explaining that true blessing belongs to those who hear God's word and put it into practice (11:28). Happiness comes from obeying His teaching. That's where we will find God's favour – not in anything else.

Lord Jesus, You are worthy of my praise. May I gladly give it among the crowd as well as in the private place. Amen.

31 July

'Fear not, little flock,
for it is the Father's good pleasure
to give you the kingdom.'
Luke 12:32

Reading: Luke 12:32–34

Jesus' interaction with women and children gives us a glimpse into the kindness of His heart. And those we read of in Scripture are but a tiny number of the multitude He touched while here on earth. For some it was miraculous healing for themselves (Mark 5:34) or those they loved (Matthew 15:28). For a few they received their dead back to life (John 11:44). But for the majority it was liberation through faith, and the realization that they were of value to God, as Jesus taught them alongside the men (Luke 10:39).

You are never the same again once you've met with Jesus.

Life with all its complexities can then be viewed through a different lens. Jesus may not change our circumstances or deliver us from the heartbreak caused by a fallen, broken world. Instead, He adds a new perspective, teaching us to look at life's big picture . . . from the viewpoint of eternity. In fact, we choose our response to the difficulties of life.

Fatalism keeps the focus on me. Wrapped in the cloak of negativism, it ensures that I keep my eyes on the circumstances, with a 'this can never change' attitude devoid of peace and joy.

In contrast:

Perseverance surrounds itself in positivity and encourages me to take my eyes off the circumstances and direct the focus towards God, which in turn leads to . . .
Acceptance, which focuses on God's big plan, including His will for my life and what He's doing in my circumstances, even if I can't see it yet. And it's in acceptance that I can find peace.

When surrounded by the needy and broken, Jesus often used the words 'Fear not', but He never promised that all their problems would suddenly disappear . . . He did promise them 'the Father's good pleasure to give [them] the kingdom', and all that means for time and eternity.

Lord, I choose today to lift my eyes from life's rubble and set my focus on You. I believe that You know what You're doing, even if I don't. Amen.

August

1 August

Jesus answered, 'It was not that this man sinned,
or his parents, but that the works of God
might be displayed in him.'

John 9:3

Reading: John 9:1–5

With ears fine-tuned like those of a bat, the beggar sensed that a group of footsteps had stopped directly in front of him. 'Rabbi?' a voice questioned. 'Who sinned, this man or his parents that he was born blind?' The man felt his face flush, embarrassed that his sin should become the topic of public conversation. 'Neither this man nor his parents sinned,' came the reply, before he had time to interrupt.

Is he saying it wasn't my fault?! The beggar was stunned into silence. 'He was born blind so that the power of God could be seen in him,' the Rabbi continued. The beggar didn't recognize the voice. All he heard was, *It wasn't my fault!* He was weary of the times his blindness had been mocked. Tired of the shouted accusations that sin had denied him sight. Now all he could hear was, *It wasn't my fault . . . nor my father's . . . nor my mother's.* It wasn't sin that had made him blind!

Too often we look for reasons when something goes wrong in our lives. Occasionally illness, or even death, occurs as a direct result of foolish or even sinful behaviour. But that is not always the case. I was once rocked by an accusation that some specific sin in my life must have caused our daughter to be born disabled. Terrified that my accuser might be right, I spent much time and many tears pleading with God to show me the sin in order that I could confess and allow my child to be healed. It was, of course, nonsense. Let's ensure that we don't foolishly cause someone else such pain.

Pain is part of life's package – perfection belongs to heaven.

Here, Jesus pointed to another reason for the man's disability: 'That the works of God might be displayed in him' (John 9:3). While we can only see the immediacy of where God has placed us, He sees an altogether different picture, where Jesus works to bring light out of darkness and joy out of pain.

Jesus, please bring clarity into the fogginess of our lives. Amen.

2 August

And [Jesus] said to him,
'Go, wash in the pool of Siloam' . . .
So he went and washed and came back seeing.

John 9:7

Reading: John 9:6–12

The blind man heard fingers scraping dirt from between the smooth stones. Something he himself did when boredom ruled. Then suddenly the beggar heard the rabbi clear his throat and . . . spit. *Spit!* Almost immediately, hands were plastering his eyes with mud made from the spittle and dirt from the road. It was disgusting! But he didn't object, allowing the man they called Jesus to cake his sightless eyes with mud before raising him to his feet.

'Go,' he commanded. 'Go and wash in the pool of Siloam.'

He knew every stone, every wall and every gutter well between where he sat and the fresh Gihon spring to which he'd been sent. His toes carefully felt for all thirteen of the steps as he made his way into the water. Jesus' words rang in his ears as he plunged his head under the cool water and rubbed and rubbed until the muck fell away from his eyes.

It felt strange at first. His eyelids felt fuller than ever before, and as the last of the mud fell away, they stretched – and then opened! *What is happening?* Shock took over as he shook the water from his head, lifting it out of the pool. Pain assaulted his eyes as the perpetual darkness he'd lived in was banished by something else. 'It must be light!' the poor man shouted as he squinted at his hands through the brightness for the first time. Then, with his legs still in the water, the beggar tilted his head back and looked at the sky stretching above him.

'Blue! So that's what my brother tried to describe when he talked about the sky overhead!' And he laughed as a little wisp of cloud dared to skip across the expanse. 'It's blue!' he exclaimed, to the bemusement of some women sitting nearby.

I can't imagine what that must have felt like, especially with the strange method Jesus used. Dirt. Spittle. Mud. Water. Let's understand, there's never anything 'usual' about Jesus. We cannot predict His ways, any more than we can challenge His methods. But we can trust His heart . . . every time!

Surprise me today, Jesus! Amen.

3 August

He answered, 'Whether he is a sinner I do not know.
One thing I do know, that though I was blind,
now I see.'

John 9:25

Reading: John 9:13–41

'There's none so blind as those who will not see,' said John Heywood back in 1546.

For the blind man – now with his sight restored – the return journey from the pool of Siloam was slow, delayed by the new sights and colours he saw with every step: the little flower pushing through the cracks; children playing; a mangy dog running across his path. Then, turning a corner, the man saw what his blindness could never have imagined. The temple! In all its splendour, the huge edifice rose towards the sky, dwarfing everything around it. The southern steps heaved with worshippers, while the gold adorning the Holy Place glinted in the sunshine ... and tears ran down his cheeks at the privilege, now his, to view its splendour.

Jesus was gone by the time he got back. In His place was a crowd – the excited and the questioning. Backslappers mixed with sceptics, believers with doubters, and the critics multiplied when he was dragged before the Pharisees. *Are you really the blind man who begged on the road to the temple? How did you get your sight back? Who did this to you?* (John 9:8–15).

However, 'The Jews did not believe that he had been blind and had received his sight' until they brought in the parents (9:18). Terrified they would be excommunicated (9:22), instead of delight they felt compelled to push their son back into the ring of condemnation (9:21). But the man had met with Jesus – he had been healed and transformed – so he would not entertain the suggestion that Jesus was a sinner, even if He had healed him on the Sabbath. 'God does not listen to sinners,' the man quipped, exposing their delusion. Now he was seeing with more than his eyes!

The Pharisees aren't the only ones who refused to see what was literally sitting on the end of their noses, are they? Perhaps we who were once 'blind' should take off the sunspecs of doubt and let the Light fully shine in us, and through us.

Lord, forgive me for refusing to see what You have made clear. Amen.

4 August

THINK ON THIS

'We know that God does not listen to sinners,
but if anyone is a worshiper of God and does his will, God
listens to him.'

John 9:31

- Read through this verse a number of times – including out loud.
- Write it out, stick it on the fridge, have it on your phone.
- Meditate on the words, then respond in praise.
- Encourage someone by sharing this verse with them today.

5 August

Moved with compassion . . .

Mark 1:41, NLT

Reading: Mark 1:40–45

Silent conversation filled Reuben's (the name I've given to the unnamed man) head and tormented his heart, tears mixing with the water he splashed on to his potter's wheel. But as he pounded clay against wood, the hopelessness of his situation overwhelmed him. What could he do? It was so unfair. No one could help him. Fate had dealt him the most vicious of blows. He felt condemned, alone and unclean as he paddled his wheel ever faster.

'Reuben . . . stop!' Clay shot across the room as his hands were pulled away from the wheel. 'Reuben . . . why didn't you tell me?' his wife asked, stroking his tear-stained face. 'I needed to prepare,' Reuben responded, 'to leave as much as possible in place for you and the children before I go to the priest.'

'The priest? You really think that it's . . . it's . . . ?' 'Leprosy, Deborah. It's leprosy! I can't hide it any longer. Just give me one more day . . . then I'll go . . .' They collapsed into each other's arms, as if holding each other could stop their world from falling apart. It should all have been so different. They should have spent many years together enjoying their simple, hard-working life. Now the future was bleak. No, it was unimaginable. What made it worse was that no one could help him. Even the Lord Jehovah had forsaken him.[30]

Life has a way of delivering the unthinkable when a moment in time suddenly catapults us into the realm of the unfair . . . or the devastating. And when the road we now walk is neither the one we set out on, nor leads to the destination we had planned, it may even feel as if God has abandoned us. We may not have to leave our homes and families as Reuben did, but the feeling of isolation is just the same. And the enemy of our souls loves to whisper his lies to our already burdened hearts. *God doesn't care. Where is He when you need Him?*

But Jesus is here. He is not distant. And if we could but glimpse the eternal, we would look into His face as the leper did that day . . . and see compassion written all over it.

Lord, may those receiving bad news today feel Your compassion. Amen.

6 August

I will sing to the LORD,
because he has dealt bountifully with me.

Psalm 13:6

Reading: Psalm 13

Lament has almost become trendy. Authors are clicking keyboards to remind us that prayers of distress litter the Bible, and not least in the Psalms. For too long we have been dissuaded from praying anything accusatory or negative, told it lacks faith and shows disrespect towards a sovereign God. For years I put on my smile to go to church while lamenting constantly before God over the suffering of my children.

But we can't put on a show for God. His compassionate heart sees our pain. Lament is a natural human response that ultimately drives us Godward, causing us to recognize our need of Him and His bounty towards us. I'm pretty sure the leper in yesterday's story would have repeated David's words.

As Reuben walked towards the caves outside town, he thought about how often he had passed the place where the lepers lived – hurrying by, hoping he wouldn't meet any of them on the way. They were unclean; a danger to society; people to be avoided at all costs. Or that's what he had thought – until now. Until he was one of them.

A sense of panic swept over him as he watched people go about their business in this city of the destitute. Men, women, boys and girls, they all looked the same: dejected, despairing and without hope. Lost. And, like the stabbing of a dagger, the sharpness of reality pierced Reuben's soul. He was no longer a man – he was a leper.

Day followed day, month followed month. Seasons came and went, leaving Reuben only with memories and a body totally ravaged by the disease that had taken him away from those he loved. Slowly drowning in a sea of helplessness, his daily prayer was that of the forgotten:

How long, O LORD? Will you forget me forever? How long will you hide your face from me? (Psalm 13:1).

But Reuben was unaware that heaven had already heard his cries.[31] He just needed to remember the final words of the psalmist's lament.

Thank you, Lord, that You desire to deal bountifully with us. As we wait, help us not to give up. Amen.

238

7 August

And Jesus stretched out his hand and touched him,
saying, 'I will; be clean.'

Luke 5:13

Reading: Luke 5:12–15

As a nurse, I've cleaned many a putrid wound in my day, but the one thing that made it a privilege to undertake such an unpleasant treatment was the thought that, *If it's tough for me, what must it be like for the patient?*

By the time this man heard about Jesus, we are told that he was 'full of leprosy' (Luke 5:12). To be described thus, it's likely he was grossly deformed, while the infected, rotten sores covering his body undoubtedly oozed a stench. We can be sure that the crowd around Jesus moved back when this man fell at the Saviour's feet. But Jesus didn't flinch.

Mark writes that instead He was 'moved with compassion' (Mark 1:41, NLT). It disturbed Him – not in revulsion, but in sincere concern ... even love. And when faced with such an overwhelming sight, Jesus saw beyond the ravages of the disease – and the breath-catching smell – to the man beneath the rags. 'And Jesus stretched out his hand and touched him ...' (Luke 5:13).

Jesus touched him! The man who had been forced to leave his family and live an isolated, threatened existence, where children were terrified of him and adults would throw stones at him. Where there were no kind words, and only fleeting memories of what a tender touch felt like. Yet, here in the dirt, with death trailing his every step, Jesus stretched out His hand and touched him! He bent over and placed His hand on him. He could have spoken words of healing and sent the man away, but He didn't. He touched him ... and I can't help but wonder: did that touch mean more to the man than the healing itself? Did it fill his every waking thought?

Today, Jesus stands with the same tender kindness, hand outstretched, waiting for us to fall at His feet ... to bring Him our hurts, hearts, and yes, even the repugnance of our sin. Know this ... He will never step away. His touch is there for the asking.

It pulls at my heart, Lord, that there is nothing that can ever hold You back from touching me and making me complete. Thank you. Amen.

8 August

Great crowds gathered to hear him and
to be healed of their infirmities.

Luke 5:15

Reading: 2 Peter 1:16–19

'Curiosity killed the cat' was a phrase often used by my parents when we were young to warn us that nosiness can get you into trouble. It was only recently that I discovered it was the first line of a couplet that finishes with: 'But satisfaction brought it back!' according to Ben Johnson in 1598.

In a nation whose direction from God through the Old Testament forbade the use of magic and divination (Deuteronomy 18:10–12), it is remarkable the number who sought cures from the multitude of magicians and fortune tellers across Israel and beyond. You can imagine the word spreading about a new magician doing the rounds who didn't charge any money, and who actually cured sick people!

Multitudes sought Jesus out of curiosity, eager to see if what they had heard was true. Was He a magician? Or as some said ... was He the Messiah? Ancient Roman pictures foolishly record Jesus waving a wand over the bread before feeding the five thousand. Yet, how far from the truth those records are. The crowds may have come to see Jesus out of curiosity, but many returned to their homes satisfied – and not merely with food.

Satisfied that He was no magician. Satisfied that He had not come to take their money. Satisfied that He did not add to their burdens. Satisfied that maybe through this Man their lives might change. And among the crowds were those who were satisfied that this Man was indeed the Son of God (Matthew 27:54).

Two thousand years later, people are still curious about Jesus. Yet, if they choose to seek Him they will come away satisfied, for 'You will seek me and find me, when you seek me with all your heart' (Jeremiah 29:13) is God's promise.

And we who know Jesus, are we still curious? Do we still seek Him every day? Is His presence our deepest longing? His name our joy and comfort? His will our own? 'For he satisfies the longing soul, and the hungry soul he fills with good things' (Psalm 107:9).

Lord and Saviour, I choose to honour You as Majesty, and seek to help others to see Your glory and be satisfied. Amen.

9 August

'According to your faith be it done to you.'

Matthew 9:29

Reading: Matthew 9:27–30

Following the crowd is not always the wisest thing to do. In fact, this is what we often tell our young people to alert them to the power wrong company can have on their lives. These two men had been part of an actual crowd; no doubt jostled, even carried along by it.

On this occasion they were following a good crowd. One that was following Jesus. Jesus had returned to Capernaum. Caught up in the thrill of all that was going on that day, they had heard this new rabbi preach, and then be criticized for mixing with the riffraff of society (Matthew 9:11). But it was what they had heard Him do that made them decide they wouldn't let Him out of their sight, which for two blind men was quite something.

There was that woman who crept up behind Jesus and was healed merely by touching Him (9:20–22). They must have shaken each other in excited anticipation, especially when Jesus told her it was her faith, not His clothes, that had healed her. As the crowd moved, they followed, but they couldn't get into the next house. The sound of clapping and shouting confused them at first, until the words 'Jesus has raised the young girl back to life!' reached them.

Determination propelled them forward. Jesus *had* to hear them. 'Have mercy on *us*, Son of David' (9:27, emphasis mine), they cried until they were brought into the house where He was staying. 'Do you believe that I am able to do this?' (9:28), Jesus asked. A simple 'Yes, Lord' was all it took for the Saviour to restore their sight and send the two men away rejoicing (9:29–30)!

Following the right crowd was vital for these men that day, but it took personal faith for them to receive what they needed from the Saviour. Some of us have been around the right crowd for many years, yet still Jesus challenges us to respond personally and positively to His question: 'Do *you* believe . . . ?'

Lord Jesus, only when we respond in faith will our eyes be opened to all You have for us. Make it a reality for someone today. Amen.

10 August

They cast their crowns before the throne, saying,
'Worthy are you, our Lord and God.'
Revelation 4:10–11

Reading: Revelation 4:9–11

At the time of writing, our nation is mourning the death of Britain's longest-reigning monarch, Queen Elizabeth II. Ten days of national mourning have seen wall-to-wall media coverage of individuals from all walks of life paying tribute to the diminutive monarch who pledged commitment to serve her nation – whether her life would be short or long – when she was only twenty-one years old. Little did she know then that she would reign for seventy years! Millions of us have admired her devotion to duty and a life of selfless service.

Multitudes travelled from every corner of the UK, the Commonwealth and across the world to take part in what is known as 'shared mourning'. Many tears have been shed and stories exchanged as sadness swept across our land.

For me, one of the most moving sights was watching the symbols of her monarchy being removed from the coffin in which her earthly remains lay. In full view of her loving family, the crown, the orb and the sceptre were removed from atop the flag-draped coffin and placed on the high altar before the casket descended from view. Queen Elizabeth II's reign was over. So was her life. And yet she is more alive now than she ever has been, having publicly declared her personal faith in Jesus Christ.

The BBC announced that Queen Elizabeth's funeral had an estimated viewing of more than four billion people worldwide.

King Jesus' earthly reign lasted a mere three years. Only a few hurried to be with Him in His death. His crown was of torturous thorn, His grave a borrowed tomb. There was no adulation at His passing; His mourners hid themselves away. But death could not hold Him. Earth became His footstool, heaven His eternal kingdom. One day every crown presented will be cast at His feet. There is only One worthy of such honour and praise . . . even Queen Elizabeth knew that.

King Jesus, You alone deserve my heart's devotion, my mouth's praise. And one day I will be thrilled to lay my crown at Your feet. Amen.

11 August

THINK ON THIS

'I am coming soon. Hold fast what you have,
so that no one may seize your crown.'

Revelation 3:11

- Read through this verse a number of times – including out loud.
- Write it out, stick it on the fridge, have it on your phone.
- Meditate on the words, then respond in praise.
- Be a doer . . . Serve someone with an act of kindness today.

12 August

And as they went they were cleansed.
Luke 17:14

Reading: Luke 17:11–14

What with *The Great British Bake Off* (a televised baking competition) and the free hours suddenly available during the Coronavirus lockdowns, millions in the UK apparently found their inner chef. Among my friends, Valerie is queen of scones, Helen is the traybake countess, Loraine is the shortbread duchess and Susie is simply the best with sponges! The one thing they have in common is that they are one-recipe women in respect of their speciality bakes. They excel at what works.

Jesus was, however, not a one-size-fits-all miracle worker, unlike the false magicians of His day. His method for successful healing differed as frequently as the faces before Him. For some, the Saviour used touch (Luke 13:10–13) or spit (John 9:6–7). Others He commanded to do what they hadn't been able to do for years (John 5:6–9). At times Jesus healed from a distance, never having seen the sick person (Luke 7:7–10). In an age of serious demonic activity, Jesus' words of authority often healed and freed those tormented physically, spiritually and mentally (Luke 4:36).

Perhaps the ten people with leprosy, who approached Jesus as He made His way to Jerusalem, had heard about the other leper who had been healed when Jesus touched him (Luke 5:12–15). Maybe the miracle-worker would touch them too – even heal them. But Jesus didn't touch them. Instead, He told them: 'Go and show yourselves to the priests' (5:14), which was a Jewish regulation to confirm healing. They didn't argue ... they simply turned and did what Jesus had commanded ... 'And as they went they were cleansed.'

The method of this miracle was different, but the one vital ingredient for all of Jesus' miracles was right there: faith! These men showed remarkable faith. They listened to Jesus' command, believed in His ability and did what He said. For Jesus, that was enough! Then, as they acted on what they believed about Him, the miracle was accomplished.

Lord Jesus, help me not to expect You to do what I need in the same way as You have done it for others. Instead, help me to listen, believe and act as You guide. Amen.

13 August

And he fell on his face at Jesus' feet,
giving him thanks.

Luke 17:16

Reading: Luke 17:15–19

Why is it so difficult for some people – perhaps even you and me – to say thank you? Gratitude ought to be in our spiritual DNA. The apostle Paul writes: 'Be thankful in all circumstances, for this is God's will for you who belong to Christ Jesus' (1 Thessalonians 5:18, NLT).

The journey from Galilee to Jerusalem was fraught with risk, its miles of desolate landscape perfect for muggings and the like. Little villages along the way provided welcome respite. Reaching one such place on the border with Samaria, Jesus and His followers were approached by a ragged band of ... not thieves ... but of people with leprosy. It must have been rather unnerving to see a literal gang of disease carriers making their way towards them. And they were shouting! Not the usual warning of 'Unclean!' (Stay away!), but of 'Jesus, Master, have mercy on us' (Luke 17:13).

And the miraculous did happen that day for those ten men whose future held nothing but destitution and a slow, lonely death. Imagine, if you can, what it would feel like instantaneously to have your health restored, your family returned, your job reinstated, your finances surer ... your death sentence lifted. Think what it would mean to be able to hug your wife, play with your children, have a meal with friends, worship with others ... and never again have strangers call you names or throw stones at you!

Surely that's a multitude of reasons to be thankful! Especially to the Man who gave you back your life. Yet, unbelievably, only one man returned to say thank you. Imagine ... only one out of ten! And the Bible says of him, 'Now he was a Samaritan' (17:16). The foreigner was teaching the most basic of human responses – gratitude – to those who should have known better.

But before we point our finger in disapproval ... what about us? Gratitude is habit-forming. Let's not miss any opportunity, whether small or great, to show our thanks and bless the giver as we do so.

Lord, show me today where I have fallen in the gratitude stakes, and help me put it right. Amen.

14 August

In that same hour he rejoiced in the Holy Spirit and said,
'I thank you, Father, Lord of heaven and earth . . .'

Luke 10:21

Reading: Psalm 100

Did you sleep last night? Will you eat today? Did you have a choice of clothing to wear this morning? Is your roof sound? Your plumbing operational? Do you have a job? Are your children healthy? Is your marriage good? If you can say yes to any of these, you have reasons to be thankful to the God who supplies our needs, for 'his mercies . . . are new every morning; great is [his] faithfulness' (Lamentations 3:22–23).

You won't be alone if you answered 'no' to some of the above, for in this world damaged by sin's fall, we all experience life's tough stuff. Just as weeds can damage what is good in the garden, so difficulty and heartache can cause pain in our lives. Weeds can be uprooted, though, by a good hoe, and thankfulness can turn our hearts Godward, where we'll be reminded that He is working on our behalf. Hasn't He said, 'I will strengthen you, I will help you, I will uphold you with my righteous right hand' (Isaiah 41:10)? A definite reason to be thankful, if ever there was one.

And yet, isn't it amazing that Jesus, the very Creator of all things good in our lives, also felt it necessary to display gratitude in His own life?

- Jesus, the Bread of life (John 6:35), gave thanks for the bread He Himself had multiplied to feed the five thousand (Matthew 14:19, NIVUK).
- He, who is our wisdom (Colossians 2:2–3) thanked the Father for giving wisdom to the childlike (Matthew 11:25, NLT).
- The One who answers our prayers (John 16:24) thanked His Father for answering His (11:41).
- At the final Passover, Jesus gave thanks to God for the representation of His death in the bread and the wine, in faithful acceptance of what was about to happen on the cross (Luke 22:19–20).

Even in suffering, Jesus showed us the importance of being thankful, for: 'Whoever offers praise glorifies Me' (Psalm 50:23, NKJV). Let's get glorifying! He is worthy.

Lord, Creator of the universe and King of my heart, I praise you from the sun's rising to its setting. Amen.

15 August

So Jesus said to him,
'Unless you see signs and wonders you will not believe.'

John 4:48

Reading: John 4:46–53

'Prove it!' is a common philosophy of life today. Yet, in an age that demands tangible evidence for everything before it can be believed, a lot of money is poured into theories that are being treated as fact. The more finance involved the greater the possibility that assumptions will be classified as fact. Unfortunately, show the same people a life changed by God and they won't believe He exists unless you prove it.

Jesus confronted a similar problem. Those in the crowd were only interested if they could see evidence that He was different from the other self-professed 'messiahs' that kept popping up – and that meant miracles. In Cana, Jesus' name was already up there in the possibility stakes. I mean . . . water into wine (John 2:1–10)! Many were still working on the theories: magic or miracle?

No wonder Jesus lamented over the situation when the nobleman asked Him to heal his son (John 4:47). The distraught father had dashed twenty miles on hearing that Jesus had returned from Judea. He wasn't about to be put off because others had their doubts. Considering his social status and employment profile, it is probable the man was a Gentile, but he certainly knew something about faith. As for many of us, desperation sent him looking for Jesus, who saw not only his despair but also his willingness to humble himself, and to believe that Jesus could indeed make his son well.

Asking soon turned to pleading. The boy was dying. The nobleman needed Jesus to come with him to Capernaum. Jesus needed the man to believe that distance was no obstacle to His power. A shaky faith had to move from maybe to certainty. 'Go; your son will live' (4:50), Jesus told him. A simple command, followed by a promise that guaranteed the earth. Yet, it was one the man was prepared to believe and act on.

Jesus' word is always His bond. That's proof enough! It was for the nobleman. It is for me.

Lord Jesus, every word You speak is a miracle of grace and life to me. May I respond as quickly as that nobleman. Amen.

16 August

'I know who you are – the Holy One of God.'

Mark 1:24

Reading: Mark 1:21–28

Some Christians seem to see demons behind every tree, attributing each dark cloud to Satan's power. Others rarely acknowledge the existence of supernatural evil in our world, choosing to ignore Scripture's warning (1 Peter 5:8). Either position is spiritually dangerous. To be obsessed with Satan's limited power dilutes our belief in a sovereign, all-powerful God. Yet, to ignore the existence of the 'mighty powers in this dark world' (Ephesians 6:12, NLT) leaves us ill-equipped to 'stand against the schemes of the devil' (6:11).

Any experience of visible demonic activity is rare to most of us today. Yet, the four Gospels are full of Jesus' daily encounters with those possessed by evil spirits. How come? Where have all the demons gone?

The three years of Jesus' ministry undoubtedly displayed the greatest demonic activity known in human history. The One promised by God in the garden of Eden to crush Satan's head had arrived in human form (Genesis 3:15). Therefore, 'the Empire of Satan focused all of its concentration on Jesus of Nazareth, it was no holds barred. This is the last opportunity to snuff out the possibility of this One who is going to crush its head.'[32]

Satan failed, as he always will. Jesus reached the cross to break the power of sin and death.

But do not underestimate the battle that continues to rage for the souls of men and women, or doubt that Satan still desires to shake the faith of each believer (Luke 22:31).

Yet, for me, what the unclean spirit said to Jesus is remarkable: 'I know who you are'! Imagine, the demons of hell know that Jesus is 'the Holy One of God' (Mark 1:24)! James takes it further in his letter by declaring that this knowledge causes them to 'tremble in terror' (James 2:19, NLT).

When were we last overwhelmed by the thought of Jesus as the 'Holy One of God'? Does it make us tremble – not in fear as the demon did – but in reverence, love and worship?

Jesus, thank you for making it possible for us to know who You are. Holy One of God, I worship you. Amen.

17 August

I trust in God, so why should I be afraid?
What can mere mortals do to me?

Psalm 56:11, NLT

Reading: Luke 12:4–7

If I had met some of the people Jesus did, or encountered some of the situations He faced, I think I would have been afraid. The demon-crazed, the disease-ridden, the angry, the powerful, the liars, the forces of nature and the forces of hell – virtually all were on His daily agenda, yet never do we read that Jesus was afraid.

Of course, Jesus knew all about being hungry (Mark 11:12), and He knew what it was like to feel exhausted and need rest (6:31). He enjoyed the company of others and socialized with friends (2:15). Jesus even had moments of indignation when He saw people cheating the poor and the temple worshippers (John 2:13–17). But He also experienced joy, especially in doing the Father's will (15:10–11). And He empathized with the grieving – openly weeping at a family grave (11:33–36). His compassion for the suffering and rejected was unrivalled (Matthew 9:20–22), especially for those isolated from home and family (Mark 1:40–42).

In many ways, Jesus was just like us. He experienced all the human emotions, even disappointment (Matthew 17:16–17). The writer to the Hebrews reminds us that Jesus 'had to be made like his brothers *in every respect*, so that he might become a merciful and faithful high priest in the service of God' (Hebrews 2:17, emphasis mine).

Yet, we never read of Jesus being afraid. Whomever or whatever He faced, He remained unafraid. Today's words from the psalmist would have resonated in the Saviour's heart. His trust was completely in the Father, whose plans He knew were only for His good. Jesus already knew that 'the Most High rules the kingdom of men' (Daniel 4:17) – God's sovereignty was never in question. No person, problem or plan of Satan could ever disrupt God's will for His Son ... not even the agony of Gethsemane (Luke 22:42).

Jesus always practised what He preached. Faith and fear cannot live together. When we fear, we lose the peace that trusting in God's sovereignty gives. He sees. He knows. He cares.

Lord, I will not be afraid. My trust is in You. Amen.

18 August

THINK ON THIS

For you did not receive the spirit of slavery to fall back
into fear, but you have received the Spirit of adoption
as sons, by whom we cry, 'Abba! Father!'

Romans 8:15

- Read through this verse a number of times – including out loud.
- Write it out, stick it on the fridge, have it on your phone.
- Meditate on the words, then respond in praise.
- Take steps to allow God's word to change you: perhaps . . . repent,
  forgive, love.

19 August

'What have you to do with me,
Jesus, Son of the Most High God?'

Mark 5:7

Reading: Mark 5:1–15

Of all men, this man had every reason to be afraid . . . but Jesus was on His way.

The man they called Legion beat his chest with clenched fists, forcing out another tormented scream. The sky may have been blue as he gazed across the Sea of Galilee from the hillside of Gadara, but the colour black was all he ever saw. The sun didn't shine in his sky. His possessors dragged him from his gaze. There was something, or someone, they didn't like – perhaps even feared – across those waters on the Jewish side of the Jordan valley.

Soon, menacing clouds gathered overhead, prematurely darkening the scene. Fishing boats started to turn towards the shore – all except one. It kept on going. The wind became a gale, whipping Galilee's waves into frenzied foam, like white horses riding on mountaintops, tossing the little boat to and fro; threatening to swallow ship and sailors alike.

Legion watched from the shore, tearing at his skin, screaming the anguished screams of the damned; somehow aware that he was about to face the greatest battle of his life. Suddenly – instantly – the sea was calm! The waves fell flat, the clouds rolled back in the sky, the gale stopped its howling. And some miles out in the middle of the lake, the light of the moon shone once more on the little vessel. The tortured man had never seen such a sight! He had no idea what had happened. But the Man on the boat did. He would soon arrive to calm another storm . . . the one raging in Legion's life.[33]

Often, we want to minister to crowds. Jesus sought out individuals. He was as interested in the 'one' as in the multitudes. The immoral woman of Samaria (John 4) and the violent, possessed man of Gadara each needed His touch and deliverance . . . so Jesus sought them out. In the same way, He knows our fears, our suffering and even our sinfulness. Yet still He seeks us, for there is no storm He cannot calm.

Precious Jesus, thank you for journeying from eternity to find me, and to calm my storm. Amen.

20 August

'Go home to your friends and
tell them how much the Lord has done for you,
and how he has had mercy on you.'

Mark 5:19

Reading: Mark 5:14–20

Wailing, Legion ran towards the little band of men heading up the hill. Pushed to his knees by the many evil residents of his life, he heard the chief voice of his possessors name the Man from the boat: 'What do you want with me, Jesus, Son of the Most High God?' From a position of worship, the demon grovelled at the feet of the One before whom even the devils tremble, imploring Jesus not to torture him.

Identifying themselves as 'Legion' to the Creator of the universe in an anguished display of torture and mayhem, a myriad of voices poured out of the man's mouth, begging Jesus not to send them away. Now powerless, the demons convulsed the man one last time before being sent to their doom . . . nearby pigs providing the perfect vehicle to transport them to a watery end! Never before had such horror echoed through Gadara.

And when the terror subsided, Legion sat in stillness at the feet of Jesus . . . clothed and in his right mind.

Thankfully, the city gate was still open when the delivered man arrived home. With firm determination he set his sights on the dwellings just beyond the town square, barely able to contain the joy and excitement that propelled him forward. Later, as his son lay in the crook of his arm, the boy heard how Jesus had come through a storm to meet with the father he had given up on ever seeing again. His Abba had been on the mind of the Son of God – and Jesus had come all that way to deliver him, to set him free . . . from his tormentors and from his fear.

Then, as the boy's father told him of the assignment Jesus had tasked him with – to go home and tell everyone what Jesus had done for him – the son determined that, one day, he too would meet Jesus. Likely, he wouldn't have long to wait.

There is still mercy with the Lord . . . still time to spread the word.

Lord Jesus, may I unashamedly tell others today of all that You have done for me. Amen.

21 August

When Jesus saw her, he called her over and said to her,
'Woman, you are freed from your disability.'

Luke 13:12

Reading: Luke 13:10–17

I love that when you read the words of Jesus, there's more going on than it first appears. Here was a woman bent double by a physical disability. For eighteen years she had only seen what was beneath her. She hadn't looked into the faces of those she loved, never mind anyone else, for many years. Neither could she gaze upon the beauty of God's creation. Pain would certainly have been her daily, unwanted, companion, while the basic activities of life would have proved virtually unmanageable.

Yet, there she was, worshipping at her local synagogue, with no apparent bitterness towards God for the dreadful disability she endured. Jesus, touched by her situation, described her as one whom Satan had bound (Luke 13:16), and He immediately healed her (13:13), calling it a loosening of her bond (13:16). His compassion was primarily for this dear woman – His desire was to set her free from the imprisonment of disability. But He also had others on His mind.

In our churches today, many are bowed low. We may turn up for services, but if our hearts and minds are manacled by sorrow, suffering and loneliness, spiritual growth becomes stunted and vision clouded. Pain dampens the ability for service, while circumstances erect a barrier that increases introspection. Just like the disabled woman, we can become prisoners – trapped and longing for freedom. Thankfully, Jesus can lift our burdened and bowed heads to remind us that He is ever-present . . . and willing to transform and set us free.

In that place of worship there was a man who also required liberation. Unbelievably, the ruler of the synagogue was indignant because Jesus had healed the woman on the Sabbath. So low was he bowed down by legalism that he missed the thrill of the miracle performed in *his* synagogue! So hypocritical was his heart that Jesus had to set him straight (13:14–16). Religiosity makes cripples of us all! It's time to straighten up.

Lord, may we never be bowed so low that we do not experience Your presence, or be so stubborn that we refuse Your healing. Amen.

22 August

God chose what is low and despised in the world . . . so
that no human being might boast in the presence of God.

1 Corinthians 1:28–29

Reading: 1 Corinthians 1:26–31

God does His best work through weak vessels.

Shepherds were the first to declare the Messiah's arrival (Luke 2:8–20), but the king wasn't told. An elderly couple recognized the baby Jesus in the temple (2:25–38), while the high priest luxuriated obliviously nearby. A crazy recluse baptized Jesus into ministry (Matthew 3:13), while the Pharisees watched from the riverbank. Uneducated fishermen, hated tax collectors and Zealots became the rabbi's students (Luke 6:13), while Jesus denounced the teaching of the religious elite. Women became part of Jesus' company (8:1–3), at a time when many Jews placed women in the same category as dogs and Gentiles.

Even the Saviour's family was different. His mother was a teenage virgin, His earthly father a working-class carpenter. Jesus didn't live among Israel's high society, but after holding refugee status in Egypt for around two years, His family settled in the northern village of Nazareth.

If you were diseased, poor, politically questionable, immoral or discredited, you were just the kind of person that drew Jesus' attention. You, the very person He could help, and Jesus, the very One you could trust. He wasn't interested in the self-sufficient, the self-obsessed or the self-righteous, because it's unlikely they would ever admit to needing a Saviour, healer or friend. Although He did not seek out the wealthy, Jesus was always happy to speak with them when they came to Him (Matthew 19:16–22).

Confessing need and declaring faith was, and still is, the one prerequisite for a life-changing encounter with Jesus. Perhaps you've looked at the list above and couldn't match those circumstances with your own, but we all have one thing in common, whether then or now: we all have souls sick with sin. Every one of us needs a Saviour.

I'm glad Jesus loves the different. I'm thrilled that He loved my disabled daughters as much as the bent-over woman in the synagogue. But I'm also glad He loves me. For I, too, am needy.

Heavenly Father, I wouldn't dare boast of anything in Your presence . . . except for Jesus. Amen.

23 August

Set your minds on things that are above, not on things that are on earth.

Colossians 3:2

Reading: Colossians 3:1–4, 15

Circumstances can have a withering effect on our lives. The physical ramifications can be many, but it's what they do to the soul that has the potential for far greater destruction. Is fatalism the best way to deal with the agonies we live with? After all, aren't these the cards we've been dealt; the life God has given us?

Fatalism and acceptance are two different things. Fatalism is passive, a shrugging of the shoulders attitude wrapped in pessimism; whereas acceptance is active, a willingness to come to terms with something for positive benefits. God is much too kind to expect us to tolerate the difficulties of life by mere fatalism . . . resigned to whatever horror invades. Instead, He wants to bring us to acceptance, with all its hope for the future. In the meantime, we are called to persevere.

Perseverance delivers the staying power that helps us to endure until we reach the place where we, too, can say: 'Your will be done' (Matthew 26:42). It requires us to shift our focus from the rubble of circumstances to the solid ground of God's sovereignty . . . to 'set [our] minds on things above, not on things that are on the earth,' as the apostle Paul told the suffering church in Colossians 3:2. But how do we get our heads around the eternal when the 'now' is crumbling around us? We choose to believe that our identity is not found in our circumstances but in our relationship with Jesus Christ.

We are children of the King! He will never abandon us; why, *even in the valley of the shadow of death*, God has promised to be with us (Psalm 23:4).

Perseverance requires that we look up from the pain, where He promises: 'You will seek me and find me, when you seek me with all your heart' (Jeremiah 29:13). Even if our circumstances remain unchanged, we start to recognize God's loving presence with us, and the burdens begin to transform in appearance . . .

'. . . because we know that suffering produces perseverance' (Romans 5:3, NIVUK).

Holy Spirit, give me the power to set my mind on things above. Amen.

24 August

'Do you want to be healed?'

John 5:6

Reading: John 5:1–9, 14

What a strange question Jesus asked the disabled man. Something dreadful had happened to him thirty-eight years previously, leaving him helpless and unable to walk. Since then, the man had lived at the pool of Bethesda, where the ill and disabled lay waiting for a miracle. What a dreadful sight this community of the sick must have been. How sad their predicament. Yet, what was worse was the belief they had in a superstition concerning this pool, situated outside the city walls, north of the temple.

Legend had it that, at a certain time, an angel would come down and disturb the water, and the first person to make it into the pool would be healed. Somehow, the waiting sick believed, without evidence, that the water was magical because of its association with the temple. The man Jesus questioned that day blamed his persistent disability on the fact that he had no one to help him into the water. The superstition had been ingrained in his psyche. He believed in absurdity because he didn't know any better . . . until he met Jesus.

Remarkably, when Jesus said, 'Get up, take up your bed, and walk' (John 5:8), the man did exactly what he was told! No questions asked. He had already proved the legend false, and now he was given the opportunity to respond to the question he had skirted around the first time. We are told little about his healing, apart from that it was both miraculous and instantaneous. Obedience and faith came from somewhere in his heart during his encounter with Jesus. 'And at once the man was healed, and he took up his bed and walked' (5:9). Foolish superstitions were no match for Jesus. Neither are they today.

It's hard to fathom that people still prefer to misplace their faith in legends and superstitions – crystals, angel figurines and amulets – rather than taking their burdens to the One who continues to transform lives today.

Lord Jesus, there is no person or thing that could ever match Your power or authority. Only the Source of Life has all we need. Amen.

25 August

THINK ON THIS

But he said, 'What is impossible with man
is possible with God.'
Luke 18:27

- Read through this verse a number of times – including out loud.
- Write it out, stick it on the fridge, have it on your phone.
- Meditate on the words, then respond in praise.
- Encourage someone by sharing this verse with them today.

26 August

He touched her hand, and the fever left her,
and she rose and began to serve him.

Matthew 8:15

Reading: Matthew 8:14–17

I was awestruck the day we visited Capernaum. There, layered beneath the more recent ruins of the ancient synagogue, were the black basalt foundations of that former place of worship. On this very structure, Jesus had taught the people of the town closest to any He could call home during His ministry. It touched me deeply to sit on those ruins and to hear Jesus speak to my heart as the Scriptures were read. In my mind's eye I could see the crowd follow Jesus down the mountain after listening to the greatest sermon ever, then stop as He took the time to heal the man with leprosy (Matthew 8:2–3), and gasp at Jesus' declaration of the centurion's faith for the healing of his servant (8:5–13).

Next, we walked to what is believed to have been Peter's house. Protected by a wall of Perspex were the ruins of what would have been a fairly large structure back then, which was a good job, given all the visitors Peter and Andrew kept bringing home when they were in town! After the mountain experience and the healings on the journey home, Peter and company arrived, no doubt pumped with equal amounts of excitement and hunger. However, a worrying situation greeted them. Peter's mother-in-law was sick. Immediately, Jesus calmed the family's anxiety and touched her hand. The fever left her . . . she was healed (8:15). No big surprise, you might think, but what came next was. She got up from her sickbed and made them all dinner!

It wasn't just that she had a crowd of hungry men to feed. The text says she 'began to serve *him*' (8:15, emphasis mine). The woman's response to what Jesus had just done for her was to use her normal everyday gifting – cooking – and worship Him with it. Peter's mother-in-law expressed her gratitude by doing what she knew best . . . she served dinner to the Servant King.

Lord, may I use what I know to worship You. May even the most trivial task I perform today be an act of service. Amen.

27 August

'But I have called you friends,
for all that I have heard from my Father
I have made known to you.'

John 15:15

Reading: John 15:13–17

Throughout my life I have been blessed with good friends. Friends with whom I have laughed and enjoyed good times. But true friends are not only fair-weather ones. They are the ones who turn up when life has been cruel, or when I've made a mess of things all by myself. True friends sit alongside when you need understanding silence, but also know when to speak a word of comfort, or the more challenging word of wisdom or rebuke.

I'm grateful for the times when they have dried my tears or brought food when sorrow filled my days. And then there's a special group with whom I have walked down many emotional journeys . . . each caring for the others by faithfully carrying their burdens in prayer to Jesus. I am blessed indeed.

Yet, I am not so foolish as to deny that friendships don't always live up to expectations – when others let us down or cause us hurt . . . or, worse still, when I have been the cause of these things. Human friendship can be exhilarating, but it is not always the case.

No one models friendship better than Jesus, and there's no better friend than He. I cannot name-drop when I speak of my friends, for they don't run with the wealthy or elite. Yet, the Creator of the Universe calls me His friend (John 15:15). The only status that matters to the Saviour concerning my friendship is whether I do what He commands (15:14). That's where this incomparable friendship with Jesus starts, and where we will find acceptance – the bedrock of any meaningful relationship.

Rejection is not in God's game plan. He won't ask us to jump through hoops to see if we're worthy of His friendship. No, He simply asks us to lean in, listen and obey, because 'friends, [all] I have heard from my Father I have made known to you' (15:15).

Lord Jesus, thank you for being my friend. Amen.

28 August

'You are my friends if you do what I command you.'
John 15:14

Reading: Genesis 18:1–5, 16–18

It seems strange to link friendship with obedience. Surely to obey someone implies that they have some degree of authority over you. Companionship with an emotional attachment is normally what we associate with friendship, rather than subservience. However, the Greek word for 'friend' used here has a much wider interpretation. Translated as 'a friend at court', it describes those nearest to the king – still subject to him, yet party to his secrets. A special relationship within the inner circle, just like Peter, James and John had with Jesus. They weren't mates or buddies in today's sense of the words, but they did enjoy friendship while recognizing Jesus' authority.

In the Old Testament, Jehovah referred to Abraham as His servant (Genesis 26:24). The first time the man from Ur heard God's call, he responded with obedience (12:1–4). Yet, he was also called 'a friend of God' (James 2:23). Such was this friendship that God shared confidences with Abraham – even what He had planned for the cities of Sodom and Gomorrah. 'The LORD said, "Shall I hide from Abraham what I am about to do . . . ?"' (Genesis 18:17). It was simply unthinkable for God to keep it from the man He had chosen to be the father of the Jewish nation. Abraham was both God's servant and His friend.

So, what are we? Jesus' servants or His friends? Surely, they are not mutually exclusive. Friendship involves both. To be a friend is to be willing to put ourselves out. It might mean dropping what we're doing to bring help, crossing town to be with them when they need us or using precious sleep time to pray for them. That makes friendship all about obeying what our heart is telling us to do for those who matter to us.

Jesus will always be our Master and we His devoted servants, but He has chosen to call us friends (John 15:15). As believers, we are part of His inner circle – trusted with His secrets. For all that He has heard from the Father He has made known to us (15:15).

Lord, may my friendships always display Your servant heart. Amen.

29 August

The friendship of the Lord is for those who fear him,
and he makes known to them his covenant.

Psalm 25:14

Reading: John 15:3–5

There are friends, and then there are 'friends' – those we are friendly towards, but with whom we don't share confidences. Acquaintances, really. Casual relationships within a group setting, or at the school gate, can't really be defined as true friendships. Real friendship necessitates commitment. It requires closeness, time and unselfish involvement in the life of another. The odd 'hello' won't cut it.

Jesus' commitment towards us oozed unselfishness well before we had any desire to reciprocate: 'God shows his love for us in that while we were still sinners, Christ died for us' (Romans 5:8). When we turned our backs, ignored His word, refused to acknowledge His person, denied His sacrifice and rejected His love for us, Jesus kept moving towards the day when He would become our Saviour and our friend. Commitment doesn't come much deeper than that.

Yet, even within the ranks of Christ's followers there are friends . . . and there are 'friends' – those who have a nodding acquaintance with Jesus. They prefer to stay on the periphery, afraid of the cost of discipleship (Matthew 16:24), yet all the while missing its blessings (19:29). Some choose not to pursue God's secrets for themselves – scantly and rarely even reading the Bible, which contains them all. Not *every* secret, you may say, and you'd be right, because the Saviour wants to give His friends every opportunity to grow deeply in their friendship with Him.

We lose so much by keeping our relationship with Jesus purely on the level of an acquaintance. Jesus desires for us to know Him. If we choose to stay close . . . connected . . . attached in our friendship with the vine (John 15:5), we have all we need, and a friendship that brings ultimate satisfaction.

Lord Jesus, I'm thankful that Your inner circle is never limited. You share Your secrets with those close enough to listen. May I always seek Your friendship above all others. Amen.

30 August

'Greater love has no one than this,
that someone lay down his life for his friends.'
John 15:13

Reading: Isaiah 53:4–6

If you were to list the qualities you would expect in a best friend, what would they be? And how does God's friendship through Jesus compare?

- **Faithfulness** – unfailing loyalty. Someone who never breaks the promises they have made you. 'Not one word of all the good promises that the Lord had made to the house of Israel had failed; all came to pass' (Joshua 21:45).
- **Patience** – the kindness to wait for another, tolerate their foibles and remain calm when we don't. 'Don't you see how wonderfully kind, tolerant, and patient God is with you? Does this mean nothing to you? Can't you see that his kindness is intended to turn you from your sin?' (Romans 2:4, NLT).
- **Sympathy** – the emotional connection needed when sorrow hits. The binding of one soul to another in response to the other's pain. The human touch in times of distress. 'Surely he has borne our griefs and carried our sorrows' (Isaiah 53:4).
- **Listening ability** – the willingness to use their ears at least as much as their mouth. The ability to identify when listening is called for, to hear the words spoken when others don't. 'You came near when I called on you; you said, "Do not fear!"' (Lamentations 3:57).
- **Trustworthiness** – one who can be relied on. Always telling the truth, honest in everything. Someone who has your complete confidence. 'The Lord is righteous in all his ways and kind in all his works' (Psalm 145:17).
- **Constancy** – someone who won't change like the weather and remains the same even when the tough times come. 'Jesus Christ is the same yesterday and today and forever' (Hebrews 13:8).
- **Forgiving nature** – tender-hearted enough to forgive when the wrong has been confessed. Willing to forgive because their love is greater than the hurt. 'For you, O Lord, are good and forgiving, abounding in steadfast love to all who call upon you' (Psalm 86:5).

I wonder, are the qualities we want in a best friend mirrored in our relationships?

There is no better friend than You, Jesus. Teach me to be a friend like that. Amen.

31 August

'As the Father has loved me, so have I loved you.
Abide in my love.'

John 15:9

Reading: John 15:8–13

Friendship means more than liking someone or enjoying their company. A deep, lasting friendship is rooted and grounded in love ... what the Bible calls *phileo* love. It's the type of love that seeks to make the other person happy by showing generosity and affection.

But as our friend, Jesus shows us more than *phileo* love. His friendship is not based on mutual interests or personality similarities alone, for His love towards us is always of the *agape* variety. *Agape* – sacrificial love – is what cements our friendship to Jesus. To become our friend, God sent His Son to a sin-cursed earth and a rebellious people, and His Son willingly and sacrificially died on the cross to reconcile us to the Father (Galatians 4:4–5). Now, that kind of love tops anything we could experience from a spouse or a good friend. Jesus' love for us cost Him His life (Luke 23:44–46), separated Him from the Father (Matthew 27:46) and sent the Son of God to the grave (27:59–60).

When it comes to friendship, there really is no comparison with Jesus. He will always be the best in the best friend line-up, because He gave His life for us. His love is unrivalled (1 John 4:10).

However, in drawing us into this sacrificial love, Jesus gives us a new commandment: 'Love one another: just as I have loved you, you also are to love one another' (John 13:34). And He's not speaking about *phileo* love. Jesus only ever used *agape* love with us, and that's what He expects from us in respect of others, especially fellow believers. We are to love sacrificially – in the same way that He loved us. True friendship always costs, but it is love that gives us the ability to put others first. For in loving one another, a selfish world will know that we belong to Jesus (13:35).

Dearest Friend, thank you that You hold nothing back in Your love for me. You have my love, Lord. My heart belongs to You. Help me to love others as You have loved me. Amen.

September

1 September

THINK ON THIS

And this is the testimony,
that God gave us eternal life,
and this life is in his Son.

1 John 5:11

- Read through this verse a number of times – including out loud.
- Write it out, stick it on the fridge, have it on your phone.
- Meditate on the words, then respond in praise.
- Be a doer . . . Serve someone with an act of kindness today.

2 September

And Jesus, looking at him, loved him,
'You lack one thing: go, sell all that you have and
give to the poor, and you will have treasure in heaven;
and come, follow me.'

Mark 10:21

Reading: Mark 10:17–22

The disciples and the women who travelled with them were undoubtedly friends of Jesus. They ate together, chatted over their day, got involved in the minutiae of the itinerant life and no doubt shared their hearts after the crowds headed for home.

Then there are those who had personal encounters with Jesus. Perhaps some of them frequently stood listening on the periphery, while others only got to interact with the Messiah once. What they did with that opportunity is telling.

Take the man we know as the rich young ruler. He actually ran to meet Jesus, fearful that he might miss the opportunity to ask Him the question that was dominating his life. 'Good Teacher, what must I do to inherit eternal life?' (Mark 10:17). Unfortunately, he squandered the chance to settle that question, failing to recognize that: 'This is eternal life, that they know you, the only true God, and Jesus Christ whom you have sent' (John 17:3).

Yet, Jesus' reaction to the questioner is very tender . . . 'looking at him, [He] loved him' (Mark 10:21). The Master saw that his question was genuine and that he had made every possible religious attempt to gain eternal life by himself (10:19–20). But the man had an idol – something he loved more than the Saviour: 'he had great possessions' (10:22). While Jesus' reply was that the man should sell everything in order to follow Him, that should never be misinterpreted as a requirement for salvation. The point Jesus was making was that there must be no rivals for His Kingship in our lives (Matthew 22:37).

Is there 'one thing' – a relationship, career, habit – that Jesus is telling you to go and sort before you can come and follow Him (Mark 10:21)? The man got to keep his wealth . . . but he went away sad (10:22). His response cost him the very thing he needed most.

Lord, forgive me if I have put some 'thing' before You. Point it out, that I might put it right. Amen.

3 September

Even my close friend, someone I trusted,
one who shared my bread, has turned against me.

Psalm 41:9, NIVUK

Reading: John 13:21–30

Seems you can get fake anything these days! Perfume. Jewellery. Handbags. Watches. You might think you've bagged a bargain, but you soon find out you've been had! Imitation products are one thing, but it hurts more deeply when we discover that those posing as friends are, in fact, phoney. Unfortunately, actors abound within what appear to be genuine relationships and godly communities.

Who would have thought that Jesus' closest friends included a hypocrite? Jesus wasn't fooled, but the other eleven were. Judas Iscariot spent the same time with Jesus as the others. In addition, he was given the important role of treasurer, even though he was stealing from them (John 12:6). He saw and heard the wondrous things the others had, and was treated with same love and kindness by Jesus. But none of the others had any idea what was in Judas' heart ... only Jesus knew (13:11). Yet, the Master kept him close, showing mercy as only He could. He even washed the betrayer's feet with the identical service He offered those who were His true friends (13:5). I have no doubt that Jesus really loved Judas and gave him every chance to change – to drop the mask in repentance and faith.

Then, as they gathered around the table together for the final time, Jesus said, 'Truly, truly, I say to you, one of you will betray me' (13:21). So convincingly had Judas deceived his friends that they had no idea whom Jesus was talking about (13:22). Even after Jesus had given them the clue about passing a sop of bread to the person concerned, they didn't guess. But Judas knew. The game was up when Jesus gave it to him and said, 'What you are going to do, do quickly' (13:27).

Appearances can be deceiving, but we cannot fool Jesus. Whatever Judas' motives, in the end he was an unfaithful friend and a disappointment to Jesus. Could there be anything worse?

Lord Jesus, my heart is sad as I consider this. May honesty be my covering and every mask dropped. Amen.

4 September

'Don't you fear God
even when you have been sentenced to die?'

Luke 23:40, NLT

Reading: Luke 23:32–43

There are days when you know things can't get any worse. For the man who uttered these words, all hope for any relief in his situation disappeared when the cross he was nailed to dropped loudly into position. His life of violent crime had finally caught up with him. He had damaged, perhaps even destroyed, the lives of many. Now it was judgement time. A Roman cross awaited.

Yet, on the day of his impending death, the criminal had no idea that Hope was hanging on the neighbouring cross. As the soldiers settled themselves down for a spot of gambling (Luke 23:34), he was about to have an encounter with Jesus, and to discover for himself that you can't meet Jesus and remain the same.

It seems that the criminal was taking in the scene of gloating religious leaders and taunting soldiers around the man on the middle cross. He heard them shout, 'God's Messiah, the Chosen One' (23:35, NLT), hatred mixed with their laughter. But it was the words of this Man they called Jesus that seized the criminal's heart. 'Father, forgive them, for they know not what they do' (23:34). And suddenly, as the criminal on the other side of Jesus joined in the ridicule, the enormity of his own sin hit him. 'Do you not even fear God . . . ?' he yelled. 'For we receive the due reward of our deeds; but this Man has done nothing wrong' (23:40–41, NKJV).

Had he heard about Jesus? Perhaps listened from the edge of a crowd? Been told about His miracles? Heard about Lazarus? I don't know. But I know this: that the naked, bloodied, dying Jesus looked at Him and, hearing the criminal's confession, granted the man's dying request: 'Truly, I say to you, today you will be with me in paradise' (23:43). Even in His anguish, Jesus cared for a soul.

Believe me, we can't do life or death without Him.

Merciful Saviour, forgive me for the times I've waited until I've reached the end of myself before calling for Your help. May Your name always be first on my lips. Amen.

5 September

'Are you not the Christ? Save yourself and us!'

Luke 23:39

Reading: Luke 12:8–10

It is interesting to hear the different reactions of people who have just left exactly the same event. The main features may be described in the same way, but often what they remember hearing or seeing differs, even to the point of making you wonder if they had actually been at the same meeting.

There were three men crucified that Friday on Golgotha. One was Jesus, the other two were criminals – guilty of heinous crimes and deserving of punishment. Both had heard the same thing, witnessed the same abuse hurled at Jesus and felt the same horror of their own impending death. Miraculously, one of those men sought salvation from the Messiah on that middle cross (Luke 23:42). But not his companion. Even though he, too, had heard Jesus pray for those who had sinned against Him (23:34), and those who had cruelly pressed Pilate to have Him condemned (Matthew 27:20), he refused to plead for God's mercy. Instead, he chose to side with the godless crowd, using his ebbing strength to hurl abuse at someone who had done him no harm (Luke 23:39).

What a pathetic sight. Side by side with the only One who could offer forgiveness and give hope for the next life, he died, unwilling to submit. Stubborn and full of pride to the end, this man watched the world go dark (Matthew 27:45), while refusing the Light of the world (John 8:12) – unaware that one day he would have to bow before Jesus (Philippians 2:10), but by then it would be too late for his soul.

The cross is past, but not its work, for Jesus continues to draw alongside, patiently waiting for the sinner to repent before it is forever too late (Hebrews 9:27). Yet, 'If we confess our sins, he is faithful and just to forgive us our sins and to cleanse us from all unrighteousness' (1 John 1:9). Death will still come one day, but so will the promise Jesus made to the repentant thief on the cross: 'Today you will be with me in paradise' (Luke 23:43).

Forgive my stubborn heart, Lord. Make it pliable, that I might respond in repentance and faith. Amen.

6 September

But, knowing their hypocrisy, he said to them,
'Why put me to the test?'

Mark 12:15

Reading: Mark 12:13–17

Pride can be a dangerous thing. Of course, it's reasonable to experience joy because of an accomplishment. But that fleeting warmth success brings should never be allowed to morph into arrogance. In history, superior attitudes over one's fellow men produced the dictators of this world. In the intertestamental era it produced the Pharisees – a group of devoted Jews who wanted to bring the people back to honouring God by strict adherence to the Mosaic Law. It started with such promise. However, by the time the Messiah arrived, the only thing it had produced was a prideful company of the superior religious who looked down on everyone and opposed the One for whom they had been waiting.

Despite the many interactions they had with Jesus, they believed themselves superior to everyone else; not only in religious fervour, but in every way. If you were poor, sick or socially isolated, they judged it was because you hadn't kept God's law. So, when Jesus came preaching love, grace and mercy . . . as well as healing the sick and fraternizing with those the Pharisees saw as unclean, it was all too much. He couldn't possibly be from God, they said (John 9:16). God was all about law . . . not love! People needed to listen to them, follow them and do what they said.

Their pride blinded them to truth, deafened them to the God of mercy, and paralysed them from walking the path to God's heaven. They only sought for those who agreed with them. A huge warning to us all. Could it be that we spend more time checking out the preacher than listening to what he is saying? Does a church have to tick every one of our theological boxes before we would worship with them? Modern-day Pharisees are no better than those Jesus called 'whitewashed tombs', adding: 'So you also outwardly appear righteous to others, but within you are full of hypocrisy and lawlessness' (Matthew 23:27–28).

Lord, help me to remember that I'm only a sinner, saved by grace. Teach me to measure truth by Your Word, not by my opinion. Amen.

7 September

For by grace you have been saved through faith.
And this is not your own doing; it is the gift of God,
not a result of works, so that no one may boast.

Ephesians 2:8–9

Reading: Ephesians 2:1–10

The Pharisees would not have been at all happy with what Paul wrote to the Ephesian Christians years later. One of their own – a former Pharisee (Acts 23:6) – Paul knew the damage done by a mind set on self-righteousness. Even though his life was devoted to the law of God, he had known nothing of the God of the law. So incensed had he become by those in the early church that he 'dragged off men and women and committed them to prison' (8:3). Can you believe it? Persecuting people who were devoted to loving God with all their being, and their neighbour as much as they loved themselves (Matthew 22:37–39).

Why? As usual, Jesus had it in one! 'Remember the word that I said to you: "A servant is not greater than his master." If they persecuted me, they will also persecute you . . . these things they will do to you on account of my name' (John 15:20–21).

Jesus' message, précised here by Paul, clearly explains that neither good works, nor attempting to keep God's law, will bring us salvation. We are simply not good enough. In fact, we are sinners (Romans 3:23). That grates, even angers, us – especially those who've spent their lives publicly demonstrating their own righteousness to the world. There's only one way to God, Jesus said, and that is by grace – God giving us what we don't deserve through Jesus' sacrifice on the cross (1 Peter 2:24). And that reaches us through the conduit of faith, explained well by the old acrostic:

F – Forsaking
A – All
I
T – Trust
H – Him

Salvation is a free gift. There is nothing I can do to earn it. I must abandon the exhausting activities of trying to gain God's favour by my own behaviour, and trust in Christ alone (Acts 16:31). Yes, it is that simple . . . and that difficult.

Lord Jesus, forgive me for the times, even now, when I continue to try to please You through activity rather than trust. Amen.

8 September

THINK ON THIS

'My Father, who has given them to me,
is greater than all,
and no one is able to snatch them
out of the Father's hand.'

John 10:29

- Read through this verse a number of times – including out loud.
- Write it out, stick it on the fridge, have it on your phone.
- Meditate on the words, then respond in praise.
- Take steps to allow God's word to change you: perhaps . . . repent, forgive, love.

9 September

Bless the LORD, O my soul,
and all that is within me, bless his holy name!

Psalm 103:1

Reading: Psalm 103

The little boy's arm shot into the air, stretching every sinew as he tried to catch the speaker's attention. The Bible lesson was about prayer, with flannelgraph figures of Daniel providing a colourful illustrative backdrop. 'Mister, Mister,' the child squeaked through clenched teeth. Unable to keep a straight face, my husband finally asked, 'Seamus, do you have a question?' 'Yes Mister,' he replied. 'Mister, can you pray in your head?'

The boy was delighted to hear that, yes, you can pray in your head . . . or out loud . . . on your own . . . with others . . . short prayers . . . long prayers . . . thank you prayers . . . asking prayers . . . all kinds of prayers, in all kinds of places. God loves to hear our voices . . . and loves to answer our prayers (1 John 5:14).

But the prayers that bless God most are praise prayers. As a Jew, Jesus would have been taught short blessing prayers, developed first by Moses when he encouraged the people not to forget the Lord (Deuteronomy 8:10–11). Used throughout the day, this form of praying was habit-forming; a constant reminder of God's goodness, focused on Him and not themselves. The word for 'bless' here means to kneel, so in blessing God we are mentally bowed in worship.

On waking: 'Blessed is he who opened the eyes of the blind.' When dressing: 'Blessed is he who clothes the naked!' For nature: 'Blessed is he who created good trees for people to enjoy.' When the thunder rolled in: 'Blessed is he whose strength and power fill the world!' Following life's difficult experiences: 'Blessed is he who has allowed us to live, and has sustained us and enabled us to reach this day.' Imagine the impact this had on those who chose to recite these prayers as a true offering of praise, focusing on God's goodness at every turn of life's experience.

Imagine what it would do to our hearts if we developed a similar habit of praise throughout the day – for the little things we take for granted. And yes, you can pray them in your head!

Bless the Lord, O my soul, and praise Him for all He has done for me. Amen.

10 September

'And when you pray . . .'
Matthew 6:5

Reading: Hebrews 10:19–23

For the Christian, praying isn't optional. When teaching His disciples about prayer, Jesus didn't say, 'If you're in the mood to pray,' or, 'When you become spiritual enough,' or even, 'If you're good at forming words.' Rather, Jesus said, 'And *when* you pray' (emphasis mine). I find that so comforting. Too often we compare our prayers with others, assessing our attempts as weak by comparison, somehow rendering them ineffective. God doesn't measure our words or how well we express them. He simply desires to hear the voices of His children. In fact, 'the prayer of the upright *is* His delight' (Proverbs 15:8, NKJV).

Yet, we seem to have overcomplicated it. Our bookshelves are heavy with advice on prayer . . . especially on how to make it simple! But when it comes to it, there's only one person who can do anything about my prayer life, and that's me. 'When you pray' simply means 'Just do it!'

And when we do, we discover:

- who God is. Bowing before the King places within us a sense of awe and reverence for His greatness (Isaiah 40:12);
- an open door to intimacy with God. 'Draw near to God, and he will draw near to you' (James 4:8). We cannot campfire with Jesus as the disciples did, but we can experience His near presence in prayer;
- we can communicate what's on our hearts . . . praise, thanksgiving, worship . . . even our questions, fears and insecurities (1 John 5:14);
- we can bring our requests to God, 'And if we know that he hears us . . . we know that we have the requests that we have asked of him' (1 John 5:15). What's meant here is not shopping lists of desires, but rather the fulfilment of learning to pray what's on God's heart for us, and for those we love (Jeremiah 29:11);
- that it's possible to simply enjoy God's company (1 John 4:9).

While our desire is to bless God's heart, we are the ultimate winners. He does not need us, but in reconciling us to Himself through His Son, He willingly loves and engages with us through prayer. That's something I do not want to miss!

Father God, may my prayer bring You delight today. Amen.

11 September

But for me it is good to be near God;
I have made the Lord GOD my refuge,
that I may tell of all your works.

Psalm 73:28

Reading: 1 John 4:9–12

I've been married for forty-five years. Yes, to the same man! And without sounding too sentimental in such a public space, I'd happily do it all over again. You see, I know my husband very well now. I get his corny jokes and know when he's up to mischief. I recognize the cues when he's feeling down or when he's concerned. I love how, after all these years, he still holds my hand when we walk together, or the way he briefly hesitates before he speaks when he wants to say something that might upset me. I enjoy the silence with him as much as the long conversations. I cannot doubt his love for me, and I trust him as much as any human being can trust another. Living without him is unimaginable.

This is intimacy.

And intimacy with God is the only spiritual experience that will truly satisfy, when He draws near to us as we draw near to Him (James 4:8). Relationship that is deep and enduring is never one-sided – it requires the attention of both parties to produce the very best. God is not needy (Acts 17:25), but we are, and His love for us is such that He chooses close relationship in order that we might trust Him. After all, we love God because He first loved us (1 John 4:10). Trust cannot happen where love has not been first, but trust is the benchmark in our relationship with God; the heart of intimacy.

Prayer is the door through which we get to know Him – the access to learning who God is, how much He loves us, and how dependent we are on Him for everything. And as time passes and we speak often, we get to know Him better. Then we can enjoy the silence where His presence is enough, and commit the difficult terrain to Him as He walks with us – our hand in His.

Lord, to know You is to love You, and to love You is to trust You. May both draw me into Your presence today. Amen.

12 September

'And when you pray, you must not be like the hypocrites. For they love to stand and pray in the synagogues and at the street corners, that they may be seen by others.'

Matthew 6:5

Reading: Hebrews 10:19–25

One Sunday morning, sources suggest that several young visitors arrived early to attend the service at the famous Metropolitan Tabernacle in London. They quickly became engaged in conversation with a man in the empty sanctuary, whom they told of their wish to hear the church's world-famous preacher, Charles Hadden Spurgeon. Seemingly unimpressed, the man spoke briefly to them, then invited them to visit the church heating plant. Strangely puzzled, they followed him downstairs. On opening the door to the church's 'heating plant' the visitors were met with the sight of hundreds of people gathered – praying! 'This is the power behind my preaching,' Spurgeon reportedly said, revealing himself to the surprised young men. 'I couldn't do what I do without what happens in this prayer meeting.'

The church prayer meeting. In spite of the biblical instruction for us not to neglect meeting together (Hebrews 10:25), the prayer meeting is usually the smallest meeting of the church week. Attendance, or non-attendance, is too often driven by how we feel, excusing ourselves with Jesus' words when he found Peter asleep when he should have been praying: 'The spirit indeed is willing, but the flesh is weak' (Matthew 26:41).

Worse still is turning up to the prayer meeting because we want to be seen by others, or to avoid what might be said if we're not there. Hypocrisy is not only the domain of the Pharisees, to whom Jesus was referring in today's verse. There is no doubt they were men of prayer, nor that they were consistent in what they did . . . and no doubt that it wasn't God they were praying to! They liked to have an audience. Jesus' response: *Don't be like them!* (6:5).

The Saviour isn't saying that we shouldn't pray in public places – He set that very example for us to follow. It's the heart behind our public prayer He's challenging. There may be others present, but it should be the audience of One that we seek.

Lord Jesus, it's Your presence I seek, Your greatness I worship. Amen.

13 September

'But when you pray,
go into your room and shut the door
and pray to your Father who is in secret.
And your Father who sees in secret will reward you.'

Matthew 6:6

Reading: Philippians 4:6–7

When you hear the word 'but', you know there's more to come – what usually follows is a contrast. Having instructed His disciples in how *not* to pray, Jesus immediately goes on to say, '*but* when *you* pray' (emphasis mine), make it private and 'pray to your Father'. No one else is to be involved. No one else knows. Not another soul will hear your words, nor stand in judgement over them. This is the ultimate in Father–daughter or Father–son experiences. It is exclusively for the audience of one – who loves you 'with an everlasting love' and who continues in 'faithfulness to you' (Jeremiah 31:3).

Jesus explains that the best place for conversation with the Father is one where you are free from interruption and distraction – where the phone won't ring or the kettle boil, or the children come calling your name. Simply pick your spot ... a bench in the garden, the kitchen table, a rock by the seaside or your early morning walk before your working day begins. Jesus usually chose a secluded hillside (Luke 5:16), but wherever you choose, one thing is certain: the Father will be waiting for you before you arrive. It's one appointment that must be in the diary. No postponements, no cancellations, for without regular prayer we only get to peek at God ... to experience Him in snippets ... to remain unfulfilled. And we will miss the rewards Jesus promises to those who pray in secret (Matthew 6:6) – including the thrill of God's presence, the joy of answered prayer and His felt peace.

And then, when we shut the door behind us, we discover that prayer follows us into the day ... continuing 'in our head', as the little boy asked at that Bible club. 'Everywhere God is, prayer is. Since God is everywhere and infinitely great, prayer must be all-pervasive in our lives.'[34]

Father God, thank you for meeting me in the secret place, where I can pour out my heart, knowing that You hear and answer according to Your will. Amen.

14 September

'And when you pray, do not heap up empty phrases
as the Gentiles do, for they think that they
will be heard for their many words.
Do not be like them,
for your Father knows what you need
before you ask him.'

Matthew 6:7–8

Reading: Psalm 23

We learn so much from children, don't we? When our grandson was very little, he was always the first one to respond to his dad's question: 'Who would like to thank God for the food?' With eyes closed in reverence – he knew to whom he was praying – and hands firmly clasped together, so as not to distract him, he would launch into his prayer for the food now sitting beneath his nose: 'Thank you, God, for the food. Amen.' That was it! The food never got cold when this little man prayed. And the next time it was his turn to give thanks he'd use exactly the same words. He is still quite young, and still loves to give thanks, but he has managed to add a few extra sentences to that oft-repeated prayer.

Were his words those 'empty phrases' Jesus was warning about? No. He was then, and is now, genuinely thankful for his food, and knows it comes from God's blessing on his family. Is it repetitive? Well, yes, but he is still learning.

Jesus doesn't condemn us for repeating ourselves in prayer. The Saviour Himself did it in the garden of Gethsemane (Matthew 26:44). Repetition isn't the problem ... but empty words are. 'This people honors me with their lips,' Jesus said later in Matthew's Gospel (15:8), 'but their heart is far from me.' Our hearts and lips need to be in sync when we pray. And long prayers don't add any merit with God. We are coming to our Father, who not only knows His children; He knows exactly what we need ... today and every day.

Did you read Psalm 23, as I suggested? Written on every line is the evidence, if you needed it, of how our Shepherd/Father knows exactly what is best for us, and how to provide it.

Kind Father, my words can never gain Your favour, but let them show You my thankful heart. Amen.

15 September

THINK ON THIS

Is anyone among you suffering? Let him pray.
Is anyone cheerful? Let him sing praise.

James 5:13

- Read through this verse a number of times – including out loud.
- Write it out, stick it on the fridge, have it on your phone.
- Meditate on the words, then respond in praise.
- Encourage someone by sharing this verse with them today.

16 September

'Pray then like this:
"Our Father in heaven . . ."'
Matthew 6:9

Reading: 1 John 3:1–3

Sometimes when I am reading God's word, one word stands out. You might think from the beginning of what's become known as the Lord's Prayer that it would be the word 'Father'. But it's the word 'our' that was first on my mind when I woke this morning. The fact that Jesus was sharing access to *His* Father with mere mortals like us touches my heart.

Their relationship was very special. The Father publicly declared His love for His Son, Jesus (Mark 1:11), and Jesus affirmed His devotion to the Father through continual loving obedience (John 6:38). It's a beautiful picture of what a parent–child relationship should look like – the very model Jesus wants us to observe and experience as members of God's family. Jesus' sonship will always be unique, as He shares the same divine nature as God (Philippians 2:6–7). But His intent was always to have us share the same Father, and all that that means for us – now and into eternity.

Although being His 'one and only Son' (John 3:16, NLT), Jesus made it possible for *His* Father to become *our* Father by adopting us into the family. We are indeed children of the King. John says: 'But to all who believed him and accepted him, he gave the right to become children of God. They are reborn – not with a physical birth resulting from human passion or plan, but a birth that comes from God' (1:12–13, NLT).

This is why, when we come to pray, Jesus reminds us that we are doing so as children of His Father ... and ours! And this Father isn't only personal, but powerful – He is *our* Father in *heaven*. 'Privilege' hardly touches the thrill that revelation should bring to our hearts.

Our Father, thank you for loving me and making me Your child . . . for giving me an inheritance that can never fade, which has already begun through Your Son. Amen.

17 September

'Hallowed be your name.'

Matthew 6:9

Reading: Isaiah 6:1–5

It's interesting to see how Jesus continues in His prayer training of the disciples. The personal and powerful Father He encourages them to address as their own is none other than the Lord Jehovah to whom they had been reciting formal prayers since childhood (Deuteronomy 6:4–5). Jesus does not finish the first line of this model prayer with 'holy is your name', using instead the term 'hallowed be your name'. The disciples were already aware of God's holiness, 'who alone has immortality, who dwells in unapproachable light, whom no one has ever seen or can see' (1 Timothy 6:16).

Rather, Jesus teaches His followers to ask that the Father's name be hallowed – treated as holy. In a world that uses God's name with disdain and disrespect, reverence should always be the tone we use to coat our words when we speak of the One addressed in both testaments as 'holy, holy, holy . . .' (Isaiah 6:3; Revelation 4:8). Both Isaiah and the apostle John record the immense privilege they had of visiting God's throne room in a vision. In vivid mental pictures they show us living heavenly creatures reverently worshipping around God's throne, covering themselves in such a way as to declare their unworthiness in the presence of the holy God.

What a challenge Jesus presents to us, who carelessly dash into God's presence as if we're calling in on a best mate, and who seldom enter His throne room with the awe and wonder He merits. When has His holiness so impacted our prayer time that all we could do was bow in His presence? And in our rush to ask – even on behalf of others – do we bow even for a moment to acknowledge who He is? After all, it is God's holiness that sets Him apart from all other beings. He is distinct, transcendent, pure. These minds of ours can only comprehend a fraction of what that means . . . yet, it should cause us to gaze in wonder, adoration and praise.

'Worthy are you, our Lord and God, to receive glory and honor and power, for you created all things, and by your will they existed and were created'.[35] *Amen.*

18 September

'Your kingdom come.'
Matthew 6:10

Reading: John 18:33–37

I wonder what the disciples thought Jesus meant when He included these words. Perhaps a few of them were thinking about the overthrow of Roman oppression. Politics was on their mind, and Jesus could very well have been the king to rule in place of Caesar and Herod. Others may have been thinking of a kingdom freed from the burdens of the law, especially the oppressive Pharisaic add-ons. But neither was what Jesus had in mind as prayers to their personal, powerful and holy Father.

Jesus, the One Paul later described as 'the blessed and only Sovereign, the King of kings and Lord of lords' (1 Timothy 6:15), was alluding to an altogether different kingdom ... an everlasting one (Psalm 145:13). In one sense, God's kingdom is already here, in that: 'The LORD has established his throne in the heavens, and his kingdom rules over all' (103:19). We don't pray that somehow God will take control of the universe – it has always been His. But rather that His royal authority would rule in every area of our lives as we enjoy the blessings of salvation, and the responsibilities that come with it. The world shouts: 'Live as you like – do your own thing!' Jesus says: 'For what does it profit a man to gain the whole world and forfeit his soul?' (Mark 8:36).

Self-life is an empty life. Kingdom life is, 'According to his great mercy ... to be born again to a living hope through the resurrection of Jesus Christ from the dead, to an inheritance that is imperishable, undefiled, and unfading, kept in heaven for you' (1 Peter 1:3–4). So, Jesus encourages us to pray for the Father's kingdom to be born in us, and then to be lived out through us ... in joyful and loving submission as His children.

Then one day, 'when Christ who is your life appears, then you also will appear with him in glory' (Colossians 3:4), and He will establish His kingdom on earth as its rightful King (Zechariah 14:9).

Bring Your kingdom, Lord. Reign in my life, that the world might see Your glory. Amen.

19 September

'Your will be done,
on earth as it is in heaven.'
Matthew 6:10

Reading: Hebrews 13:20–21

In her small kitchen, my mum had an extending table that could magically transform the seating capacity from four to six places when needed. 'Magically' is perhaps the wrong word to use about said transformation, as the meal could sometimes be prepared more quickly than enlarging the table! For a start, it always required two people to perform the action – one at either side, pulling and shaking it to force it apart. Then, if you managed to retrieve the midsection from its hidey-hole without nipping your fingers, the real work began . . . that of aligning the little brass pins into the counterpart holes before securing tiny hooks underneath to stop it coming apart in the middle of the meal!

'It's all down to alignment,' my husband would quip, as if I hadn't worked that out for myself! 'You need to work on both sides at the same time.'

That's exactly what Jesus was speaking about when instructing us to pray: 'Your will be done, on earth as it is in heaven' (Matthew 6:10). Alignment. My will needs to come together with His for the divine plan of hallowing *His* name to occur. That requires both of us to work together. God's will is already set – He 'desires all people to be saved and to come to the knowledge of the truth' (1 Timothy 2:4). In this one succinct sentence we can identify God's will for humankind to be reconciled to Himself through Christ (2 Corinthians 5:18), and that we should know Him, for He is truth (John 14:6).

So, the crux of the matter is: how can I align my will to His? It involves the 'S' word. Submission. It doesn't happen by vaguely hoping that what I desire will fit with His will, but rather that I deliberately embrace God's desires for myself. It might mean subjugating my stubbornness, standing down my pride or confessing my selfishness. But in choosing to accept His sovereign control over my life, earth and heaven merge together into the beautiful plan of God.

Heavenly Father, You have my heart. Make it Your throne, that my words and deeds might reflect Your will. Amen.

20 September

Jesus said to them, 'My food is to do the will
of him who sent me and to accomplish his work.'

John 4:34

Reading: John 8:25–30

Jesus was the embodiment of what He taught. God's will was accomplished on earth as in heaven (Matthew 6:10) as the Saviour demonstrated the loving-kindness of God to everyone He met (Titus 3:4–5). Obedience to the will of God was Jesus' very lifeblood. Even in the garden of Gethsemane, when He struggled with the horror of what lay ahead, He declared: 'Nevertheless, not my will, but yours, be done' (Luke 22:42). The Lord's Prayer is not merely one to copy; it shows the intimate communication between the Son of God and His Father. No one knew more about God's will in heaven than He did, and no one did more to bring it to earth than Jesus.

Jesus' will was fully aligned with the Father's. And if we are to follow His example, there is help available:

- **God's word is key.** God chooses to speak to us through His written word: the Bible. It makes us 'wise for salvation through faith in Christ Jesus' (2 Timothy 3:15). It is God-breathed, 'profitable for teaching, for reproof, for correction, and for training in righteousness . . . [that we might be] equipped for every good work' (3:16–17). There is no better way for God to reveal His will to us than through His word. He is a speaking God, but if we want to hear Him we must open the book! And if we are to see His will accomplished, we must 'be doers of the word, and not hearers only' (James 1:22).
- **Wisdom is available.** There is much still to learn. Whether we are new believers or have been a long time on the road with Jesus, remember: 'If you need wisdom, ask our generous God, and he will give it to you. He will not rebuke you for asking' (James 1:5, NLT).
- **Jesus is our companion on this journey.** He won't lead us astray. Setting aside our own personal wishes to prioritize His expands His kingdom in our hearts and delivers the same joy Jesus felt when doing the Father's will (Psalm 40:8).

Teach me, Lord. I want to hear You and do Your will. Amen.

21 September

'Give us this day our daily bread.'

Matthew 6:11

Reading: Exodus 16:9–18

Having left the truck further down the hill, we made our way up a winding grass path towards Jimmy's Camp. As we approached a small clearing, an unwalled platform on stilts with a leaf roof came into view. Beyond the rickety building was a densely forested area concealing dozens of Karen refugee families, or what was left of them following the massacre of their tribespeople in Myanmar. Within minutes of reaching the desolated site, people began to arrive from the jungle. Haggard faces atop skinny, poorly clothed bodies piled under the wooden platform and sat on the rough ground in complete silence. Even the babies made hardly a sound. We smiled our greetings into traumatized, empty faces. It was heartbreaking.

We presented each family with a bag of food and a few other essentials. Their response was muted, so fearful were they that strangers might turn them in to the Thai police. At least we knew they would eat that night, and we could only pray the same for the following day.

Most of us have no idea what real hunger feels like. We say we're 'starving' when all we mean is that we haven't eaten since lunch. When Jesus taught the people to ask God for their daily bread, many of them had little access to food. During Israel's desert wanderings there were more than a million souls to feed, and God taught them to look to Him for their daily needs. That was all He promised . . . two small meals per day (see today's reading). But it was enough to keep them alive, and to prove His faithfulness towards them.

In the Western world, greed is the bane of our age. We never seem to have enough, and are always looking for more – of everything. Jesus reminds us to trust God for what we need daily. Thanks to His providence we rarely need to pray for bread, but we can ask God to provide for our world's starving. And for ourselves we can pray daily for the provision of grace, patience, kindness and love to live for Him in these days.

Father, we are blessed indeed with food, shelter and all we need. Keep us faithful in praying for others. Amen.

22 September

THINK ON THIS

And the world is passing away along with its desires, but whoever does the will of God abides forever.

1 John 2:17

- Read through this verse a number of times – including out loud.
- Write it out, stick it on the fridge, have it on your phone.
- Meditate on the words, then respond in praise.
- Be a doer . . . Serve someone with an act of kindness today.

23 September

'And forgive us our debts,
as we also have forgiven our debtors.'
Matthew 6:12

Reading: Micah 7:18–20

The Lord's Prayer isn't as simple as you think at first glance, is it? The repetition at school assembly, or even in a church service for that matter, pales with inadequacy when we consider what Jesus is encouraging us to say and do as we approach our Father in prayer. These words are part of the serious stuff of praying. This is where righteousness meets honesty and expects action.

We will never be sinless in this life (1 John 1:8), although we should not wilfully lead sinful lives (Romans 6:1–2). Therefore, it is imperative that we daily ask forgiveness from the Lord, which involves the clearing of the debt and guilt associated with it (1 John 1:9). Sin impacts our fellowship with the Father in the same way a cloud hides the sun's brightness from us. He is still there ... but our behaviour interrupts our relationship with God, resulting in unanswered prayer (Isaiah 59:2). How could God trust us with answers to prayer if we hold on to the very things that grieve Him?

Jesus makes it clear that forgiveness is essential for a healthy soul – not only God's forgiveness of us, but our forgiveness of others. He is not saying that a forgiving spirit earns us the right to be forgiven ... for God's grace is a free gift (Romans 3:24). But rather, once we recognize the enormity of our own sin, we should be willing to forgive the sin of others against us (Ephesians 4:32). At times this is hard, even proving a stumbling block for those of us deeply hurt by another. Remember that our forgiveness does not absolve that person from the personal responsibility for their sin – but it does free us up to enjoy the full life God has for us. What greater reward could there be for ridding our hearts of bitterness than restoration with our Father, and basking in His peace?

'Who is a God like you, pardoning iniquity ... [delighting] in steadfast love.' (Micah 7:18)

Heavenly Father, teach me to love the sinner as You do, for none of us could stand if it were not for Your mercy. Amen.

24 September

'And lead us not into temptation,
but deliver us from evil.'

Matthew 6:13

Reading: Psalm 141:3–4, 8–10

The Father we pray to is a God who leads us:

- in the way everlasting when we ask Him to show us our sin (Psalm 139:24);
- along the right path when we are surrounded by our enemies (Psalm 27:11, NLT);
- beside still waters when we need to rest (Psalm 23:2);
- along an unfamiliar path when we can't see the way ahead (Isaiah 42:16, NLT);
- until we die, for He is our God forever and ever (Psalm 48:14, NLT).

Therefore, it follows that Jesus teaches us to pray that God would lead us away from evil. While our old sinful nature draws us towards what is not good for us, we need God's wisdom to help us choose what is righteous and God-honouring. Our days are full of choices – from the simple ones, like what we will eat or where we will go, to those that affect our eternal souls. Will we choose obedience or disobedience; faith or doubt; belief or unbelief . . . godly living or sinful desires? Jesus encourages us to pray: *God rescue me from making the wrong choice . . . don't let evil suck me in.*

These are things we can't do without God's enabling. We cannot resist the evil one by ourselves. The instruction to 'resist the devil' in James 4:7 is preceded by the command to 'submit yourselves therefore to God'. Only when we get them in the right order will we see the devil 'flee from [us]'. God works with us on this one – recognizing that our weakness is the first step towards trusting Him and experiencing His strength. Trusting God is habit-forming. The more we trust, the more likely it is that we will send Him to answer the door when temptation comes knocking. He alone has the power to deal with the evil one.

God who subdues the thunder, wind and storm, give me the strength to avoid every place where temptation would seek to overwhelm me. Help me to submit my will to Yours and exchange my desires for Yours. Empower me by Your Spirit to experience victory today. Amen.

25 September

'For Yours is the kingdom and the power
and the glory forever. Amen.'

Matthew 6:13, NKJV

Reading: 1 Chronicles 29:10–13

If you are reading from one of the newer versions of the Bible, you might be wondering where this sentence came from. No, I didn't make it up; later translators excluded some text from the work of their earlier counterparts. Mine is not to reason why here, but I cannot ignore these tremendous words of praise that bring to a close the teaching of Jesus' model prayer. They sum up the theme of the prayer and remind us again of the magnificence of the One to whom we pray:

Our Father in heaven: personal – for He has graciously adopted us into His family through the sacrifice of His Son; and powerful – creator of the universe (Jeremiah 10:12).

Hallowed be your name: holy – distinct, transcendent, pure; His name higher than that of any earthly sovereign.

Your kingdom come: present throughout eternity, and now born in and lived through us until the day Christ comes and makes the earth His footstool (Psalm 110:1).

Your will be done, on earth as it is in heaven: heaven and earth merging together as we submit to His will . . . just as Jesus did (John 4:34).

And also remind us of the graciousness of His provision for us:

In giving us our daily bread, faithfully meeting our needs.

In forgiving our sins and clearing the debt they should have incurred, while encouraging our relationship with Him through our forgiveness of others.

In leading us away from temptation and delivering us from the evil one, as the only One with the power to defeat Satan and give us the power to reject sinful practices.

Is it any wonder that I'm glad these words remain as a postscript of praise to the One to whom we pray? There is no better way to conclude our praying than by affirming, with thankfulness, that the kingdom belongs to our Father, and the power and the glory none can supersede.

Precious Father, my heart bows in gratitude and awe that You allow us – sinners, saved by grace – to enter Your Holy presence at all! May I never take it for granted. Amen.

26 September

'For where two or three are gathered in my name,
there am I among them.'
Matthew 18:20

Reading: Acts 2:42–47

'No man is an island entire of itself,' wrote the seventeenth-century poet John Donne.[36] Not a new thought, as at creation God said that it wasn't good for us to be alone (Genesis 2:18). People need people, whatever our individual personality. If Jesus needed people, then who are we to think we don't?

While private prayer was the Saviour's daily practice, there were times when Jesus prayed with others (Luke 9:18, 28), specifically Peter, James and John. These close companions were also privileged to share in the important events of His life (Mark 5:37–42; Matthew 17:1–2). They were the ones taken aside from the others in the garden of Gethsemane to pray with Jesus (Matthew 26:36–38). Yes, Jesus was mentoring the future leaders of the church, but it was more than that – He prayed with them ... and trusted them with His heart.

Praying with another grows our personal prayer life as we learn from them through their knowledge of God and openness with Him. The power of our praying is also enhanced as we share together in our love and worship of the Lord: 'Iron sharpens iron, and one man sharpens another' (Proverbs 27:17). Excitement breeds excitement, and dynamics change as 'me' is surrendered from the top prayer spot. Praying with someone else requires trust – fear of gossip can be the biggest hindrance to partnering in prayer – but that works both ways, therefore reducing vulnerability. It's a beautiful experience that doesn't need to be time-consuming, and the rewards are immense.

Most important is the need to pray with our marriage partner. However busy family and work life is, those few minutes carved out of the day are critical. You might even find out some important information that had slipped under the radar! And don't just pray for your children ... pray *with* them ... about everything. You'll be rewarded by the thrill of hearing them speak to the Father for themselves. Nothing gives greater joy!

Lord Jesus, help me to treasure the privilege of praying with others. Strengthen my marriage and our family as we prioritize prayer with each other. Amen.

27 September

'For truly, I say to you, if you have faith like a grain
of mustard seed, you will say to this mountain,
"Move from here to there," and it will move,
and nothing will be impossible for you.'

Matthew 17:20

Reading: Matthew 17:14–20

'I tried it, and it didn't work,' said my husband as he came through the door. 'What did you try?' I replied, noticing the glint in his eye. 'I was travelling along the motorway,' he said, tongue firmly in cheek, 'and as I am a man of faith – to say nothing of being a minister of the gospel – I stared at Slemish Mountain and told it to move!' Before I could interrupt, he continued: 'You'll never guess what–' 'It never moved,' I interjected. 'Now, what do you say to that?' he replied. 'Does God answer the prayer of faith or not?'

Of course He does! But it wasn't the instant translocation of some natural elevation that was primarily on the Saviour's mind. Rather, it was frustration with His disciples for failing to exercise faith for a child's healing that resulted in this particular analogy (Matthew 17:16). Earlier, Jesus had given His disciples the authority to do the miraculous (10:1, 8), but it appeared that they didn't have the requisite faith to carry out His bidding on this occasion.

These men knew plenty about mustard seeds. They were tiny. But once planted they had the potential for enormous growth, even when planted in poor soil. We are told that 'without faith it is impossible to please him' (Hebrews 11:6), yet in His kindness Jesus reminds us of what He can do when we display even the tiniest semblance of trust in Him. For once planted in our hearts, faith can grow and become a mighty force for God. A seed never stays a seed when it is sown in the right place.

Then the mountains we see moved by the prayer of faith will be the rubble of hurt, disappointment and pain. Stone by anguished stone will be broken and removed by our miracle-working God as He works with us through believing prayer.

Lord God, let's move some mountains today! Together we can! Increase my faith. Amen.

28 September

And even when you ask, you don't get it
because your motives are all wrong –
you want only what will give you pleasure.

James 4:3, NLT

Reading: 1 John 5:13–14

My elderly mother had been in hospital for several weeks following a fall that had inflicted major injuries. Other long-standing medical conditions were causing her condition to worsen, and for the first time in her ninety-two years she was becoming seriously confused. In one of those rare clearer moments, she squeezed my hand, made eye contact and spoke firmly. 'Catherine,' she said as tenderly as she could. 'You're not praying right.' I had no idea what she was talking about. 'Pray that God will take me home . . . don't pray that He will heal me.' I couldn't stop the tears as she pulled my hand towards her face to give me a cheek hug. 'It's time,' she said.

I agreed. Her frail body had had enough, but while I couldn't approach God with her request, the best I could do was pray for God's will to be done. Mum's motivation wasn't wrong in seeking an end to her suffering, but ultimately God's perfect will is what we should seek . . . no matter the circumstances. He knows best.

James, the brother of Jesus, was writing to the diaspora – those Jews scattered from Israel because of their faith in Jesus. There were problems afoot; not merely due to persecution, but also because of serious personal and church disruption caused by self-centred attitudes and behaviour (James 4:1). They were not living as Christians should.

When selfishness seeps into our prayer life, it can destroy it. God is not there to satisfy our selfish desires. He cannot be cajoled or browbeaten into giving us what we want. James reminds us that wrong motives lead to wrong praying. And 'when our praying is wrong, our whole Christian life is wrong . . . the purpose of prayer is not to get man's will done in heaven, but to get God's will done on earth.'[37]

However, there is a difference between sinful motivation and misdirected motivation. Thankfully, God sees our heart and answers accordingly.

Lord Jesus, teach me to ask according to Your will, and not from selfish desire. Amen.

29 September

THINK ON THIS

'Before they call I will answer;
while they are yet speaking I will hear.'
Isaiah 65:24

- Read through this verse a number of times – including out loud.
- Write it out, stick it on the fridge, have it on your phone.
- Meditate on the words, then respond in praise.
- Take steps to allow God's word to change you: perhaps . . . repent,
  forgive, love.

30 September

Likewise the Spirit helps us in our weakness.
For we do not know what to pray for as we ought,
but the Spirit himself intercedes for us
with groanings too deep for words.

Romans 8:26

Reading: Romans 8:26–30

This verse brings such comfort, doesn't it? I could feel myself sigh with gratitude as I typed it out. So often I wonder if I prayed enough, used the right words, included everything I needed to say, hadn't been selfish or rushed, asked in God's will . . . or even prayed at all that day. There seems to be so much to remember that I forget that I am praying to my Father. That he sees my heart and knows what is behind each prayer . . . or lack of it. He doesn't merely test my motivation to see if I need to be corrected, or if I'm praying out of selfishness, but to identify where He can help me to pray prayers that He can answer.

God loves to answer our prayers, telling us: 'Call to me and I *will* answer you, and *will* tell you great and hidden things that you have not known' (Jeremiah 33:3, emphasis mine). In fact, God loves us, full stop (31:3). Praying is not a daily exam we have to take. It is the best bit of our relationship with our Father, where we get to communicate with each other. And He even has a solution for times when I run out of words.

And that has happened too many times to count. Usually, it's when I'm in a difficult place; when my broken heart doesn't know how to pray or what to ask for, or when tears have dried up my words. And when all I can say is, 'I don't know what to say, Lord,' He replies with, 'That's okay . . . I have Someone to step in. One who knows what to ask for.' And He whispers 'Peace' to my heart as the Spirit gets to the business of interceding for me (Romans 8:26). Our heavenly Father has every situation covered. I love that about Him.

Your love and generosity blows me away, Lord. Is it any wonder that I'm lost for words, precious Saviour? Amen.

October

1 October

'Take care then how you hear.'

Luke 8:18

Reading: Luke 8:16–18

I have the greatest admiration for teachers. The skill they have in assessing who among their class of thirty pupils is hearing what they are being taught, or merely listening to the words as they fly over the top of their heads, is admirable. If only we could all learn in the same way. A good teacher needs to engage different teaching methods depending on ability, without damaging any of their students.

Jesus was one such teacher. A great storyteller, He engaged His listeners with images that would not only throw light on His sermon, but also would stay with them long after He had gone. Easily identified everyday items such as sheep (John 10:27) and bread (6:35) were His daily show-and-tell method of teaching, especially early in His ministry.

However, there came a point when the Saviour's methods changed, and He began to use parables (Mark 4:33–34). Parables use a whole story, with strong characters and rich imagery, which can require deeper explanation to draw out a spiritual lesson; more so than a specific word or phrase. They are much more than an earthly story with a heavenly meaning, particularly for those listening. They required explanation (Luke 8:9–10), which Jesus gave to those who were already accepting of who He was, and of the truth He spoke.

Jesus always sifts out the spiritually hungry from those seeking self-gain rather than kingdom living. His concern is for those prepared to hear with spiritual ears and to act on what they hear; something that produces its own rewards. 'Take care then how you hear,' Jesus said, 'for to the one who has, more will be given, and from the one who has not, even what he thinks that he has will be taken away' (8:18).

Hearing God's word is a serious matter, involving both privilege and account-ability. Treat it flippantly and we lose. Seek it out and absorb it, and God will give us more. In the parables, Jesus tests our commitment to Him. So then, are we hearing . . . or merely listening?

Holy Spirit, give me the humility and submission required to truly hear what You are saying to me. Amen.

2 October

So faith comes from hearing,
and hearing through the word of Christ.

Romans 10:17

Reading: Luke 8:4–15

Jesus is in farming mode as He launches into what is usually called the Parable of the Sower. It could just as easily be called the Parable of the Seed or the Parable of the Soil, since parables always involve more than one thought. The Jews explained a parable as sitting in a house where you can look out of different windows and see something different from each one.

There are three equally important views from these windows: that of the Sower, the seed and the soils. How wonderful to know that the Sower (Jesus) spreads the seed far and wide. How else would the word of God (the seed, Luke 8:11) have taken root in our hearts (the soil, 8:12)? This is no haphazard sowing; it demonstrates Jesus' desire for the 'gospel of the kingdom' to be 'proclaimed throughout the whole world as a testimony to all nations' (Matthew 24:14).

Soil cannot grow anything without a seed, nor can a healthy plant develop unless it is tended. We shouldn't assume that our hearts are the good soil spoken of in Luke 8:15. Fruit is not guaranteed. What happens to the seed is determined by the quality of the soil. So, what's my heart like? I need to be careful who walks over it, for they might destroy the seed God has planted (8:12), while fair-weather faith quickly dies at the first clap of thunder (8:13). Roots need to grow deep if they are to produce something beautiful, so there's no room for the weeds of self-centred living. If we don't deal with them, they will cause catastrophe (Hebrews 12:15).

On one occasion, our green-fingered neighbour watched me struggle with the weeds in our little patch. Trying to be helpful, he said: 'You know, Catherine, if you take a few minutes every day you'll find the garden doesn't get so out of control.' That's good advice for tending our souls too.

Lord Jesus, help me to treasure and nurture the 'seed' planted in my heart. May it bear fruit and become the means of seed-spreading elsewhere. Amen.

3 October

'And the seeds that fell on the good soil represent
honest, good-hearted people who hear God's word,
cling to it, and patiently produce a huge harvest.'

Luke 8:15, NLT

Reading: 1 Thessalonians 5:16–22

My heart melted the first time our newborn daughter closed her tiny hand around my finger and held on tightly. In the emotion of the moment, it felt like an expression of love from this tiny child . . . a special symbol of bonding between us outside the womb that had been building while she grew inside my body. She needed me. I loved her. We connected. It was more than my finger she held . . . she had my heart.

I refused to allow the midwife in me to declare that actually this clinging to my finger was merely one of the many involuntary, instinctive reflexes that appears at birth and disappears around six months of age. It's called the palmar reflex. How clever of God to allow such a beautiful action to initiate the important bond between mother and child . . . and everyone else who gets close enough to stroke her hand.

It was deemed medically unfortunate that Cheryl never lost that reflex – a sign of her neurological condition. But for me it was always beautiful that, for the many things she couldn't do, she was still able to cling tightly to my finger. Even in brokenness the bond never faltered.

Jesus explains the importance of clinging to Him through attention to His word. In those early days of trusting, it almost seems like an involuntary action to respond to the seed that has been planted in our hearts. Our new-found faith is exciting, exhilarating and different from anything we've experienced before, but it is fragile. The enemy of our souls seeks to destroy it by any and every means possible (Luke 8:12). Our permanent spiritual reflex should be to push those roots ever deeper and hold fast to the One who planted the seed in the first place . . . a planting paid in His blood (Ephesians 1:7).

Lord Jesus, may my instinctive reflex always be to trust You. Make my grasp of Your word strong and the bond between us unshakeable. Amen.

4 October

And Jesus said to him, 'You go, and do likewise.'
Luke 10:37

Reading: Luke 10:25–37

Often, it's not our words that betray us, but the motivation behind them. Why we say what we do is as important as how we listen. Words laced with untruth or selfish desire are always 'fake news', to use the term correctly.

Jesus was an expert at spotting the motivation behind a conversation. There's no trick or test that he can't see through, yet He always gives us the opportunity to say the right thing. We call that grace. And this lawyer was no exception. Jesus answered his question about how to receive eternal life (Luke 10:25), but when he foolishly tried to justify himself (10:29), the Lord had to take the lawyer into parable house to examine the question for himself. The answer was one the lawyer would find uncomfortable.

The main characters in the story are the man who was violently mugged, the two religious travellers and a Samaritan. It's called the Parable of the Good Samaritan, but it could equally be called the Parable of Prejudice. We like to think we're not prejudiced; that it doesn't matter if people don't look like us or think like us ... until the issue is staring us in the face. We may even use religion – like the priest and the Levite did (10:31–32) – as our excuse for not becoming involved in a situation needing our help or involvement. Helping a 'half dead' person might render them ceremonially unclean. Anyway, someone else was bound to come along soon and help the injured man. It wasn't their responsibility. Oh, no! But what about the Lord's requirement 'to do what is right, to love mercy' (Micah 6:8, NLT)?

The 'somebody else' mentality cripples the church even today, and should leave us personally embarrassed. The lawyer was undoubtedly horrified that a hated Samaritan was the hero in Jesus' story, and worse still, he had to admit that Jesus was right (Luke 10:37). The view from parable house is often rather more challenging than we would like.

Forgive me, Lord, for the times when I haven't done the right thing because of prejudice or spiritual arrogance. Change my heart. Amen.

5 October

'If a kingdom is divided against itself,
that kingdom cannot stand.'

Mark 3:24

Reading: Mark 3:22–27

My husband and I like to watch the occasional TV quiz show. There's one thing that rattles me though. How can you tell a player who only answers two out of ten questions correctly, 'You're a good player'? It doesn't seem to make sense, does it?

Even more nonsensical is the religious leaders' accusation that Jesus cast out demons by Beelzebub, the prince of demons (Mark 3:22)! Where is the logic in that? Jesus responded to the absurd rumours they were spreading by challenging them directly: 'How can Satan cast out Satan?' (3:23). Oh, I'd love to have heard their replies, but I'm guessing they didn't have any . . . especially as Jesus enlightened them further about their folly.

Accomplishment involves teamwork, Jesus explained, citing the futility even of Satan – if he were stupid enough – to rebel against himself. That kind of strategy guarantees failure. While Satan is not so foolish as to set himself up for such a downfall, the master liar (John 8:44) uses that very tactic to cause havoc in churches, in families and in any situation that requires people to be unified in purpose.

Division, feuding and dispute are never healthy signs for success, but they are the perfect breeding ground for disaster. Paul, writing to the Romans, was on the same page as Jesus. 'I appeal to you, brothers,' he said, 'to watch out for those who cause divisions and create obstacles contrary to the doctrine that you have been taught; avoid them' (Romans 16:17). I would like to add in one more comment . . . let's make sure we are not that person. It is not clever. In fact, it is positively sinful!

Lord Jesus, show me if I am ever the cause of dissention within Your family. May I willingly work together with others for the extension of Your kingdom, and for the glory of Your name. Amen.

6 October

THINK ON THIS

'The kingdom of heaven is like treasure hidden in a field,
which a man found and covered up.
Then in his joy he goes and sells all that he has
and buys that field.'

Matthew 13:44

- Read through this verse a number of times – including out loud.
- Write it out, stick it on the fridge, have it on your phone.
- Meditate on the words, then respond in praise.
- Encourage someone by sharing this verse with them today.

7 October

From that time Jesus began to preach, saying,
'Repent, for the kingdom of heaven is at hand.'
Matthew 4:17

Reading: Luke 3:7–14

It is amazing what you uncover when you're clearing out a house. It was an emotional experience when the time came to divest a certain little red-brick bungalow of all my mother's belongings, Dad having died four years earlier. There's something sad about handling what has been precious in the life of someone you love and relegating it to boxes. While less personal, it can also be disturbing what you discover when you begin to remove things more structural.

Mum always had a lovely kitchen, but the cupboards were dated and had to come down during the renovation. However, we were unprepared for what we found hidden behind them – lumps of cement, wire castoffs and sockets the fitters had decided not to use. The cabinets were concealing a veritable rubbish dump! So much had to be removed before the new kitchen could be built.

Right from the get-go, Jesus' message was of repentance (Matthew 4:17). If we are to experience anything of God's kingdom on earth and the eternal one that lies ahead, the rubble of our sin needs to be removed ... before the new life Jesus promises can begin (John 10:10). That happens through repentance – admitting the presence of sin in our lives with heartfelt sorrow, and changing our life's direction to that of following Christ (Romans 10:9). But repentance isn't only visited when we're in need of salvation; rather it's a place we should return to again and again to receive the sanctifying power of Jesus Christ, until the day when we will be made sinless forever (Philippians 3:12).

However, those whose sin is as obvious as the nose on their face aren't the only ones who need to repent. We cannot forever conceal what often lies underneath the cover of clean living and even Christian testimony. There comes a time when the aesthetics have to come down – 'If we say we have no sin, we deceive ourselves' (1 John 1:8) – and deal with the reality. Thankfully, Jesus is in the reconstruction business (2 Corinthians 5:17).

Forgive me, Lord, when my pride attempts to hide the truth. Keep me honest and always willing to seek Your forgiveness. Amen.

8 October

'If you then, who are evil,
know how to give good gifts to your children,
how much more will the heavenly Father
give the Holy Spirit to those who ask him!'

Luke 11:13

Reading: Luke 11:5–13

The Campbells are list people. (Well, I am, and I could name others, but I won't!) From shopping lists to to-do lists, reading lists, call lists and packing lists, and of course – the pièce de résistance – the Christmas gift list. If I was going to be away during the years I looked after Mum, you could be sure of a snigger from my substitutes at the lists of reminders left for them.

Jesus had a little list of His own when teaching His disciples about the importance of persisting in prayer. It wasn't a long list – just three words (Luke 11:9). Ask. Seek. Knock. Perhaps you could say that, if you keep at it, you'll eventually get what you want. It seems pretty obvious, but remember that parables are never completely straightforward. They require us to look more closely. While Jesus makes it clear that He wants us to be persistent in our praying, it becomes evident that the response is not determined by how hard we knock on heaven's door, but on God's generosity.

God is not some handy ATM handing out answers at the push of an 'ASK' button. Our Father specializes in giving good gifts (11:13), but He is the one who determines what is best (James 1:17).

In the community these men came from, withholding hospitality brought shame – hence the reason for the late-night request and its eventual response. Neither man was glowing in this; protecting reputations likely pipped the priority stakes over generosity. Perhaps the Parable of the Faithful Father might have been a better title for the story. God does not play the badgered neighbour here, but the generous, good Father, giving us what we need out of the storehouse of His great love. He has nothing to prove.

Heavenly Father, I can come to You at any time of the day or night, and it will never be too late for You to hear my prayer. Thank you. Amen.

9 October

'And when he has found it,
he lays it on his shoulders, rejoicing.'
Luke 15:5

Reading: Luke 15:1–7

There are some parts of Scripture that we think we know well, perhaps with such familiarity that we tend to skim over them. The Parable of the Three Lost Things may be one of those. But such action makes us the losers. Described by some as 'the gospel in the Gospels', this parable describes not only the intensity of Jesus' love for the lost, but of the value He places on each individual.

On this occasion, Jesus was surrounded by those the Pharisees saw as sinners (Luke 15:2). They even had their own classification – 'the People of the Land' – whom Pharisaic regulation dictated were to be avoided at all costs. Strict Jews believed there would be joy in heaven – not over the repentant, but over the destruction of sinners by God! So, Jesus took them into parable house, and the view from His teaching brought delight to those who recognized they were lost, while those blinded by self-righteousness left disappointed, angry and full of hate.

How thrilled the shepherds must have been to be included ... even to have this new rabbi depict them as main characters in the story (15:4). Every villager knew the importance of trusting what few sheep they had to the combined flock for the shepherd to care for them and keep them from danger. Each sheep was important to its owner and, if lost, the shepherd had to produce the fleece as evidence of its death.

Knowing this, the villagers must have thought Jesus' final words revolutionary. Heaven would rejoice over a repentant sinner (15:7)! God's Shepherd valued them such that He would seek for them, leave comfort behind and choose to put His life at risk for the People of the Land! And as if that wasn't enough, Jesus tenderly 'lays it on his shoulders' (15:5) and heads home, delighted.

I wonder, did they get it? For what lay behind the search wasn't just rescue, but the purest of love for the lost. Do *we* get it?

Lord Jesus, I am constantly amazed by Your great love for the unlovely ... including me. Thank you. Amen.

10 October

'Rejoice with me . . .'
Luke 15:9

Reading: Luke 15:8–10

Given their attitude to shepherds, the sheep analogy would have been lost on the Pharisees. But mention the word 'coin' and their ears would have pricked up. The Pharisees loved coins, laughing in Jesus' face when He taught about the impossibility of serving both God and money (Luke 16:13–14). They had tried it, but greed gave them away (Matthew 23:25). Would Jesus speaking about a woman losing a coin grab their attention with more success than the shepherd losing a sheep? Highly unlikely. But Jesus never gives up on any of us.

Instead, He continued to address the importance of the value of what was lost, and the intense desire of the searcher to find it. The woman mentioned (how wonderful of Jesus to use women in His parables – something that would have disgusted the Pharisees) had lost a coin. It is not clear whether the anxiety caused by the loss was due to her financial circumstances or because the coin was important to her for other reasons. The fact that one of ten coins is mentioned could signify that she had lost part of her marriage headdress, which would have consisted of ten drachmas attached to a silver chain. Undoubtedly precious beyond monetary value alone. I totally understand her anguish, having shed many tears over losing my wedding ring early in our marriage.

Giving time to describe the woman's frantic search among the dried reeds and rushes covering her beaten-earth floor, Jesus once again shows us that what is lost cannot be found without the involvement of a diligent searcher.

In Jewish thought, this was quite outrageous. God might forgive the sinner who comes begging, but He would never go seeking that sinner Himself. They believed that seeking love was not in Jehovah's nature. Yet, God has always demonstrated just that . . . right from Adam and Eve (Genesis 3:9) until now (Luke 19:10).

Celebration with friends and family follows the finding of what she had lost, but it is nothing compared with the party there is in heaven when even one sinner repents (Luke 15:10)!

Seeking Saviour, I rejoice with You over those You have found, and pray for those known to me who are still lost. Amen.

11 October

'And he arose and came to his father.
But while he was still a long way off,
his father saw him and felt compassion,
and ran and embraced him and kissed him.'

Luke 15:20

Reading: Luke 15:11–24

The third lost thing in this parable is not a thing, but a son. Sadly, the son's lostness was entirely his own wilful, selfish decision (Luke 15:13). It was no accident that he ended up away from the father's protection and provision (15:12), and found himself about as far down as a Jewish boy could sink (15:15). He got there all by himself. And no one went in search of him. The Father let him go, but he lovingly kept watch for the prodigal to return (15:20). How serious is the rebellion of our hearts (Jeremiah 17:9), and how deep the consequences of our sin (Luke 15:16).

Yet again, it is the father's love that is central to the story. Jewish communities didn't take lightly the shame brought on them by individuals. Not only a disappointment to his father, this wayward son had brought disgrace on the whole village. Neither would have been lost on Jesus' listeners.

Watching for his younger son, likely daily, was as much about protection as it was about love. The father never gave up on him. Then, seeing him in the distance, he did something no father from the East would ever do – he ran! – humiliating himself in the process. But that's not all. His boy, according to Deuteronomy 21:18–21, deserved the judgement of stoning by the community. Knowing this, the father put himself between the lad and any potential stone throwers by wrapping his arms around him (Luke 15:20). He was willing to take the punishment his son was due.

Can't you almost hear the gasp of the crowd as the picture exploded in their minds? Who would ever be willing to take the punishment for their sins ... and love them while doing it? Oh yes ... there was One ... and soon they would see it happen for themselves.

Lord Jesus, I am astounded by Your willingness to take the punishment for my sin, and beyond grateful for such a demonstration of love. Amen.

12 October

'But he was angry and would not go in.
Therefore his father came out and pleaded with him.'

Luke 15:28, NKJV

Reading: Luke 15:25–32

It is probable that the Pharisees were okay with most of what Jesus was saying. They loved to hear people being told they were sinners. They didn't much like the rabbi's thoughts on Jehovah demeaning Himself by searching for them, but at least Jesus wasn't getting at them for once. But Jesus wasn't finished. Instead, He had come to the cringeworthy part. He was returning to the reason He had started the story: their accusation that He was keeping bad company (Luke 15:2).

The behaviour of the older son following the return of his brother was truly disgraceful. Yes, it's commendable that he wasn't the one who ran away. And yes, he was a dutiful son in his work and commitment to his father (15:29), but it appears that is where his virtues stopped. He was deeply loved by the father (15:31), but there is no evidence of that love being returned. Duty was the older son's mantra. His outward actions appeared blameless . . . but his heart gave him away. He was a sinner just like his reprobate brother, but was unprepared to admit it. His glowing account of all he had done was merely a display of self-righteousness, pride and selfishness. He hadn't cared about the brother when he ran away, and he wasn't about to show any joy at his return.

When he didn't turn up at the welcome home party, the father didn't send a servant to bring him in, but went himself to plead with his angry firstborn (15:28). But nothing this kind, loving father could say would dull his son's fury or coax an iota of forgiveness out of him (15:29–30). Alone, the older son stood sulking outside and missed the joy.

Self-righteousness is the foundation upon which unforgiveness is built. The attitude of 'I'm always right' or 'I didn't do anything wrong' sets us up for a hard heart. Hard, unforgiving hearts are what tear apart families, churches and, worst of all – our own relationship with our heavenly Father.

Father, give me a heart like Yours . . . willing to forgive and full of grace. Amen.

13 October

THINK ON THIS

'For the LORD your God is gracious and merciful
and will not turn his face away from you,
if you return to him.'

2 Chronicles 30:9

- Read through this verse a number of times – including out loud.
- Write it out, stick it on the fridge, have it on your phone.
- Meditate on the words, then respond in praise.
- Be a doer . . . Serve someone with an act of kindness today.

14 October

And Jesus said to them, 'Can the wedding guests fast
while the bridegroom is with them?'

Mark 2:19

Reading: Song of Solomon 4:9–11

Jesus didn't come to patch up the old religious system. He came to introduce a new covenant between God and humankind (Jeremiah 31:1); to establish a new spiritual kingdom.

When questioned by some of John the Baptist's disciples, along with the Pharisees, about why His disciples didn't fast, He launched into wedding speak. Hadn't John the Baptist already spoken of Jesus as the bridegroom, and about his own joy being complete because he was the bridegroom's friend (John 3:29)? The Jews were described in the Old Testament as God's bride (Isaiah 54:5) – the marriage analogy of total commitment used as an illustration of His faithfulness to them. To their shame, they had frequently behaved in an adulterous manner, as they tried to add other gods – lovers – to the relationship (Jeremiah 31:32).

The result was that their religious experience had become more like a funeral than a wedding. Their continual striving at the impossible task of keeping the law had reduced what God had intended to be joyous into misery.

But right now, the Bridegroom was actually present . . . with them. This was to be an occasion of celebration, Jesus explained; an occasion to feast, not to deny yourself (Mark 2:19)! Jesus was instituting a new marriage agreement – not based on the 'bride' being good enough, but on what the Bridegroom could do for her. The old way wasn't working.

God wants life with Him to be like a wedding feast, and Jesus invites us to join Him there. There's a party to be enjoyed! Salvation is the 'I do', if you like, of being in a committed relationship with the Bridegroom. Once the ceremony is over, life begins with the privilege of taking on Christ's name and enjoying His love and protection. For even when the party is over and storms come our way – as they do – He will partner us through every step. This Bridegroom will never leave us . . . as the apostle Paul testifies (Romans 8:38–39).

Lover of my soul, I cannot adequately express the gratitude I have for all You sacrificed for me. I love You, Lord. Amen.

15 October

'No one sews a piece of unshrunk cloth on an old garment.
If he does, the patch tears away from it . . .
and a worse tear is made.'

Mark 2:21

Reading: Hebrews 8:6–7; 13

Having discussed the delights of wedding celebrations, Jesus went on to explain the benefits of 'new-for-old' versus 'mend-and-make-do'. He is always so practical in His illustrations, using pictures that resonate with men and women. Few men would have been patching clothes, but they probably knew quite a bit about wineskins!

There is no doubt that Christ's teaching impressed the religious up to a point, but the Pharisees wanted something they could add to what they were already doing. They didn't want to abandon what made them look good spiritually. Surely Jesus didn't need to introduce a new way of doing religion to make pleasing Yahweh possible? But patching things up was foolish, and it obviously wasn't working. The burden of additional rules they had made up was weighing the people down (Matthew 23:4), and helping no one in their quest for peace with God.

Jesus was establishing a new covenant – no longer dependent on the temple's daily animal sacrifice, but written in His own blood (Luke 22:19–20). In this covenant between God and man, God's law would be written 'not with ink but with the Spirit of the living God, not on tablets of stone but on tablets of human hearts' (2 Corinthians 3:3). Jesus had not come to bring together the old and the new, but to fulfil the old *in* the new (Matthew 5:17). Salvation is not a patch-up job; rather, it is a receiving of Christ's new robe of righteousness – the covering for our sin (Isaiah 61:10). Neither is salvation pouring what is new into what is not fit to receive it, which would have resulted in disaster (Mark 2:22).

'Therefore, if anyone is in Christ, he is a new creation. The old has passed away; behold, the new has come' (2 Corinthians 5:17).

Holding on to dead religion instead of living spiritual truth is just about one of the saddest things any of us could do. Let's embrace the new and celebrate Jesus!

Forgive me, Lord, if I am holding on to self-righteous practices instead of embracing Your full, free salvation. Amen.

16 October

They received the word with all eagerness,
examining the Scriptures daily
to see if these things were so.

Acts 17:11

Reading: Mark 4:33–34

As an author, I love that Jesus used illustration and parable to plant deep spiritual truths in the minds of those who took His teaching seriously. The Saviour's time on earth was short, and while there was always opportunity for genuine seekers to listen to Him, Jesus specifically planned to teach those He would be leaving behind (Mark 4:34). After all, they would be carrying on the work after He had returned to the Father (16:15). It was time to get serious.

Coming from a strict, rule-driven religion, the followers of Jesus were accustomed to having Scripture interpreted for them, but that was frequently flawed. By using parables layered with meaning, Jesus was showing them the importance of looking for something deeper than the obvious. They were learning that story is most powerful when it intersects with God's story.

The Jews had understood Yahweh as the God of their nation, but Jesus was introducing Him to them as a personal God. These revolutionary parables became transformational as Jesus' followers recognized themselves within them. They were the lost ones, the needy ones, perhaps even the rebellious ones or the unforgiving ones. But, unlike the Pharisees, Jesus didn't leave them there. For in these amazing stories Jesus also reveals what God is like, and shows the intensity of His desire for individuals to come to repentance (Acts 17:30). Discovering that the Father loved them brought light into spiritual darkness and sunshine into dreary lives.

But how could these ordinary, unschooled disciples (4:13), or we today, for that matter, understand Jesus' teaching? They, and every Christian since, were given this promise: 'But the Helper, the Holy Spirit, whom the Father will send in my name, he will teach you all things and bring to your remembrance all that I have said to you' (John 14:26). And He never misinterprets!

Holy Spirit, my heart is willing to learn. Teach me the truths Jesus wants to bring to fruition in my life. Amen.

17 October

All Scripture is breathed out by God and profitable
for teaching, for reproof, for correction,
and for training in righteousness.

2 Timothy 3:16

Reading: 2 Timothy 3:10–17

What do we do with what we learn from God's word? Is it a case of 'in one ear and out the other'? Are we learning to take Jesus' teaching earnestly – praying for the spiritual discernment needed from the Holy Spirit to understand it better? Or have we chosen a one-hour-a-week fix to listen to preaching, yet miss the thrill of hearing God speak directly to us.

If what Paul says in today's verse is true, and Scripture actively works in our lives to produce godly living, shouldn't we take it more seriously? Jesus spoke in parables to those who were committed to His teaching, but profound truths aren't merely for deep thinkers or the intellectually superior. With the help of the Holy Spirit, the Bible becomes alive in the hearts of all of those who read it. But what comes next? What do we do with what we know and experience because of Christ's teaching? We never seem to have a problem sharing about a hobby or a holiday. We talk about it, don't we?

Jesus has made it our responsibility to pass on what the Bible teaches (Mark 16:15). We are to 'gossip the gospel'; to help others understand that the Bible is not a boring book by speaking about it and living its message. We are not to be ashamed of the clear teaching of Scripture, even if some do not accept it. But we should take care to communicate clearly – neither softening its message to make it more acceptable, nor muddying the waters of understanding by complicating it unnecessarily.

And we don't need to have vast Bible knowledge before we can share with others what Christ has done for us. The early believers didn't have all the resources we have today, yet they spread the good news everywhere they went (Acts 13:49). Two millennia later it reached your heart and mine!

> *Come and hear, all you who fear God,*
> *and I will tell what he has done for my soul.*[38]
> *Amen.*

18 October

'For I have given them the words that you gave me,
and they have received them and have come
to know in truth that I came from you;
and they have believed that you sent me.'

John 17:8

Reading: John 16:29–33

The Bible is God letting us in on His secrets, while at the same time showing us His heart and His plans. Daniel experienced this after he received from God the interpretation of King Nebuchadnezzar's dream in a vision (Daniel 2:19). He goes on to say that God 'reveals deep and hidden things; he knows what is in the darkness, and the light dwells with him' (2:22). And yet God chooses to share these mysteries with us, even encouraging us to tell others.

Jesus' prayer in John 17 is another instance where what could have been kept secret is shared openly. Although Jesus frequently went to a solitary place to speak with His Father (Mark 1:35), on this very important occasion He chose to let the disciples listen in. I, for one, am so glad that He did, because this prayer also included petition for us! 'I do not ask for these only,' Jesus said, speaking of the disciples, 'but also for those who will believe in me through their word' (John 17:20). Think of it . . . all that Jesus requested of the Father for His faithful followers while on earth, He also desired for those who had yet to believe.

The Saviour had just finished telling the disciples that He was leaving them (John 16:28), and that the world He was leaving them in would cause them hardship. Not exactly a cheery speech, yet Jesus concludes by reminding them that: 'I have said these things to you, that in me you may have peace . . .' urging them to, 'take heart; I have overcome the world' (16:33).

Jesus was headed for the cross. Fear, and even panic, filled their hearts. His followers needed to hear this prayer, for its memory would surely sustain and strengthen them for whatever lay ahead. We need to hear it too. That's why He has allowed us to listen in.

Thank you, Lord, that Your love for us is no secret, and that one day You will bring us to glory. Amen.

19 October

For it is impossible for the blood of bulls and goats
to take away sins.

Hebrews 10:4

Reading: Hebrews 10:1–10

The path from the upper room to the garden of Gethsemane was one the disciples knew well. But on this occasion, it must have felt surreal underfoot. All kinds of emotions undoubtedly swirled around as they walked. It was difficult to take in everything Jesus had said. He'd talked to them nonstop, as if He were trying to squeeze every last thing He wanted to tell them into that Passover meal they had just enjoyed together. *Enjoyed?* Well, it always started with a lament over the long-ago enslaving of God's people in Egypt, but it usually ended in celebrating God's deliverance on that night when the blood of a lamb was sprinkled on the doors of the Israelites' homes, protecting those inside from God's judgement of death (Exodus 12:13). They would have remained slaves in a far-off land had it not been for the blood of that innocent animal.

But strange things had happened in the upper room before they left. The blessing Jesus spoke over the meal was of His own blood being shed . . . of His own body being broken. A different kind of sacrifice was about to be offered. Jesus explained it as 'my blood of the new covenant, which is poured out for many for the forgiveness of sins' (Matthew 26:28). In accepting that morsel of unleavened bread from the Saviour Himself, symbolizing Christ's bodily sacrifice, each was personally confessing their sins and their need of His forgiveness . . . being 'sanctified through the offering of the body of Jesus Christ *once for all*' (Hebrews 10:10, emphasis mine).

No longer would individuals seek God's forgiveness through the national sacrifices prescribed by Mosaic Law. Never again would they have to work to obtain God's favour. This time the annual walk, normally associated with attendance at sacrificial festivals, was not filled with the singing of celebration. The confusion and sadness filling the air was suddenly broken by Jesus praying . . . and He was praying for them!

Lamb of God, thank you for being willing to shed Your blood that I might go free!
Amen.

20 October

THINK ON THIS

'And this is eternal life,
that they know you, the only true God,
and Jesus Christ whom you have sent.'

John 17:3

- Read through this verse a number of times – including out loud.
- Write it out, stick it on the fridge, have it on your phone.
- Meditate on the words, then respond in praise.
- Take steps to allow God's word to change you: perhaps . . . repent, forgive, love.

21 October

'I glorified you on earth, having accomplished
the work that you gave me to do.'

John 17:4

Reading: John 17:1–5

Jesus knew that a band of soldiers was approaching, but He continued to move forward, while the words of the greatest prayer ever prayed rang in the ears of those who followed Him.

The prayer began almost as a continuation of the Saviour's talk around the table, but now it held the sharp note of reality. Jesus wasn't talking about the future, but about the present when He said: 'Father, the hour has come' (John 17:1). Jesus had always worked to a timetable. Even His birth occurred at exactly the right time (Galatians 4:4). And here He was praying about the final stage of the plan: His death, resurrection and return to heaven.

He was affirming to His Father that the work He had been given to do was finished (John 17:4). He had established the new covenant, preparing the disciples to continue the work after He'd gone, and had demonstrated God's love in miraculous ways. However, the ultimate work of the cross still lay ahead. When he said, 'Glorify your Son that the Son may glorify you' (17:1), Jesus was requesting the strength to be victorious in the trial ahead. While to humanity the cross was a symbol of shame and defeat, to Jesus it was the glory of God – because God was revealing the greatness of His love in willingly sacrificing His own Son for the salvation of humankind (Romans 8:32). That was the perfect demonstration of God's splendour – the true glory of the Father.

The driving force of Jesus' life had always been to glorify God, even in death. Before He prayed for those given to Him by the Father (John 17:2), Jesus asked for the strength to glorify the Father one final time. But that would only be possible if He could do so in a manner worthy of the Son of God – something His Father alone could empower.

This is surely the ultimate in selfless praying . . . asking for God's strength that we might glorify Him.

Heavenly Father, help me to be like Jesus . . . to seek Your glory above all else. Amen.

22 October

'And now, Father, glorify me in your own presence
with the glory that I had with you
before the world existed.'

John 17:5

Reading: Ecclesiastes 3:11, 14–16

One of the most profound truths that has blessed my life is knowing that now is not all there is. As I write, it has been a very short time since I stood beside my mother only minutes after God had called her home. Her final journey had been harrowing, and I was glad, as I looked at her peaceful face, that now is not all there is. I regularly stand by a gravestone, on which the names of our two beautiful daughters are etched in gold, and each time I am glad that now is not all there is.

As Jesus went towards His arrest, and the horror of all that was to follow, that very thought was on His mind. Now is not all there is. He was thinking of home . . . the 'beyond' of the cross, and even the resurrection. He was thinking of returning home, of being with His beloved Father once more. In His presence . . . enjoying the relationship He'd had with Him before the world even existed (Colossians 1:17). It was this very thing that enabled Jesus to say a short time later in the garden of Gethsemane: 'Not my will, but yours, be done' (Luke 22:42). No one knew better than Jesus that now is not all there is.

Our finite minds cannot begin to take in what the dwelling place of God is like. Even Paul said that: 'No eye has seen, nor ear heard, nor the heart of man imagined, what God has prepared for those who love him' (1 Corinthians 2:9).

What comfort it must have brought the Saviour that soon He would be welcomed home by the Father (John 17:5). What comfort it ought to be to us that God 'has put eternity into man's heart' (Ecclesiastes 3:11); a longing to be with Him, fulfilled only when Jesus returns or takes us home.

Thank you, Jesus, that – because of You – now is not all there is. There is glory ahead! Amen.

23 October

'I have manifested your name to the people
whom you gave me out of the world.'

John 17:6

Reading: John 17:6–8

In the Old Testament, God revealed His name to Moses when He called the prince-turned-shepherd to return to Egypt to rescue the Hebrew slaves. Moses, extremely unhappy that he should be asked to engage in such a perilous mission, dared to ask of the Almighty what name He should say had sent him. 'Say this to the people of Israel: "I AM has sent me to you"' (Exodus 3:14). Such was the powerful intent behind this name – I AM – that it was instantly recognized as belonging to the One for whom nothing was impossible. *I AM everything you will ever need*, God was saying, *through all the dangerous journey ahead.*

In biblical times, a name wasn't simply what you were called; it revealed your nature, and often indicated some family or national circumstance around the time of your birth. God, however, had never been born. He is eternal, holy and powerful . . . making Him worthy, not only of His name, but of worship.

To reveal the power of that name, Jesus took the 'I AM' and revealed God's nature by using it to describe Himself: 'I am the bread of life' (John 6:35); 'I am the light of the world' (8:12); 'I am the good shepherd' (10:11), to name but a few. Then when Jesus said to the questioning Philip, 'Whoever has seen me has seen the Father' (14:9), the pieces all came together. 'I and the Father are one' (10:30) was confirmed by the life Jesus had lived before them for the previous three years.

The Jews trusted the great I AM to protect and provide for them as a nation. Jesus was confirming that He was all His disciples would ever need. After all, the Father had gifted each one to His Son (17:6). So, we have no need to fear . . . Jesus has it covered.

Lord Jesus, thank you for showing us the nature of our heavenly Father, the power in His name, and His loving provision for our every need. Amen.

24 October

'I am praying for them. I am not praying for the world
but for those whom you have given me,
for they are yours.'

John 17:9

Reading: John 17:9–12

It is unlikely that this was the first time the disciples heard Jesus praying for them, whether beside a campfire or around a table. But this was different. Jesus was praying for them for the very last time. This was serious – the disciples were listening in to God's Son speaking to His Father about 'keep[ing] them in your name' (John 17:11), because He wouldn't be with them for much longer. I'm sure they later wished they could have asked Him to explain all that He had included in His prayer.

One thing was certain. Something dreadful was about to happen to the Master, but instead of planning how to remove Himself from impending doom, His only concern appeared to be for them.

'Holy Father, it's time for me to leave this world behind. I'm blessed in that I am coming to You, but they must stay in this world. Great I AM, protect their hearts for Yourself – keep them safe' (my paraphrase of John 17:11). During His years with them, Jesus had demonstrated the Father's pure nature to them in person. Through God's word we are privileged to see much more. We get to dwell 'in the shelter of the Most High' and to 'abide in the shadow of the Almighty' (Psalm 91:1).

Protection for those He was leaving behind was key in Jesus' request, but so was unity. Jesus wanted His disciples to 'be one, even as [He and the Father] are one' (John 17:11). His followers were going to need each other in order to continue His work. Therefore, it was paramount that they loved each other in the same way Jesus had loved them (13:34). A tall order indeed, which is why Jesus asked the Father for it ... not only for His immediate companions, but for every believer who followed in the future (17:20).

Lord Jesus, I cannot love others the way that You love me, except for the Holy Spirit living in my heart. Create in me a heart desirous of unity. Amen.

25 October

'But now I am coming to you,
and these things I speak in the world,
that they may have my joy fulfilled in themselves.'

John 17:13

Reading: John 17:13–16

As I write, I can see the rain falling outside my window. The skies are grey and the wind is whipping the tree branches that border our back garden. To add to this miserable day, I seem to have caught the flu, and am feeling sorry for myself. But my heaviness of heart is about more than bad weather and temporary sickness. In a few hours' time we will attend the funeral service for the daughter of dear friends.

It will be a service of thanksgiving for a remarkable young woman who had faced enormous challenges in her short life. Now she is free. Free from pain and disability – enjoying the liberty and healing of heaven. Her bravery and resilience are an example to us all. I do not weep for her, but for those who loved her most and will miss her lovely presence in their lives. I know that precise feeling, for grief is but a measure of our love. The greater our love, the deeper our grief.

In the middle of all that Jesus was praying for His disciples, He asks 'that they may have my joy fulfilled in themselves' (John 17:13). Having spent a considerable amount of time warning them of the hatred and persecution they would face in the future (15:18–20), Jesus assures them 'your sorrow *will* turn into joy' (16:20, emphasis mine).

In context, Jesus was specifying sorrow caused by persecution, but He gives us joy in every sorrow. Joy is not dependent on happenings, but rather on the promises in God's word, as well as the indwelling presence of the Holy Spirit. I could not have survived the death of both of our daughters were it not for the overflowing love and peace spoken by the Lord to my heart through the Scriptures (Isaiah 43:2).

May the words of Jesus bring joy to the broken hearts of my friends today, and to all who sorrow: 'Blessed are those who mourn, for they *shall* be comforted' (Matthew 5:4, emphasis mine).

Lord Jesus, thank you that You desire for us to experience Your joy in every situation. Amen.

26 October

'Sanctify them in the truth;
your word is truth.'

John 17:17

Reading: John 17:17–19

As Christians, our thoughts, words, habits and actions are to be different from those around us. We are no longer to live in order 'to satisfy [our] own desires . . . for the Scriptures say, "You must be holy because I am holy"' (1 Peter 1:14–16, NLT).

However, the word 'sanctify' means more than 'holy'; it means 'different' or 'separate'. This is not a lifestyle any of us can manage on our own, which is exactly why Jesus prayed specifically for His disciples to be gifted with these qualities through the truth. That truth Jesus specifies as God's word.

Doesn't it thrill you that the Bible is more than a good read . . . more than wholesome principles to live by? It's neither a how-to manual on spirituality, nor a pick-'n'-mix of advice, but a whole library of life essentials. A history book, it catalogues the account of humanity from creation – especially the story of God's own people, the Jews (2 Samuel 7:24). Regarding law, the Bible's legal section is the foundation for natural, moral and civil law within society, family and church (Psalm 19:7). It has a fine poetry section that does more than romance us with creative beauty – providing stunning imagery of the greatness of God, and words for us to use in worship (Psalm 29:2). We discover in the books of prophecy what God reveals of His plans for this world, especially in relation to His merciful plan of redemption fulfilled in Jesus Christ (Isaiah 7:14). For teaching in righteousness, alongside the record of Jesus' earthly ministry and sacrificial death, there never has been, nor ever will be, a more complete textbook (Romans 15:4).

It is little wonder then that Jesus prays that our lives may be transformed and ordered by its contents. In its pages we discover the Author's loving heart. In each paragraph we hear Him speak into our spiritual and human need. God's word is living and powerful, graceful and true, and it came to us embodied in Jesus, for: 'In the beginning was the Word, and the Word was with God, and the Word was God' (John 1:1)!

Living Word, how amazing that You not only live in me, but also speak to me through the Scriptures. Amen.

27 October

THINK ON THIS

You will show me the way of life,
granting me the joy of your presence
and the pleasures of living with you forever.

Psalm 16:11, NLT

- Read through this verse a number of times – including out loud.
- Write it out, stick it on the fridge, have it on your phone.
- Meditate on the words, then respond in praise.
- Encourage someone by sharing this verse with them today.

28 October

'The LORD bless you and keep you;
the LORD make his face shine to upon you
and be gracious to you;
the LORD lift up his countenance upon you
and give you peace.'

Numbers 6:24–26

Reading: John 17:20–23

There is one Bible bookshop in Northern Ireland where it's unlikely you'll leave without someone saying, 'Goodbye, the Lord bless you.' Some folks may think it's a bit corny, but I love it. The staff care about those who come through their doors, and particularly that God will bless their customers' lives in ways that will meet their need.

Today's verses are known as the Aaronic blessing, but it was God who told Moses to pass on to the priest the words to be used to bless them (Numbers 6:23–26). Jehovah wanted the people to know that it was He who gave the blessing; He was the giver of grace; He the One who looked upon His people with favour . . . and He alone who could grant peace to their troubled souls.

Then, when Jesus included in His prayer those who would believe in Him in the future (John 17:20), He was displaying a heart like His Father had done all those years earlier. He assures us of our importance to Him. We are one with Him (17:21); recipients of His glory (17:22); unified to show Jesus to the world (17:23). But in reminding us that the Father loves us, even as He loves Him (17:23), Jesus leaves us without any doubt of our worth or our place in God's family.

Let's face it, there are some days, more than others, when we all need to know that we are loved. Perhaps you've had one of those weeks when nothing has gone right: the flu has struck you down; the online hackers have done their worst; sorrow has been nipping at your heart. Then when you've reached an end of yourself, we read those words again . . . straight from God's loving heart:

'The LORD bless you and keep you;
. . . be gracious to you;
. . . and give you peace.'
Numbers 6:24–26

And then, Lord, suddenly I believe I can face the day . . . because of You. Thank you. Amen.

29 October

'Father, I desire that they also,
whom you have given me,
may be with me where I am,
to see my glory . . .'

John 17:24

Reading: John 17:24–26

Last words are rarely forgotten, especially if spoken by someone we love or greatly admire. They linger in the mind and cause the heart to respond in ways that might suddenly interrupt what we're doing with a gush of unexpected emotion. That final 'I love you' or 'I'm proud of you' – spoken despite the weakness of the human frame – means more than at any other time. It never leaves you. How dreadful to miss that gift to the heart because of physical distance or lack of time. But how much worse if the last words between us are spoken in anger or thoughtlessness. Words you can no longer take back, paired with those you will never be able to say, result in painful regret.

Unfortunately, life isn't like the movies, where emotional farewells with family gathered at the bedside seem to go on forever, until the dying father sees the last family member walk through the door. Instead, final moments are sometimes messy, always sad and, at times, disappointing.

But Jesus didn't disappoint. It's likely that some of the disciples didn't realize His words would be His very last . . . until the soldiers dragged the Saviour away from them. He'd told them so many times that He would be leaving them, but they never thought it would be like that. They thought they would have more time . . . a common mistake. However, Jesus' last words were not of despair but of glory. A glory He wanted to share with those He loved and who were committed to Him.

The glory we share with Jesus now is incomparable to what we will experience one day in heavenly places, for: 'If we have died with him, we will also live with him; if we endure, we will also reign with him' (2 Timothy 2:11–12). He has made it clear: 'I desire that they . . . may be with me where I am, to see my glory' (John 17:24).

Lord Jesus, these are words I will never forget, and I look forward to that time when the promise is fulfilled, and I can walk with You in glory. Amen.

30 October

Through him we have also obtained access by faith
into this grace in which we stand,
and we rejoice in hope of the glory of God.

Romans 5:2

Reading: Romans 5:1–5

Sometimes we use words that we don't quite understand. John 17 is littered with the word 'glory', but what is its relevance? Glory is usually associated with honour earned through achievement ... ask any Olympian. But it also means magnificence, wonder, splendour and beauty. Is it any wonder then that glory is attributed to Jesus? And when we see who He is in His glory, our faith grows.

What exactly do we see when we glimpse the glory of God? We see that:

- God's glory is eternal, 'for from him and through him and to him are all things. To him be glory forever' (Romans 11:36). Of man's glory, Peter says: 'All flesh is like grass and all its glory like the flower of grass' (1 Peter 1:24). There is simply no comparison;
- the joy of God's glory far outweighs any suffering we will ever have to experience. 'For I consider that the sufferings of this present time are not worth comparing with the glory that is to be revealed to us' (Romans 8:18);
- God's glory shows its power in the '[measuring of] the waters in the hollow of his hand' and in 'mark[ing] off the heavens with a span' (Isaiah 40:12). Could there be anything greater? Well, apart from raising Christ from the dead 'by the glory of the Father' (Romans 6:4).

And this barely touches the surface – climaxed for us in the realization that we will share in this glory, this splendour, this magnificence, because we are 'justified by faith' and 'have peace with God through our Lord Jesus Christ' (Romans 5:1). Our access to the sure hope of His glory is only possible by standing in His grace (5:2).

From grace to glory! What a hope. 'And hope does not put us to shame, because God's love has been poured into our hearts through the Holy Spirit who has been given to us' (5:5). God's giving never stops and His love never fails.

I stand in wonder, Lord, awestruck by Your greatness. Praise Your holy name. Amen.

31 October

'Remember what I told you: I am going away,
but I will come back to you again.'

John 14:28, NLT

Reading: John 14:18–21

The person who first said 'Out of sight, out of mind' knew very little about the human mind. It's a fallacy. While we may not have to deal face to face with the person who has moved away or passed away, our minds ensure that they can never fully be erased. The intensity of such recall, however, is determined by our relationship with them.

Jesus was out of the disciples' sight after the brutal arrest in the garden of Gethsemane, but He was never far from their minds. How could they ever forget the scene at Calvary? When He appeared to them after the resurrection, some dared to believe that this was the return of which He spoke, but Jesus was speaking of His return to the Father (John 20:17). Yet, the Saviour had promised that while He would not be bodily present with those who loved and followed Him, He would be 'with you *always*, to the end of the age' (Matthew 28:20, emphasis mine). The Holy Spirit would see to that; initially through His permanent indwelling at salvation (Ephesians 1:13), and also through His enabling us to live in a right way (Galatians 5:22–23) and to witness for Christ (Acts 1:8).

More than 2,000 years later, this age of grace has still not come to an end, and the promise of Jesus' presence with us has not faltered once. He is a Man of His word, as many of us have proved. I cannot wait to meet my Saviour in person, but until then I listen for His speaking voice from the pages of His word (Hebrews 1:1–2) and enjoy the sense of His presence as I wait in prayer or walk in the sunshine . . . or more especially, when the dark circumstances of life close in (Isaiah 43:2).

Jesus is out of sight . . . but He need never be out of mind.

'So we can confidently say, "The Lord is my helper; I will not fear; what can man do to me?"' (Hebrews 13:6).

The closer we become, Lord Jesus, the more deeply I sense Your presence. Thank you for the assurance that You will never leave me. Amen.

November

1 November

Now when they saw the boldness of Peter and John,
and perceived that they were uneducated,
common men, they were astonished.
And they recognized that they had been with Jesus.

Acts 4:13

Reading: Acts 4:5–13

Take it from me . . . book titles are important. However, there are times when you don't get it quite right.

The Acts of the Apostles was the second book in a series, whose author was Luke. In the Gospel named after himself, Luke purposed to write an organized account of Jesus' life and ministry (Luke 1:3–4), which he achieved masterfully, right up to Jesus' ascension (Luke 24:50–53). You might think that was the end of Jesus' story, but it wasn't, because Luke clearly explains that: 'In the first book, O Theophilus, I have dealt with all that Jesus *began* to do and teach' (Acts 1:1, emphasis mine).

So, it follows that Luke's second volume records what Jesus *continued* to do and teach after His ascension. While not bodily present, Christ is neither absent nor inactive today. His presence is felt, and His work continues through His followers because of the amazing gift of the Holy Spirit, promised immediately before He left them (Acts 1:8). The title of Luke's second volume, named some 100 years later, should surely be 'The Acts of Jesus Christ' or at least 'The Acts of the Holy Spirit', for we can be sure that these 'acts' could never have been accomplished by mere men alone.

Peter and John's healing of the man outside the temple (3:1–10) got them into trouble. But it was their preaching of the resurrected Jesus afterwards that resulted in their arrest and appearance before the country's supreme court, which included the high priest. It was obvious that even in death Jesus could not be silenced . . . but then, as Peter eloquently told them, 'Jesus Christ of Nazareth . . . whom you crucified . . . God raised from the dead' (4:10). He is still very much alive!

Interestingly, their judges were astonished by the teaching of these uneducated fishermen and were forced to conclude 'that they had been with Jesus' (4:13)!

And the story is not finished, Lord Jesus, for You are still at work in and through me. May others recognize that I have been with You. Amen.

2 November

'Whether it is right in the sight of God to listen to you
rather than to God, you must judge,
for we cannot but speak of what
we have seen and heard.'

Acts 4:19–20

Reading: Acts 4:15–21

Some people never learn! There were chief priests and elders present who had previously tried to stop Jesus' teaching in the temple by challenging His authority to do so (Matthew 21:23). They didn't get away with it then, and Peter, having learned well from Jesus, told his judges in no uncertain terms that God's authority trumped theirs, after they threatened the disciples not to do it again. The evidence was clear for everyone to see. The man who had been healed in the name of Jesus (Acts 3:6–8), was the prime witness in their case, along with a crowd of very excited eyewitnesses. The judges had no choice but to release Peter and John (4:21).

The council had hoped that a warning might intimidate these followers of Jesus, but that was never going to happen. After all, what they had personally witnessed and heard could not and would not be forgotten. This was the first of many occasions when choosing God's law over human authority called for protest. And if the laws of the land today stand in direct opposition to the word of God, then we cannot, nor should we, remain silent. But we must have a biblical mandate before we protest or defy those who have God-given authority over us.

Peter and John had been present when Jesus told them: 'Go therefore and make disciples of all nations' (Matthew 28:19). The message had to be preached . . . not hidden as the Sanhedrin had instructed.

However, protesting today is never to be motivated by personal whim or inner frustration, nor should it be carried out in anything but a Christlike manner. Later, Peter wrote of the importance of obeying those whom God has put in authority over us (1 Peter 2:13–7), while Paul said we are 'to avoid quarrelling, to be gentle, and to show perfect courtesy toward all people' (Titus 3:2).

Lord Jesus, we are Your witnesses to a watching world. May we be fearless, yet gracious, in our stand for You and Your Word. Amen.

3 November

THINK ON THIS

And when they had prayed, the place in which they were
gathered together was shaken, and they were all filled
with the Holy Spirit and continued to speak
the word of God with boldness.

Acts 4:31

- Read through this verse a number of times – including out loud.
- Write it out, stick it on the fridge, have it on your phone.
- Meditate on the words, then respond in praise.
- Be a doer . . . Serve someone with an act of kindness today.

4 November

And with great power the apostles were giving their
testimony to the resurrection of the Lord Jesus,
and great grace was upon them all.

Acts 4:33

Reading: Acts 4:31–35

It is remarkable to read what happened when Peter and John returned from prison to their friends. They had previously hidden behind locked doors for fear of receiving the same treatment from the religious court as Jesus had (John 20:19). Now they responded with incredible spiritual maturity, recognizing God's sovereignty as the One who created the universe, and in whose safe hands their lives rested. What a way to pray when danger threatens us.

Then, after reminding God of the wickedness of the plot against His Son – more for themselves than for God – they affirm His plan in it all (Acts 4:24–28). Jesus had taught them well. Their praying honoured God before they prayed for themselves. Yet even their request for God's help was not for physical protection, but to enable them 'to continue to speak your word with all boldness, while you stretch out your hand . . . through the name of your holy servant Jesus' (4:29–30).

What had happened? Were these really the people who were virtually afraid of their own shadows just weeks earlier? Yes, they were the same people physically, but they were completely 'other' in all the ways that counted for God's kingdom.

The Holy Spirit had come . . . just as Jesus had promised. And just as He had promised, they did 'receive power when the Holy Spirit [had] come upon [them] . . .' (1:8). Everything had changed. They were unafraid of the authorities; unafraid of their own inability; unafraid to carry out Christ's great commission. And we read that the miracles they thought would stop because Jesus was no longer with them just kept on coming (4:30).

For when they prayed, God came . . . and they knew it! And when God came, He gave them all they needed to do what Jesus had asked of them (4:31).

Great power to testify that Jesus was alive!
Great grace to live selfless and thoughtful lives towards others, as Jesus had (4:33–34).

Living Lord Jesus, may great power and great grace be seen in my life through Your Holy Spirit. Amen.

5 November

'Remember the word that I said to you:
"A servant is not greater than his master."
If they persecuted me, they will also persecute you . . .'

John 15:20

Reading: Acts 6:8–12; 7:55–60

'**Suspected Islamic terrorists have killed 15 Christians in Obi county, north-central Nigeria** . . . 'The herdsmen during the invasion of our village shot randomly at our people who were sleeping in their houses.'

'**Two evangelists in Eastern Uganda have been beaten and slashed with knives after leading several Muslims to Christ** . . . We were beaten because of taking the gospel of our Lord and Saviour Jesus Christ to that purely Muslim community.'

'**A group of Muslims attacked an Orthodox church in Beit Sahour, a predominantly Christian neighbourhood near Bethlehem, throwing stones and injuring several people** . . . What happened in Beit Sahour was horrific.'

'**If we must die for our faith in Jesus, that is what we must do,**' said local Christians in Burkina Faso despite the persecution.'

All the above are direct quotes from a recent edition of a monthly Christian newspaper.[39] Christians are suffering, even dying, today – right now, this very minute – for their publicly professed faith in Jesus Christ as their Saviour. Persecution didn't end with the early church. Stephen may have been given the title of the first Christian martyr, but he would not be the last.

He was also in charge of the first 'foodbank' in history – tasked to manage the distribution of food to the needy widows of the church so the apostles could get on with preaching the word (Acts 6:1–4). It was a menial job, but one that Stephen took very seriously, and which saw him identified as a man 'full of grace and power' (6:8). Food management didn't bring him to the attention of the authorities, but his preaching and miraculous acts did. So, by using lying witnesses and the farce of a trial (does that bring someone else to mind?), Stephen was accused of blasphemy and stoned to death (7:58–60).

This servant was indeed not greater than his Master . . . but you can be sure of one thing: his martyrdom will be avenged (Revelation 6:9–11).

One day, Lord Jesus, You will avenge Your slain witnesses. May their persecutors seek Your forgiveness before that awful day comes. Amen.

6 November

And we know that for those who love God
all things work together for good,
for those who are called according to his purpose.

Romans 8:28

Reading: Acts 8:1–8

I found this verse very difficult to come to terms with for a few years in my life. My husband and I had our lives all planned for the service of God – believing it would be foreign missionary service. Then our first child was born with a medical diagnosis that would close the doors to overseas work and bring anguish to our hearts.

The oft-quoted Romans 8:28 only served to deepen my hurt. How could anything good come out of this – for Cheryl, or for us? Years later, from the vantage point of hindsight, it's nothing short of miraculous how God has worked in my life, through what I had initially looked on as disastrous. Thousands have received God's comfort and peace because He had me stand in that dark and painful place, and then share with others what I had learned. He tenderly showed me that His heart was for me, and then patiently taught me what it means to really trust God.

I can't imagine how Philip the evangelist must have felt when he watched his friend Stephen executed. How could his death possibly help the church to grow? Immediately following Stephen's death, 'there arose . . . a great persecution against the church in Jerusalem', and Philip, along with many others, 'were all scattered throughout the regions of Judea and Samaria' (Acts 8:1). Philip had to leave everything behind and seek a place of safety. How could this 'work together for good'?

First, Jesus didn't stay in Jerusalem – He went with Philip, empowering him through the Holy Spirit. Then what happened through this bunch of refugees? They had themselves a revival in Samaria! Luke records: 'So there was much joy in that city' (8:4–8).

Sometimes the Lord has to shake us, surprise us or even allow us to be hurt, in order that He might do more for us than we could ever dream possible.

Teach me, Lord, that acceptance brings both peace and power. Amen.

7 November

So be truly glad. There is wonderful joy ahead,
even though you must endure many trials
for a little while.

1 Peter 1:6, NLT

Reading: 1 Peter 1:6–9

Some Bible verses never leave you. They become evidence to your broken heart that the Lord really does know what you are going through. More than that – He cares about your pain, for in the middle of a sentence that speaks of sorrow He includes the most unexpected of promises: 'There is wonderful joy ahead' (1 Peter 1:6, NLT).

It certainly didn't feel like that when our six-week-old baby was diagnosed with the same neurological condition as her older sister. How could this happen to us again? As I held our beautiful little baby in my arms, I knew that her condition would follow the same pattern as her sister's. She would never walk, talk or hold her own head up, nor would she get the chance to enjoy the things other children did.

My response to God was far from godly. I hurt, and I hurled stones of disappointment towards Him. Yet, I had learned many wonderful things from God during those six years with Cheryl – one being that God speaks through His word. I knew He would speak into my pain, but I had to open the book for that to happen. Lack of concentration turned me in the direction of short daily devotionals.

A single verse of Scripture at the top of each page was all God needed to remind me that He was still in control. He took me to 1 Peter, where I read that the trials I had to endure were likened to purifying gold in a furnace (1:7). It is the fire that removes the blemishes and causes the gold to shine . . . and to God my faith was far more precious than any yellow metal; it was of eternal value. But it would still take the fire to complete the work He wanted to do in my life.

But then, 'what we suffer now is nothing compared to the glory he will reveal to us later' (Romans 8:18, NLT).

Lord Jesus, I look forward to the day when all that will be left of my trials is joy. Amen.

8 November

Keep yourselves in the love of God.

Jude 21

Reading: Jude 17–23

Decisions, decisions! Our lives are full of them.

Jude presented his own dilemma to the recipients of his letter. He wanted to write to them about the salvation they all shared, but his choice of subject matter fell on something even more pressing. Jesus' half-brother was very concerned about the false teachers who had wormed their way into the churches, and whose teachings were contrary to what Christ had laid down (Jude 4). His short communication is packed full of advice that would rid them of false teachers and keep them in safe in God's love (20–21).

Jude was faithful in his writing of the letter. Others faithfully delivered it, while the leaders of the various churches played their part by publicly reading it and teaching its contents. But the decision to hold fast to Christ and His salvation, including rejecting false ways, was down to the response of those who heard it. What would they do? What are we willing to do today, when the problem of false teachers is just as great as it was back when Jude decided to drop the more encouraging message for a scathing attack on those determined to lead believers astray?

Decide on these three things first, and everything else will slide into place.

Choose to follow Christ. 'Believe in the Lord Jesus, and you will be saved' (Acts 16:31).

Choose to remain in Him for everything you need. 'Abide in me, and I in you. As the branch cannot bear fruit by itself, unless it abides in the vine, neither can you, unless you abide in me' (John 15:4).

Choose to love Christ completely. 'And you shall love the Lord your God with all your heart and with all your soul and with all your mind and with all your strength' (Mark 12:30).

You see, some decisions aren't so difficult after all. It is all about keeping the main thing the main thing.

Lord Jesus, I never want to stray far from Your love, for You will always help me to do what's right. Amen.

9 November

For to me to live is Christ, and to die is gain.

Philippians 1:21

Reading: Philippians 1:19–26

Believe it or not, I saw the first Christmas tree of the season back in October! But today I saw lots of them bedecking front windows, along with multiple blow-up, lit-up figures of snowmen and Santas cramping tiny lawns, and whole rows of houses covered with twinkling coloured lights. I think it's fair to say that some people are a bit obsessed with Christmas . . . or could it be it's the trappings they love?

Without wanting to sound like Scrooge, I hereby declare my love of Christmas, including the efforts of others to brighten the dark days of winter. Christmas is indeed the most wonderful time of the year, but my heart is saddened that millions will celebrate without any thought of the One behind it all (Luke 2:11). 'It's a family time,' most will say. 'It's a time for people to get together.' 'It's party time!' 'Time for celebration!' All true, but each description misses the mark by some distance.

Jesus wasn't born to provide us with an excuse to party – any more than our life's goal should be to get a good job, fall in love, own a nice house, produce beautiful children, have some money in the bank or enjoy an annual holiday in the sun. All perfectly reasonable aims to have in view, but they make lousy structures on which to build our lives. You see, those things have a habit of crumbling beneath our feet . . . of promising more than they can deliver.

The apostle Paul had it right when he clearly declared his lifetime goal: 'For to me to live is Christ' (Philippians 1:21). Christ wasn't just first in his life; He *was* Paul's life. For him, living without Christ wasn't an option, even though it would undoubtedly have made things easier. Neither was Christianity an add-on to Paul's already busy life. It was everything – after which all else correctly fell into place. And death? Paul claimed it as life's ultimate prize, since to 'be with Christ . . . is far better' (1:23).

Lord Jesus, may my life's goal be to live for You. That way I will never be the loser. Amen.

10 November

THINK ON THIS

Instead, we will speak the truth in love,
growing in every way more and more like Christ,
who is the head of his body, the church.

Ephesians 4:15, NLT

- Read through this verse a number of times – including out loud.
- Write it out, stick it on the fridge, have it on your phone.
- Meditate on the words, then respond in praise.
- Take steps to allow God's word to change you: perhaps . . . repent, forgive, love.

11 November

Therefore God has highly exalted him and
bestowed on him the name that is above every name,
so that at the name of Jesus every knee should bow,
in heaven and on earth and under the earth.

Philippians 2:9–10

Reading: John 4:21–24

Sometime ago, our daughter-in-law was sitting in a London café where she had stopped for a cup of coffee. Her attention was suddenly interrupted by a sharp knock on the window beside her. From the street a man smiled, waved and mouthed the words, 'See you later.' She happily returned the greeting with a silent nod.

She quickly became aware of the attention suddenly directed towards her. Folk around her were whispering, pointing at her. Who was she? Was she famous? I mean, why would that famous actor be arranging to see her later? Susie smiled, letting the celebrity-spotters enjoy their fun. They had correctly identified the window-tapping actor, but had got her all wrong. She wasn't his relative or his date, or an actress they should keep an eye out for. She simply knew him because she was giving his young children singing lessons!

Celebrity watching and following has become not only a hobby for millions but a huge source of income for brand promoters, as well for as the celebrity. It is worship by another name.

Jesus had many followers while He lived among us. Some, like the celebrity watchers of today, were only there to see what He was going to do next (John 6:2). Others came because they wanted something from Him (Matthew 19:2). But only those who recognized Jesus' deity worshipped Him – from the Magi (2:11) to the disciples (14:33) to the women rushing from the empty tomb (28:9) to the repentant doubter (John 20:28).

But one day that will all change. Whether we are sceptics, doubters, rejecters, atheists, religious or truly born again of God's Spirit, each one of us will bow in worship before the One whom God has highly exalted, and whose name carries more kudos than anyone who has ever lived (Philippians 2:9–10)!

Let's not wait until then . . . Jesus is worthy of our worship right now.

My head, heart and all that I am worships You, King of kings, and Lord of all. Amen.

12 November

But our citizenship is in heaven,
and from it we await a Saviour,
the Lord Jesus Christ.

Philippians 3:20

Reading: 2 Corinthians 5:3–10

Do you ever feel as if you don't belong here? Has the country we call ours become a disappointment? Is the government making decisions that totally turn on its head the moral authority our forebears once exercised? Have we become weak on justice, but strong on personal opinion? Do we act as a community concerned about the individuals within it, or do we seek only what is right for me and mine? Does the way we feel about our national identity drive us to prayer? Perhaps it should.

As I write, the World Cup is in full swing. Although some issues may have side-tracked the competition somewhat, it all comes down to the sport of kicking a ball around a field. Yet, there is something magnificent about watching thirty-two flags fluttering in the breeze that reminds us of the multiplicity of citizens represented. And as diverse as the flags are the cultures they denote. Yet, on occasions like these, all fans like to be seen as ... and to sound ... patriotic. There are no football supporters at the World Cup hiding where they are from!

Paul reminds us that although we live under the flag of an earthly country, we are citizens of heaven. Just as Philippi was a colony of Rome, so we, as members of Christ's church, are a colony of heaven on earth. And while here we should behave in a manner befitting our citizenship. You might not wear a T-shirt identifying your allegiance – although you can if you wish (an emoji would be useful here!), but the fact that we are followers of Jesus should be easily recognized.

So then ... how do I represent my King? Does my behaviour sit well with my citizenship? Do I commend Christ's kingdom to others? Am I excited about the day when I will finally get to go home?

King of heaven, the Royal Standard is flying from my heart, for I am certain that You are in residence there. Amen.

13 November

And my God will supply every need of yours
according to his riches in glory in Christ Jesus.

Philippians 4:19

Reading: Philippians 4:14–20

When we reach life's extremities God never forgets us. It is not in His nature.

Paul was in prison when he wrote this encouraging letter to his friends at Philippi, where he had founded the very first church in Europe (Acts 16:12–15). His opening remarks were full of gratitude, and his affection for them was obvious (Philippians 1:7–8). Even though Paul had spent a short spell in their local jail, the Philippians eagerly accepted the gospel message and readily supported Paul's missionary endeavour, both prayerfully and financially (4:15).

There was no online banking back then. Money took time to get where it was going! However, Paul never complained when things got tight – he had learned to be content whether in plenty or in need (4:12). When things were tough, Paul experienced the very thing he was reminding the Philippians of: that God supplies our every need (4:19). Yet, in context, Paul's words concerned the generous gift that had just arrived from the Philippian believers in the care of Epaphroditus. The apostle was thanking them for their kindness (4:18). They had blessed both him and God's work with their sacrificial giving . . . and he was assuring them that God is no man's debtor.

'Remember the words of the Lord Jesus, how he himself said, "It is more blessed to give than to receive"' (Acts 20:35). God doesn't ask for anything more from us than He already does in abundance. In fact, His practice is to 'open the windows of heaven . . . and pour down for you a blessing until there is no more need' (Malachi 3:10). And God's supply is unending because it is taken out of His many 'riches in glory in Christ Jesus' (Philippians 4:19). That's one supply that is never in danger of running out!

We can never outgive God, but we could bless the heart of one of His servants today through the joy of giving (2 Corinthians 9:7).

Thank you, Lord, for Your constant kindness towards me. Give me a generous heart like Yours, that I might be a conduit of Your blessing to others. Amen.

14 November

Him we proclaim, warning everyone
and teaching everyone with all wisdom,
that we may present everyone mature in Christ.

Colossians 1:28

Reading: Colossians 1:9–14

Paul was passionate about everything he did. And he certainly didn't take lightly his faith in Jesus Christ, nor the calling subsequently placed on his life. This man, who had once spent his days hunting down the followers of Christ to drag them off to prison (Acts 8:3), then spent all that was left of his life putting himself in danger in order that Christ's name would be known. What made the difference? Paul had encountered Jesus on the road to Damascus (9:1–19). After that, everything changed ... including his name. But not his passion ... that was redirected into telling people about Jesus everywhere he went.

Yet, no matter how hard he tried, Paul and his few faithful companions couldn't possibly get the gospel to Europe's millions all by themselves. But they didn't give up. Even when imprisonment quite literally chained Paul to Rome, the apostle took to writing letters. His burning desire was for those who had experienced salvation through faith in Jesus Christ to grow to spiritual maturity (Colossians 1:28). Young plants don't produce fruit, but those abiding in Christ do (John 15:5). And it would be mature fruit-bearers who would continue the job of disciple-making long after Paul had gone.

I wonder how long it would take the people in our company to recognize what we are passionate about. Our families? Our jobs? Our hobbies? Our favourite foods? Would they ever guess that we are passionate about Jesus? We are certainly not Paul, Peter or James, but we don't need to be. We have the same Lord living in us, the same experience of His grace, the same wonderful gospel to proclaim, the same Saviour to serve.

But do we have the same passion they did?

Lord Jesus, there is no one like You. Forgive me if my witness doesn't follow my passion. There are no excuses. Amen.

15 November

For God in all his fullness
was pleased to live in Christ, and through him
God reconciled everything to himself.

Colossians 1:19–20, NLT

Reading: Colossians 1:19–23

When it comes to writing a book, I have discovered that the most difficult part happens before page one begins. A plan is essential. What is the book about? Into which genre does it fit? Who is the book aimed at? What is your proposed word count . . . your planned chapter content? Will it fill a gap in the market, or as one wise editor once said, 'Would it bless the world more by remaining as a tree?' Will people read it . . . and buy it? What do you hope to achieve by writing it?

The writers of the New Testament epistles – Paul, Peter, James, John and Jude – wrote at different times, and for different readers and reasons, but they all had one common goal: to make much of Jesus. He was their main theme. In fact, it's barely possible to read a paragraph without finding the Saviour mentioned. Achievement in their eyes was making Christ known and seeing believers built up in their faith. Something that still happens to this very day.

Christ was central in their writing, because Christ is supreme in His person (Colossians 1:15), in His works (1:16) and in His sacrificial love for us (1:20). Yet, the content of these letters is too personal to be categorized merely as a theological textbook. Strong men, not normally given to the softer emotions, frequently included the word 'beloved' to describe those they were writing to. This overflow of affection indicates the compulsion of Christ's love in them (2 Corinthians 5:14) – that 'we love because he first loved us' (1 John 4:19). So, whether they wrote to settle arguments, to correct wrong teaching or to encourage the crestfallen, these letters were bathed in the love of Jesus.

What a challenge! Think what difference kindness would make to those conversations we find perplexing, or to those for whom rejection is the norm. The old proverb still stands: 'A gentle answer deflects anger, but harsh words make tempers flare' (Proverbs 15:1, NLT).

Lord Jesus, may all my communication with others be coated with Your love. Amen.

16 November

Beloved, if God so loved us,
we also ought to love one another.

1 John 4:11

Reading: 1 John 4:7–12

Not all nicknames are affectionate. It doesn't take much imagination to guess why Jesus gave John and his brother James the nickname 'Boanerges' – 'sons of thunder'. Rather explosive, zealous characters, filled with ambition, the brothers didn't have the word 'measured' in their vocabulary. They were passionate about Jesus from the start, but knew little about grace and humility.

It is possible that the nickname was given, or reinforced, when the brothers wanted to call down fire from heaven to burn up a Samaritan village that had refused hospitality to Jesus. Rather extreme? Absolutely. The Master set them straight. 'You do not know what manner of spirit you are of,' Jesus countered. 'For the Son of Man did not come to destroy men's lives but to save *them*' (Luke 9:55–56, NKJV).

Passion is a great motivator for others, but it needs to be moulded in the right way if it is going to lead others in the right direction. The brothers were neither political nor religious zealots, and Jesus had three years to transform the Boanergeses' weaknesses into strengths; their sharp tempers into loving, selfless personalities. Under Jesus' mentorship, John became known as the disciple whom Jesus loved (John 13:23). His fervency now tempered by that love; the hothead was transformed into an outspoken apostle of love – not thunder.

Could it have been the new commandment that Jesus gave them before His arrest that did the final work of transforming grace in John's life? Jesus said: 'Love one another: just as I have loved you, you also are to love one another. By this all people will know that you are my disciples, if you have love for one another' (13:34–35). Or was it the blood that dripped from the Saviour's broken body onto the ground where John stood at Calvary that convinced him love was stronger than anything else? Whatever it was, John was never the same. God's message of love is mixed into all his writings because Jesus had loved him first . . . warts and all.

Loving Saviour, may others know that we belong to You by our love for one another. Amen.

17 November

THINK ON THIS

Dear friends, we are already God's children,
but he has not yet shown us what we will be like
when Christ appears. But we do know that we will
be like him, for we will see him as he really is.

1 John 3:2, NLT

- Read through this verse a number of times – including out loud.
- Write it out, stick it on the fridge, have it on your phone.
- Meditate on the words, then respond in praise.
- Encourage someone by sharing this verse with them today.

18 November

So Christ has truly set us free.
Now make sure that you stay free,
and don't get tied up again in slavery to the law.

Galatians 5:1, NLT

Reading: Galatians 5:1–6, NLT

'Daniel do it!'

When our grandson was a toddler, these three words were his mantra: 'Daniel do it!' He had discovered that doing things by himself was exciting, but it got to the point where he wanted to do everything without help. It meant that putting on socks took an age, and if the heel wasn't in the right place it had to be left that way . . . because of 'Daniel do it!' He felt invincible. That nothing was too hard for him. It was so cute, and the round of applause that followed his many successes made him even more determined to do it alone. What wasn't easy, however, was trying to convince this two-year-old that some things were too dangerous to manage without Mummy or Daddy. 'Daniel *can't* do it!' was hard to accept.

We are a strange lot, us humans. When it comes to blame, we love to point the finger at someone other than ourselves. But when it comes to salvation, we'd really rather sort it out for ourselves. 'I can do it!' becomes our very own mantra. 'I will reach God in the way that I want.' 'I'm good enough.' 'I can do it!' But the hard truth for each of us is that, on our own, we can't meet God's requirement for holiness: 'For all have sinned and fall short of the glory of God' (Romans 3:23). The best thing to do is to give in, because 'God can do it!' This should be our mantra . . . 'God can do it!' Or rather, 'God has done it!'

'For all . . . are justified by his grace as a gift, through the redemption that is in Christ Jesus' (3:23–24).

At the cross Jesus did it! We have been set free! But Paul reminds us it's time to act like it. The shackles of legalism and self-righteousness have been removed. It's time to leave the prison; time to stop trying to impress God and move into the liberty Christ obtained for us.

Lord Jesus, You did it! Thank you. Amen.

19 November

Blessed be the God and Father of our Lord Jesus Christ,
who has blessed us in Christ with every spiritual blessing
in the heavenly places.

Ephesians 1:3

Reading: Ephesians 1:3–10

I will never forget the day I visited the ruins of the ancient city of Ephesus. It comes close to the top of my list of life's greatest experiences. Having been escorted through a very average-looking entrance, we turned left and the vista that spread out before us was breathtaking! I could hardly believe what I was seeing. So successful was the excavation that my vivid imagination transported me back in time.

We had entered through what would have been the rural side of Ephesus – the Upper City – where wealthy dignitaries and Rome's legislators had lived in fine houses and conducted civic affairs. Many of the ruins we observed had been built around AD 2. But when I stepped onto the shiny black stones of the Lower City I was walking on the very street Paul would have traversed, standing beside the agora where Priscilla would have bought her daily necessities, and had the place believed to have been Demetrius's silver shop pointed out to us (Acts 19:24). But I felt sorry that our touring companions were missing the heart of what had happened amid these ruins.

I wished the guide had told them about Demetrius and his silversmiths' union, who nearly caused a riot because the Christian converts weren't buying his silver idols any more. And how the huge Roman theatre still casting its shadow over Demetrius's shop almost became a place of lynching for God's servants (19:28). But most of all I wished they had been told that Ephesus wasn't merely about the Roman Empire and the magnificent buildings, but that God had visited this notable city with an abundance of His grace, and had blessed its believing inhabitants 'with every spiritual blessing' (Ephesians 1:3).

But as I remember Ephesus, I am challenged to stop throughout the day . . . and to consider personally – one by one – the spiritual blessings afforded to us in Christ Jesus. That tops my list!

Lord, there is never enough time to count the blessings You have lavished on us, but I'll give it a go! Amen.

20 November

Therefore be imitators of God,
as beloved children.

Ephesians 5:1

Reading: Ephesians 5:15–21

Family resemblances can be fascinating, such that when you meet someone for the first time you are curious of their family origins. And it's not only because they look alike. No, it's the mannerisms that remind you of their relative. The way they cock their head when they laugh; how one lip curls higher than the other when they smile; the same intonation on certain words; their short steps or long strides when they walk.

To become like someone in their mannerisms, you have to spend a long time with them. And children spend a lot of growing-up time watching their parents and older siblings. We all learn from others, especially those closest to us. We even become imitators of what they do and say. While each of us strives for individuality, we can't always shake the family mannerisms ... but we can be cautious about the ones we're passing on to the little ones in our care.

On first read, Paul's instruction to 'be imitators of God' is quite startling. How can we imitate God? That's a big ask! But, in context, the apostle is simply asking this of us from our connection as His 'beloved children'. He's encouraging us to spend time with God, just as a child loves to spend time with their earthly father. If we do, we will see His loving heart of grace, which in time will be seen in our own lives. We will experience His forgiveness and learn how to forgive those who have wronged us. And mercy will become more commonplace when see the way God holds back from us the judgement we deserve. Imitating happens with presence ... and, in the words of David, 'in your presence there is fullness of joy; at your right hand are pleasures forevermore' (Psalm 16:11).

Jesus said, 'Whoever has seen me has seen the Father' (John 14:9). Do people see Him in us?

Heavenly Father, imitating You shouldn't be scary – not when it entails being in Your presence. Thank you for letting me sit with You. Amen.

21 November

And if Christ has not been raised,
your faith is futile and you are still in your sins.

1 Corinthians 15:17

Reading: 1 Corinthians 15:12–19

There are some things in Christianity that are non-negotiable. Like it or not, some doctrines really are black-and-white. That may sound dogmatic, but there is no getting away from it; Christianity is not a pick-'n'-mix religion.

The fundamentals of the Christian faith are set in stone – immovable.

- **The virgin birth . . . non-negotiable.** 'His mother, Mary, was engaged to be married to Joseph. But before the marriage took place, while she was still a virgin, she became pregnant through the power of the Holy Spirit' (Matthew 1:18, NLT).
- **The deity of Christ . . . non-negotiable.** 'In the beginning was the Word . . . and the Word was God' (John 1:1).
- **Jesus' atonement for sin through the blood of the cross . . . non-negotiable.** 'In him we have redemption through his blood, the forgiveness of our trespasses, according to the riches of his grace' (Ephesians 1:7).
- **The bodily resurrection of the Lord Jesus . . . non-negotiable.** 'He is not here, for he has risen, as he said. Come, see the place where he lay' (Matthew 28:6).

The new believers to whom Paul was writing found it hard to shake what was ridiculed as nonsense in their Graeco-Roman society. They believed Jesus rose from the dead, but the idea that they would also be resurrected was laughable . . . especially for the educated among them (1 Corinthians 15:11–12). And that remains a problem today. If you believe in the resurrection, you can expect to be accused of being less than intelligent.

But Jesus' reputation depends on this truth. A lying Saviour cannot be trusted, and a dead one cannot save. Jesus' resurrection is essential for our justification, 'He was delivered over to death for our sins and was raised to life for our justification' (Romans 4:25, NIVUK). If we are to be presented to the Father one day – justified; just-as-if-I'd never sinned – then Jesus' resurrection is as important as His death. Disbelieving the resurrection makes a nonsense of our faith, so let's embrace it unashamedly (Romans 10:9).

Lord Jesus, whatever others say, I confess that You are a living, resurrected Saviour. On that truth I stake my salvation. Amen.

22 November

Who shall separate us from the love of Christ?
Shall tribulation, or distress, or persecution,
or famine, or nakedness, or danger, or sword?

Romans 8:35

Reading: Romans 8:31–39

The Covid-19 pandemic was probably the greatest illustration of the effects of human isolation that the world has ever experienced. While each country devised its own set of rules in the war against a clever, vicious and unseen enemy, one plan was universal: isolation. Heads of government addressed their nations as though announcing a war, declaring that people must stay apart from others – families from families; friends from friends; communities from communities. Even at times of serious illness and death, people were separated from loved ones. Essential, we were told . . . but also cruel beyond imagination.

While we all tried novel ways of keeping in touch with loved ones, the separation – and especially the lack of human touch – has had a huge impact on us all. As the years pass, research is showing how detrimental – physically, emotionally and societally – those periods of lockdown were.

Our family was fortunate, in that we sustained no personal loss to the disease, but I was shocked by how much I missed people . . . especially our grandchildren. My husband and I received 'paper hugs', comprising of a cutout of their hands with a long strip of concertinaed paper connecting each one. 'When you need a hug, Granny,' the children explained, 'stretch it out and wrap it around you . . . and pretend it's us.' Not quite the same, but rather ingenious!

God created people to be together. As a Trinity, He created us in His own image (Genesis 1:26) to be relational. In Christ, He adopted us as members of His family (John 1:12) to be together . . . with other believers, yes, but also as sons and daughters with Him. And Paul explains to God's family that whatever we are going through – difficulty, disaster, distress or disease – no one can separate us from the love of Christ (Romans 8:35–39). Absolutely no one!

Jesus is always with us. Always loving us. Never abandoning us. Never distant. We cannot be separated from His love . . . period.

Lord Jesus, I place today into your hands, in the assurance that whatever happens Your love is non-negotiable. Amen.

23 November

For the Lord himself will descend from heaven
with a cry of command, with the voice of an archangel,
and with the sound of the trumpet of God.
And the dead in Christ will rise first.
1 Thessalonians 4:16

Reading: 1 Thessalonians 4:13–18

The Greeks of Paul's day had serious negativity about death. Although Christ's resurrection would have been central in the preaching and teaching of Paul and his companions (Acts 17:3), the new Christians had become deeply concerned about some of their group who had died (1 Thessalonians 4:13). They had been told that Jesus would return, but now they feared that those who had died since they first responded to the gospel would miss the benefits of Christ's return. As any tender pastor would, Paul wrote this beautiful letter to allay their fears and confirm the hope – the confident expectation – that Christ was returning for those who had died as believers . . . as well as Christians still alive (4:16–17).

You'd think that today's society would have gained a little wisdom along the way. Sadly, that's not the case. The godless teaching of atheistic evolution – we came from nowhere; we are here for no reason; and when you're dead, that's it – has spread an utter hopelessness about life beyond the grave.

However, believers are assured that, while it is normal to grieve, we should not do so without hope: 'For since we believe that Jesus died and rose again, even so, through Jesus, God will bring with him those who have fallen asleep' (4:14). And it will be no sedate affair. There'll be noise . . . lots of it! The Kingly command, the voice of an archangel and the call of the trumpet will ensure that the no one sleeps when King Jesus arrives to take His people home! The dead in Christ are privileged to rise first – soul and body reunited once more – closely followed by those of us who are still alive. 'Together . . . we . . . will be caught up in the clouds to meet the Lord in the air' (4:17, NLT).

Do I hear a hallelujah?

Lord Jesus, You have defeated death and promised that one day we will rise with you in glory. Hallelujah! Amen.

24 November

THINK ON THIS

Therefore, since we have been justified by faith,
we have peace with God through our Lord Jesus Christ.

Romans 5:1

- Read through this verse a number of times – including out loud.
- Write it out, stick it on the fridge, have it on your phone.
- Meditate on the words, then respond in praise.
- Be a doer . . . Serve someone with an act of kindness today.

25 November

Give thanks in all circumstances;
for this is the will of God in Christ Jesus for you.

1 Thessalonians 5:18

Reading: 1 Thessalonians 5:12–24

Do you ever wonder if there's a simple version of what God's will should look like for us as followers of Jesus? There are times when Paul is wordy, then there are times when he just gives us the bare bones. Yet, in each instruction we see Jesus, because living out God's will is living like Him. We are to:

- Live lives full of peace (1 Thessalonians 5:13), as Jesus has given us His peace (John 14:27).
- Be firm with the disorderly but patient and kind with those who lack spiritual or physical strength (1 Thessalonians 5:14). Jesus did this, and more (Acts 10:38).
- Don't seek revenge, but rather seek to do good to everyone (1 Thessalonians 5:15). Didn't Jesus tell us to turn the other cheek rather than seeking retaliation (Matthew 5:38–39)?
- Always be joyful (1 Thessalonians 5:16), because Jesus has promised that although sorrow will come, our grief will be transformed into joy (John 16:20).
- Develop a rolling prayer life (1 Thessalonians 5:17). Jesus could do nothing without the Father's help (John 5:19). If it was a necessity for the second person in the Godhead, shouldn't it be the same for us (Luke 6:12)?
- Grow a gratitude attitude . . . whatever is happening. It is God's will for us in Christ (1 Thessalonians 5:18). A thankful heart brings light into every situation.
- Don't extinguish what the Spirit is doing or resist what God is saying. Make sure you check out everything you hear and then hold firmly to what is good (1 Thessalonians 5:19–21). Let's remember that it is the Spirit who guides us into all truth (John 16:13).
- Reject every form of evil (1 Thessalonians 5:22), but don't be anxious about getting everything right because Christ will faithfully present us blameless before the Father when He returns (Jude 24).

Knowing God's will was straightforward as far as Paul was concerned. But for me it is most encouraging to know that the Helper 'dwells with [me] and will be in [me]' (John 14:16–17).

Lord, I want to do Your will. Thank you for sending Your Spirit to help me. Amen.

26 November

But in these last days
he has spoken to us by his Son.

Hebrews 1:2

Reading: Acts 13:46–49

The Christmas biscuit tin, perched on the top shelf of Mum's store cupboard, begged me to lift it down. It had been patient. I had taken a long time to retrieve it from where it had probably been sitting for decades. The old brown, sellotaped paper covering the front had been my reason for leaving it almost until last. This tin promised treasure. 'Letters from around the world' was beautifully written in my mother's unmistakable handwriting.

The section of the New Testament known as the Epistles is a bit like a memory box of written treasures. Each one is written either to an individual or to the church at a specific location. Thirteen of the twenty-one letters were written by Paul, to encourage the young churches he had founded on his missionary journeys. They were sermons on parchment, carefully carried by hand across land and sea by faithful partners in the gospel, often taking months to reach their destination.

Today, we can type a message and, with the click of a key, it reaches the other side of the world before our machine has ceased whooshing! Wouldn't Paul have loved that? Or maybe not ... You can't hurry ink onto parchment. And letters written thoughtfully touch hearts and garner a more considered response than an impersonal, send-to-all electronic note. Somehow, a messenger making his way from a distant port creates more excitement than a 'you've got mail' pop-up.

However, the speed at which the gospel message can travel today, often from a more comfortable setting than the deck of wooden ship, is amazing. 'Long ago, at many times and in many ways, God spoke to our fathers by the prophets, but in these last days he has spoken to us by his Son' (Hebrews 1:1–2). And what a treasure He has now placed in our hands to pass on. Let's not put a lid on it or relegate it to the top shelf!

Thank you, Lord Jesus, for the person who brought the gospel's treasure to me. Help me to keep passing it on. Amen.

27 November

To all those in Rome
who are loved by God and called to be saints:
Grace to you and peace from God our Father
and the Lord Jesus Christ.

Romans 1:7

Reading: Romans 1:1–7

Hardly in through the door, I was greeted with much excitement and an envelope waved in my face. 'Granny, Granny,' our little granddaughter repeated, 'I had to write a letter for homework last night, but the homework isn't finished until I post the letter!' So, with little brother in the buggy, we headed to the Post Office, one excited girl bouncing alongside. It wasn't a simple matter of dropping it into the postbox. We had to go inside, buy the stamp, attach it and then post it in the box. 'There's a lot to do when you write a letter, Granny,' she commented on the way home. 'Yes,' I replied, 'but imagine the thrill Grannie Liz will have when it arrives.'

I can only begin to imagine what it must have been like for members of the early church to receive a letter from someone God had appointed to teach them about Jesus – someone like Paul (Romans 1:1). That was one church meeting you wouldn't want to miss!

We have the four Gospels, detailing every aspect of Jesus' life and teaching when He was here on earth, including the details of His birth, death, resurrection and ascension. But there is so much more we need to learn about Christ, and how to do life as a Christian. Much of this came by letter to the scattered believers of the early church, and to those whom Jesus said would believe in Him through their witness (John 17:20). Twenty-one letters in total! And what a treasure they are.

We get to open them . . . read them . . . and, whether in Rome, Belfast or anywhere else, Paul reminds us that we are loved and called by God . . . and blessed by Jesus with both grace and peace (Romans 1:7). What could be more personal? Or more inspiring?

Each letter reminds us that Jesus is very much alive, and still pouring out His blessings!

There will always be more to learn about You, and from You, Jesus. Teach my eager heart. Amen.

28 November

And let them offer sacrifices of thanksgiving,
and tell of his deeds in songs of joy!

Psalm 107:22

Reading: Psalm 107:1–9

Every country has its own national festivals and cultural traditions, but I have to admit to feeling a little jealousy over America's annual Thanksgiving Day. There is something special about a country setting aside a day in which to thank God for His blessings. Perhaps some of its citizens just look at it as a day off work to engage in overeating and watching their favourite sport, but the principle of thanksgiving to God is fixed nevertheless.

On 6 January 1941, a joint resolution of Congress in the USA wrote into law the fourth Thursday of November as a national holiday of Thanksgiving, following similar declarations from presidents as far back as George Washington in 1789. Said president assigned the day as one to render to God sincere and humble thanks for His kind care and protection of the people of America.

In fact, Thanksgiving Day can be traced further back to 1621, when a band of English pilgrims, having crossed the Atlantic on the *Mayflower* in search of religious freedom, celebrated their first harvest in the new land. Theirs was indeed costly praise, since only fifty-one of the original 102 pilgrims survived that dreadful journey and the subsequent harsh winter in America. They certainly knew the meaning of offering 'a sacrifice of praise to God . . . lips that acknowledge his name' (Hebrews 13:15).

Hardship helps us to focus on what is important – allowing the frivolous to slip from our sight, and to see who God is and praise Him for His mercy towards us. Praise concentrates our mind on God and connects our heart with His. Thanksgiving, however, focuses on what God does, and begins when we acknowledge the immense value of even the simplest of God's gifts . . . like sitting around the table with family and enjoying good food.

But oh, what thankfulness should pour from our hearts when we think how 'the God and Father of our Lord Jesus Christ . . . has blessed us in Christ with every spiritual blessing in the heavenly places' (Ephesians 1:3).

Father, may my heart be grateful every day for Your goodness, not just on one day a year. Amen.

29 November

And over his head they put the charge against him,
which read, 'This is Jesus, the King of the Jews.'

Matthew 27:37

Reading: Ephesians 1:19–23

Monarchy invariably divides opinion. Those of a more socialist disposition believe
the monarchy to be a drain on the nation's wealth; an old-fashioned, past-its-time,
upper-class firm. In contrast, many see the monarchy as great value for money, as
their endeavours bring both esteem and investment to the nation.

Here in the UK, we are privileged to have a royal family that works incessantly for
the good of its citizens – representing the country in a multitude of ways, as well as
boosting the profile of many charitable causes. Their lives are not their own ...
duty always comes first. And they refuse to defend themselves from any, and all,
assaults on their reputations in the media. But even with all of this, their royal
position is as nothing compared to the One we worship as King of kings and Lord
of lords (1 Timothy 6:15).

The false accusation that Jesus intended to become King of Israel led to His crucifixion. The written charge for which He was executed – 'King of the Jews' – was
hung on the cross above Jesus' head, while the crown of thorns which cruelly
pierced His brow mocked the truth. Jesus was King indeed, but he was no earthly
ruler. "My kingdom is not of this world,' He had told Pilate, adding: 'You say that
I am a king. For this purpose I was born and for this purpose I have come into this
world – to bear witness to the truth' (John 18:36–37).

King Jesus was setting up His kingdom in the hearts of men and women who
would hear the truth, believe the truth and trust the truth for salvation (14:6). He
alone is our Sovereign. Worthy of our allegiance, service and worship. And worthy
of the throne He was given when He returned to the Father. 'So then the Lord
Jesus, after he had spoken to them, was taken up into heaven and sat down at the
right hand of God' (Mark 16:19).

*King of heaven, as Your humble servant I gladly bow low in Your presence and give
You praise, for You alone are worthy. Amen.*

30 November

But of the Son he says,
'Your throne, O God, is forever and ever,
the scepter of uprightness is the scepter of your kingdom.'

Hebrews 1:8

Reading: Hebrews 1:1–14

Can you visualize the day when the Son returned from earth to be greeted by heaven's hosts? I wonder, did they get excited when they heard the news that Jesus was on His way? He had been gone for so long . . . thirty-three years! But then there are no clocks in heaven. Surely they missed Him? Did they wait for every report of Him during those years He had spent away from home? And when the announcement came of His soon return, did the rustling of angelic wings cause a breeze of praise to sweep through heaven? The Son was coming home! He had completed His task and remained obedient until the end . . . which was really a beginning. Were the throne, the sceptre and the crown made ready for the coronation? Did the choir practise? Did the trumpets blast triumphantly?

I don't know. But I hope so.

I do know this: the Father was pleased. For when Jesus had made 'purification for sins, he sat down at the right hand of the Majesty on high' (Hebrews 1:3). The Saviour who had nowhere to lay his head on earth (Matthew 8:20) now had a royal throne to occupy. And concerning the Son, God said:

- 'Your throne, O God, is forever and ever' (Hebrews 1:8), confirming Jesus' eternal deity;
- 'The sceptre of uprightness is the sceptre of your kingdom' (1:8), indicating that Christ's authority will never end;
- '[God] has anointed you with the oil of gladness beyond your companions' (1:9). Humanity's rejection will forever be transcended by incomparable joy;
- When everything perishes, 'You remain . . . and your years will have no end' (1:11–12). Jesus is unchangeable and immovable; totally secure.

And as 'all God's angels worship him' (1:6), Jesus once more picks up the majesty He had laid aside to become 'Immanuel . . . God with us' (Matthew 1:23). Once more, the King of kings is in His rightful place.

Lord Jesus, I look forward to the day when You will return to earth . . . not as a baby, but as a conquering King. Amen.

December

1 December

THINK ON THIS

But you, O Bethlehem Ephrathah,
who are too little to be among the clans of Judah,
from you shall come forth for me
one who is to be ruler in Israel,
whose coming forth is from of old,
from ancient days.

Micah 5:2

- Read through this verse a number of times – including out loud.
- Write it out, stick it on the fridge, have it on your phone.
- Meditate on the words, then respond in praise.
- Remember why Jesus came by reading a chapter of Luke's gospel each day until 24 December.

2 December

'I see him, but not now;
I behold him, but not near:
a star shall come out of Jacob,
and a scepter shall rise out of Israel.'

Numbers 24:17

Reading: Matthew 2:1–6

'Cheryl is the donkey in this year's nativity,' said the note in our daughter's school diary. 'That's a bit of a demotion from an angel, Sweetheart,' I chuckled. 'But then you'll not be able to run off the stage like last year's donkey.' Oh, the delights of Christmas productions at a special needs school!

Who could have imagined how God would use Daniel after he was taken by force to Babylon? Fearless, wise and faithful to God above all else, the youth became God's mouthpiece to a pagan world. God gave Daniel the interpretation of King Nebuchadnezzar's dreams, including that God's kingdom would one day destroy all previous man-made kingdoms (Daniel 2:44–45). After this prophecy, the king made Daniel ruler 'over the whole province of Babylon and chief prefect over all the wise men of Babylon' (2:48).

Do you think Daniel kept quiet about the God of heaven before this group of Babylon's finest? Of course not! The school of the Magi had begun, and from it – some 500 years after Daniel had prophesied concerning the Messiah (9:24–27) – some of them made the long journey from Persia to Bethlehem. Known as the Prophecy of Seventy Weeks, mathematicians tell us that it accurately pointed forward to Christ: the King who would rule the nations of the earth.

Were the Magi who searched for Jesus pagan? Probably. But aren't we all before we find Him? Did they recognize the promised star in the sky as that from the Hebrew writings we now know as Balaam's Fourth Prophecy in Numbers 24:17? Absolutely. Is it any wonder they got so excited by what they saw at the very time Daniel had prophesied the arrival of the King of the Jews, or that they travelled the long journey of approximately 600 miles to meet Him?

What is more surprising, however, is that the chief priests and scribes in Jerusalem didn't bother to travel the five miles to Bethlehem to welcome their Messiah!

Forgive me, Lord, for displaying any carelessness towards you, for You are the King of my life. Amen.

3 December

And behold, the star that they had seen when it rose
went before them until it came to rest
over the place where the child was.

Matthew 2:9

Reading: Matthew 2:7–12

God always has a plan. It may not be the one we expect, but we inevitably discover that it is the right plan, at the right time.

It's unlikely that Daniel would have seen his capture by the Babylonians as a good plan. But he did not waver in his commitment to the Lord Jehovah, even though there were times when it threatened his life (Daniel 6). God had a plan to make Himself known to the Babylonians, and He used Daniel to execute it by humbling a proud king (4:37).

God's plan for Gentiles to meet His Son was also fulfilled, because hundreds of years earlier Daniel had given their ancestors all they needed to seek out King Jesus when the time was right. These 'wise men' followed the prophecy, and the star led them all the way to Jerusalem – where they almost lost it, because they thought a king would be born in a palace. Thankfully, the star reappeared when they left Herod's palace and led them to their destination (Matthew 2:9).

This was not a star as we know it, for it led them day and night. While scientists have tried to class it as a cosmic event or the alignment of planets, it appears the guiding star was just as supernatural as the virgin birth. Theologians have likened it to the Shekinah Glory that led the Israelites through the wilderness – a pillar of cloud by day and a pillar of fire by night (Exodus 13:20–22). However, one thing is certain: this wasn't just any star, it was *His* star (Matthew 2:2). Indisputably part of God's plan (Numbers 24:17).

'His star' led them to Bethlehem. 'And going into the house, they saw the child with Mary his mother, and they fell down and worshiped him' (Matthew 2:11). And the Magi's journey began with a plan involving the captivity of a nation, and one individual: Daniel.

Thank you, God, that You have a plan for my life . . . one that involves meeting Jesus. Amen.

4 December

When they saw the star,
they rejoiced exceedingly with great joy.

Matthew 2:10

Reading: Psalm 98

I don't like the word 'fine'. It is nondescript. If I ask my husband to comment on something I'm wearing and he responds with, 'It's fine', then it's likely I'll go and change. 'Nice' is better, but 'lovely' hits the spot. Many of the words we use every day are functional, but if you are hoping to evoke an emotional response it's important to use the right words. While overuse of adjectives may dilute the desired effect, used properly they can transform the ordinary into the extraordinary.

Because of the grace and goodness of God we can experience joy in the everyday. Like that sense of satisfaction when we come in from the cold to a heated room, or on tasting a well-filled sandwich. Then there's that rush of delight when an unexpected kindness comes unbidden or when the local florist delivers a surprise bouquet. For me, the sound of our grandchildren laughing is surely one of life's heart-warmers. How blessed we are when joy visits us in the ordinary.

Apparently, according to someone else's count, the Bible uses the word 'joy' more than 200 times. But it only requires two hands to count the uses of 'great joy'. But then Christmas requires the exuberant. It's when Jesus took centre stage – when God became man; when he 'emptied himself . . . being born in the likeness of men' (Philippians 2:7). There is nothing ordinary about Christmas. That's why every-thing about it produces *great joy*!

When the angel shook the sleep from the shepherds' eyes that night, he declared that he had 'good news of great joy' (Luke 2:10) for them. Why? Because a Saviour had been born (2:11). There is nothing ordinary about that!

And the wise men 'rejoiced exceedingly with great joy' when they saw the star (Matthew 2:10). A star that had guided them for more than 600 miles to meet with Jesus . . . There is nothing ordinary about that!

Let's not make the extraordinary ordinary this Christmas. If we do, we'll miss the *great joy* it can deliver to our hearts when we put Jesus at centre stage.

Extraordinary Saviour, thank you for the great joy You have brought to my life because You came. Amen.

5 December

And she gave birth to her firstborn son
and wrapped him in swaddling cloths
and laid him in a manger.

Luke 2:7

Reading: Luke 1:39–45

The real Christmas story was nothing like the one we roll out every year or sing about in the annual carol fest. Bethlehem was far from still when the exhausted Mary and Joseph arrived in town. The census had made sure of that. A cacophony of noise greeted the newlyweds; the narrow streets heaved with people. Market traders bartered noisily with travellers seeking goods for their stay in the town they had left behind years earlier.

Rome was counting heads. Collecting the tax of a reluctant nation was their game. Even the little town of Bethlehem was overrun with soldiers.

And the beautifully carved figurines gracing our homes elegantly tell a story distant from reality. There was nothing sanitary about Christ's birthplace; nothing cute about animals too close to a woman giving birth. Dusty travel clothes and the lack of washing facilities are a far cry from the Christmas card pictures of the 'holy' family. Hopefully, Joseph, who had never known Mary intimately, had help from local midwives during the long, traumatic birth of the Son that God was placing into his care.

The rogue of Christ's birth was hardly the innkeeper, whom we love to berate. No, Judea's king was the real monster of the piece. Already the murderer of his wife, sons and mother-in-law, Herod felt so threatened by the young child that he ordered the death of all little boys under two years old in Bethlehem.

There is not much tinsel in this story. No glamour for the King of kings. Instead, Jesus was born into the mess of poverty, family difficulties and political instability. He experienced life in the raw. He understands our pain. He didn't look down on us; He lived among us. And when the time came for the baby in the manger to become the Christ on the cross . . . He didn't hold back there either.[40]

Babe of Bethlehem, thank you that there is nothing I go through that You don't already understand. You are King of hearts, including mine. Amen.

6 December

For if, because of one man's trespass, death reigned
through one man, much more will those who receive
the abundance of grace and the free gift of righteousness
reign in life through the one man Jesus Christ.

Romans 5:17

Reading: 2 Corinthians 9:6–9

Across Germany today, children will race to the front door before sitting down to breakfast. Last night they will have carefully cleaned their winter boots and left one of them at the entrance of their home in preparation for Sankt Nikolaus's visit during the night. With a rush of excitement, the door will be opened and there, filling their boots, will be small gifts of shiny wrapped chocolates and Christmas titbits. All in memory of a man of God who lived during the third century AD. A man whose generosity is demonstrated by his wish to bring joy into the lives of others, and especially children.

Nikolaus was born in Patara, now modern-day Turkey, to wealthy parents who raised him to love God as a devoted Christian. Sadly, they died when he was still young, leaving him a substantial inheritance. Having been taught Jesus' words to the rich young ruler – 'If you would be perfect, go, sell what you possess and give to the poor, and you will have treasure in heaven' (Matthew 19:21) – Nikolaus kept nothing for himself. Instead, he used his entire inheritance to help the needy and the suffering.

He was made Bishop of Myra while still a young man, but suffered dreadful persecution under the Roman emperor Diocletian. Following his release from prison, Nikolaus took up his life of service once more, showing special kindness to the many poor children around him, as well as to the sailors who lived very difficult lives at sea.

Nikolaus died on 6 December AD 343, and while there are many unlikely tales attributed to this man of God, the greatest legacy he has left is that of a generous heart and selfless life. And yet, even that bears no comparison to the legacy given to us by God in the person of His Son, Jesus. God's gift is simply indescribable (2 Corinthians 9:15, NIVUK)!

Thank you, God, for the gift of Jesus. Thank you, Jesus, for Your selfless love. Give me a generous heart. Amen.

7 December

'I have no silver and gold,
but what I do have I give to you.'

Acts 3:6

Reading: 1 Peter 4:7–11

As I write, every news bulletin announces more gloom. Prices have rocketed. Public service strikes are bringing the country to a standstill. And practically everyone you speak to is saying the same thing: 'We'll have to tighten our belts this Christmas.'

Yet, I can't help but wonder if it has taken a pandemic or a recession, or both, to bring things back into proper perspective. The festive season has way outgrown what it was meant to be. Parties, dinners, shows and the excessive amount of money spent on gifts is in stark contrast to the humble surroundings that welcomed the incarnate Jesus that first Christmas. Could it be that God is shouting in our ears: 'Stop treating the trappings as the main event!'?

Last night, I spoke at a 'Welcome Christmas' event for women, and was shown what true gifting is all about. Ladies had given their precious time to decorate the room, bake shortbread and cook a simple meal, while others ensured no one felt left out in that busy room. But you know what my favourite thing was? One lady had spent hours tying a shiny ribbon around each book that every lady was going to take home as a gift. It was a beautiful blessing.

Peter and John met a needy man sitting outside the temple one day. The man was begging for a few coins, but neither apostle had any money. Instead, they gave him a much greater gift . . . healing in the name of Jesus (Acts 3:6–8). You see, we don't need to be wealthy to bless someone's life. Small Christmas gifts are not a sign of meanness. It's how we give them that makes the difference to the recipient.

Peter, writing later, reminds us that: 'As each has received a gift, [we are to] use it to serve one another, as good stewards of God's varied grace' (1 Peter 4:10). I wonder how we will use ours this Christmas. Might it even introduce someone to Jesus?

Lord, help me to remember that 'small' can be a beautiful blessing to someone if it's given from a heart of love. Amen.

8 December

THINK ON THIS

'He will be great and will be called
the Son of the Most High. And the Lord God
will give to him the throne of his father David.'

Luke 1:32

- Read through this verse a number of times – including out loud.
- Write it out, stick it on the fridge, have it on your phone.
- Meditate on the words, then respond in praise.
- Encourage someone by sharing this verse with them today.

9 December

'And the glory of the LORD shall be revealed,
and all flesh shall see it together,
for the mouth of the LORD has spoken.'

Isaiah 40:5

Reading: Isaiah 40:3–5

Spiritual snobbery is an unfortunate flaw within the worldwide Church. Too much time is spent in declaring our group to be right, especially when it comes to tradition. There is no biblical mandate for mere tradition. And therefore, no justification for criticism from one wing of the church towards others who keep to a liturgical calendar. 'You leave the commandment of God,' Jesus said, 'and hold to the tradition of men' (Mark 7:8). It is important to note that church tradition stands or falls where it meets biblical authority. Yet, there are many who live in faithful obedience to God's word through the form of traditional worship.

I am part of the church that does not formally celebrate Advent, and that's sad, because the richness behind this tradition is God-honouring.

The four Sundays leading up to Christmas prepare our hearts for the celebration of Christ's arrival. In a world where we know little of waiting (think Amazon Prime!), Advent reminds us of the first longing for the Messiah to come, encouraging patience. Where would we be if God had not been patient with us, waiting for us to come to repentance (2 Peter 3:9)? His patience can be spelled: M-E-R-C-Y. In remembering this, our hearts are also pointed towards Christ's second coming, for He will return (Revelation 22:12). And it is mercy that keeps us waiting (Matthew 24:14).

Advent also provides us with the opportunity to remember purposefully, to plan stillness into the otherwise frenetic season called Christmas. To consider the grace of a loving God in keeping His promise to us by sending His Son as a baby, in order that He might experience human life before sacrificing that life for us (1 Timothy 1:15).

Our lives are full of traditions at Christmas that have nothing to do with Jesus. Why not start an Advent one that will turn our hearts towards Him? Be creative or contemplative, practical or prayerful . . . but make it all about Jesus

Patient, kind God, may all my Christmas traditions focus on Christ. Amen.

10 December

The people who walked in darkness
have seen a great light;
those who dwelt in a land of deep darkness,
on them has light shone.

Isaiah 9:2

Reading: 2 Corinthians 4:1–6

Advent simply means a 'coming' or an 'arrival'. It involves taking time to prepare spiritually for Christmas – rejoicing through reflecting on Christ's coming, while looking forward to His second coming. Encouraging ourselves to say 'no' to the things that distract our spiritual worship at this special time of the year, and 'yes' to the gift God has given us in His Son.

While we might regard the Advent wreath as simply a lovely decoration for our front door, it signifies so much more. Every other tree gives the appearance of death as it sheds its foliage and stands barren against the cold winter sky, but the evergreen stands resplendent. And as the days shorten and the temperature drops, the evergreen reminds us of the eternal nature of God, His unfailing love for us and an eternal life with Him, made possible because of Jesus.

On each of the four Sundays before Christmas, a candle is traditionally lit on the evergreen wreath to represent Jesus as 'the light of the world' (John 8:12) and to set the focus for that week of preparation. Three purple candles symbolize Christ's royalty as the King of kings (1 Timothy 6:15); one rose-coloured candle lit on week three represents joy; and one white candle lit on Christmas Day reminds us of Christ's purity.

Week 1: the Prophets' Candle is lit, declaring the hope found in Christ through the fulfilled prophecy of His coming (Isaiah 9:2).
Week 2: Bethlehem's Candle is lit, signifying the preparation made for the coming of Jesus (Isaiah 40:3–5).
Week 3: the rose-coloured Shepherds' Candle is lit to help us rejoice at the good news of the Saviour's birth (Luke 2:10–11).
Week 4: the Angels' Candle is lit, reminding us of the adoration of the heavenly host over God's love for us (John 3:16–19).
Christmas morning: the white Christ Candle is lit, recognizing that He alone is pure enough to take away our sin (2 Corinthians 5:21).

Lord Jesus, help me to say 'no' to anything that would distract me from worshipping You. Amen.

11 December

'Ah, Lord GOD!
It is you who have made the heavens and the earth
by your great power and by your outstretched arm!
Nothing is too hard for you.'

Jeremiah 32:17

Reading: Luke 1:30–37

No other six words can bring such comfort to our needy souls and broken lives as those spoken by the prophet Jeremiah: 'Nothing is too hard for you.' They are echoed later by the angel Gabriel to Mary: 'For nothing will be impossible with God' (Luke 1:37).

The God who has no beginning, yet who gave us a beginning when He created this beautiful universe for us to inhabit, brought into being the God-child – His Son Jesus – in the womb of a virgin.

He created it out of nothing: 'In the beginning, God created the heavens and the earth' (Genesis 1:1). Then, having interacted with His creation for thousands of years through the law, the prophets and supernatural intervention, He became part of it when 'the Word became flesh and dwelt among us' (John 1:14). Yet, He remained the uncreated One. The incarnation is mind-blowing yet beautiful, for in it we see the loving heart of God towards us. There was no other way for sinful people to be reconciled to a holy God than for Him to take on human flesh and die in our place. 'And there is salvation in no one else, for there is no other name under heaven given among men by which we must be saved' (Acts 4:12).

As Genesis 18:14 says, 'Is anything too hard for the LORD?':

- Abraham and Sarah had a child when they were very old, just as God had promised (Genesis 21:2);
- Moses and the children of Israel walked across the Red Sea on dry land, exactly as God had promised (Exodus 14:16);
- God stopped the rain for three-and-a-half years when Elijah prayed . . . and when he prayed for the rain to return it poured! (James 5:17–18);
- God told a teenage virgin that she would have His Son (Luke 1:35). 'And she gave birth to her firstborn son . . . and laid him in a manger' (2:7).

Could there possibly be anything in your life that is too hard for the Lord?

Lord God, thank you for consistently proving that, with You, absolutely nothing is impossible. Amen.

12 December

And he came to her and said,
'Greetings O favored one, the Lord is with you!'

Luke 1:28

Reading: Luke 1:26–38

As Christians, we often mess up – especially regarding beliefs that we like to own theologically. Take Mary, for example. She was never meant to become a doctrine, or to have theologians argue over her, or to have historical councils debate and deliberate about her. She was certainly never meant to be worshipped ... or ignored. I would even go as far as to say that Mary is probably the most misunderstood person in the Christmas story.

Evangelicalism, Catholicism and Orthodoxy have disagreed over the woman described as the 'mother of God' for more than 500 years. 'Theotokos' ('God-bearer') was the name given to Mary by the Council of Ephesus (AD 431), affirming her as the woman who had carried God in her womb and given birth to Him ... but she was not the source of God. Jesus was divinely pre-existent; she merely the woman to whom God had given the unspeakable privilege of mothering His Son (Luke 1:31–32).

Then in AD 780, a gargantuan theological shift occurred in the Second Council of Nicaea, transferring the focus from the supernatural incarnation of Christ to the veneration of Mary as 'Mother of God' and 'Queen of heaven'.

Mary would have been dismayed. She, the teenage mother who never sought position or worship during her lifetime, was chosen by God for her godliness but not for her sinlessness, 'for all have sinned ...' (Romans 3:23). Only the Son she bore – fully God and fully man – was sinless (1 John 3:5). The angel called Mary 'favored' – approved – by God. But Jesus he referred to as great; the Son of the Most High; heir of the throne of David, whose kingdom would be eternal (Luke 1:32–33); and, 'holy – the Son of God' (1:35). It's not difficult to decide which should be worshipped.

There is no doubt that Mary was very special, but she was only what God intended her to be ... no more, no less. That's all He asks of any of us.

Lord Jesus, thank you for the bravery and commitment of Mary. May I accept Your will for me with the same grace. Amen.

13 December

But when the right time came,
God sent his Son . . .

Galatians 4:4, NLT

Reading: Galatians 4:4–7

On the Malay Archipelago – a tropical landscape of more than 1,000 islands – grow some of the world's tallest trees. They are dipterocarps, and often live for centuries. The tropical floor, many metres beneath the forest canopy, is home to a multiplicity of seed-hunting animals, making reproduction difficult for the trees. But the dipterocarp uses a cunning plan to foil the seed-hunters – one that's all down to timing. It can be more than a decade before the trees suddenly produce enormous numbers of seeds . . . all at the same time. Then one day they drop billons of winged seeds – like little helicopters – to the ground below, ensuring that the glut is too much for their predators, and some of their seeds survive to take root and sprout. It all happens when the time is right.

This wonder of nature shouldn't take us by surprise because its Creator is a master timekeeper.

The world had been waiting for the promised Messiah for a very long time. Such was the wait that some questioned if He would ever come.

But then, just when the time was right:

- When Rome's oppression once again ignited a longing in the Jews
  for a Messiah;
- When there was a common Greek 'trade' language spoken throughout
  the empire;
- When Roman road-building was at its peak, allowing for much easier
  travel;
- When the world was relatively peaceful;
- When people recognized that they were unable to keep the Old
  Testament law, and were ready to appreciate Jesus' atoning sacrifice;
- When Old Testament prophecy was all coming together . . .

When everything was culturally and religiously ready to receive and spread the gospel message . . . then the time was right, and so, 'The Father sent his Son to be the Savior of the world' (1 John 4:14, NLT).

Heavenly Father, You are never too early or too late. Help me to accept this truth in my own life, and not to grow impatient in the waiting. Amen.

14 December

And the angel answered him, 'I am Gabriel.
I stand in the presence of God,
and I was sent to speak to you
and to bring you this good news.'
Luke 1:19

Reading: Daniel 9:20–23

That first Christmas was undoubtedly one of the best times in all eternity to be an angel. Up to this point there had been a lot of dark stuff. Adam and Eve had been expelled from the garden of Eden. Guard duty there would have been tough (Genesis 3:23–24). The first murder had happened (4:8). Generation after generation, sin spread – overwhelming humanity, with Satan doing all in his power to frustrate God's purposes. Oh, how the mighty have fallen. Satan, once an angel of light – 'fallen from heaven' – dared to 'ascend above the heights of the clouds', believing he could make himself 'like the Most High' (Isaiah 14:12–14).

Yet, in this dark history of selfish, sinful twists and turns, the angels see – even engage in – God's unfolding plan to rescue His much-loved creation. They observe a few chinks of light in this dreadful saga: watching the ark rise on the gushing flood to carry Noah and his family to safety (Genesis 7:18); seeing Moses lift his staff above the Red Sea and watch its waters part to allow the fleeing Hebrews to escape slavery and certain death (Exodus 14:16).

Only four words in Scripture are attributed to the archangel, Michael, commander of heaven's hosts (Jude 9). Gabriel, on the other hand, was often tasked with presenting God's words directly to the recipients, such as the reassuring message he delivered to a distraught Daniel: 'And I have come to tell it to you, for you are greatly loved' (Daniel 9:23). God's love for His people didn't begin with Jesus. The angels had witnessed it since the dawn of time.

Yet, nothing was more splendid than the gathering of angels to hear it announced that the time was finally right ... that God was sending His Son, in human form, to earth. Salvation would arrive as heaven's most precious gift. And while the angelic choir rehearsed for the shepherds, Gabriel slipped away. He had a few people to speak to!

Lord, the angels proclaimed Your arrival. May that be my goal this Christmas. Amen.

15 December

THINK ON THIS

Great indeed, we confess, is the mystery of godliness:
He was manifested in the flesh,
vindicated by the Spirit,
seen by angels,
proclaimed among the nations,
believed on in the world,
taken up to glory.

1 Timothy 3:16

- Read through this verse a number of times – including out loud.
- Write it out, stick it on the fridge, have it on your phone.
- Meditate on the words, then respond in praise.
- Be a doer . . . Serve someone with an act of kindness today.

16 December

'Joseph, son of David,
do not fear to take Mary as your wife,
for that which is conceived in her
is from the Holy Spirit.'

Matthew 1:20

Reading: Matthew 1:18–25

My father always referred to my husband as 'the quiet man', especially in the early days of our courtship. The Frasers enjoyed talking and Philip wasn't used to competing to get a word in edgeways. He's a good listener, but he often jokes about how his best talking is done when surrounded by the wood of a pulpit!

The man tasked with raising God's Son through childhood and into manhood was a quiet man. We hear no words from Joseph in the four Gospels. The nearest we get to any conversation involving him is the part spoken by the angel during a dream about his pregnant fiancée, Mary. Yet, much strength can be displayed by a quiet man. I'd love to have more information about Joseph, but God obviously felt it was enough for us to know that this man had great integrity.

Back then, betrothal was a legal commitment, therefore a pregnant fiancée would have brought great shame on her family and future husband. Jewish law could have condemned Mary to death for her presumed infidelity, but because Joseph 'did not want to expose her to public disgrace, he had in mind to divorce her quietly' (Matthew 1:19, NIVUK). Joseph was no stranger to mercy and grace.

How reassuring it must have been to this carpenter to have an angel intrude on his dream to confirm that Mary had not been unfaithful but was pregnant by the Holy Spirit (1:20). God placed His Son in the care of a kind, gentle, godly . . . quiet man. How measured and lovely was Joseph's response? 'He did what the angel of the Lord had commanded him and took Mary home as his wife' (1:24, NIVUK).

God can use any of us: the confident; the talker; the shy; the quiet. Few would have thought that a quiet carpenter from Nazareth would have been given such an important job in the great plan of salvation.

Thank you, Lord, for people like Joseph, who quietly and faithfully do all you ask of them. Amen.

17 December

'Be still, and know that I am God.'
Psalm 46:10

Reading: John 14:25–27

There is a fluorescent yellow sticky note covering the light switch in my husband's study, on which is written one word followed by an exclamation mark: NO! Unfortunately, the innocuous-looking switch underneath throws our whole upstairs into disarray when you press it. It trips all the lights and sends us into darkness! So, until the electrician turns up it's one to stay away from.

There are times when I would like to attach a bright yellow sticker, replete with the same warning, over the month of December! This month has the propensity to set off a chain reaction of stress that causes turmoil. As a list person, you can imagine the length of my to-do list at this time of the year. Gift shopping . . . and wrapping. Menu planning . . . and food shopping . . . and cooking. Card writing . . . and catching the last postal dates. Meeting up with friends. Concerts. Carol services. Visiting . . . including cemetery visits. Christmas decorating . . . and keeping up the family traditions. And . . .

But wait, are these really things we should dread? They are supposed to be the special delights surrounding the celebration that is our Saviour's birth . . . meant to add to our joy. The word 'holiday' takes its root from 'holy day' – a day to pause . . . to meditate . . . to take time out to worship . . . 'To be still, and know that [He] is God' (Psalm 46:10). Could it be that we need a reset? To reorder our priorities? Perhaps – dare I say it? – to cross some of the things off our lists that are only there because they always have been? And maybe to add some new traditions that involve time alone with the One who is meant to be the focus of this party we call Christmas?

Christmas is about the coming of Jesus, the 'Prince of Peace' (Isaiah 9:6). Let's make much of Him this Christmas – make sure His name is frequently on our lips . . . the laying aside of His majesty close to our hearts . . . His giving nature displayed in all we do.

Let's ensure that He is not left off the list. Rather, that He is at the top of it.

Lord Jesus, we were the reason You came. May my heart display the gratitude You deserve. Amen.

18 December

Thanks be to God for his indescribable gift!

2 Corinthians 9:15, NIVUK

Reading: Philippians 2:8–11

I can often be heard calling to my husband in his study: 'Philip! What's the word for . . . ?' or 'Have you a better word for . . . ?' Even authors need to search for words – terms that are not merely correct, but also descriptive and engaging.

Paul got it so right when he wrote about Jesus – God's gift – to the church at Corinth. He didn't try out all the other words in his vocabulary. There was nothing more appropriate than 'indescribable'.

'Although the Spirit employs the highest human colors our language affords – analogies, metaphors, titles, types, parables, poetry, and more – the painting is of *him* whose riches the Spirit himself calls "unsearchable," *him* whose love surpasses knowledge (and therefore language), *him* of whom the world itself is too small a library to contain all the books documenting his wondrous deeds.'[41]

Yet, to . . .

- the sinful, He is Saviour;
- the sad, He is Comforter;
- the lonely, He is Friend;
- the sick, He is Healer;
- the rejected, He is Lover;
- the widow, He is Husband;
- the confused, He is Guide.

And in the darkest night, the mere whisper of His name – *Jesus* – can calm our troubled soul. When life collapses around us, we call from beneath the rubble and discover He is there with us in the dirt. And when that final valley stretches before us, His name – *Jesus* – brings the comfort none other can. There is no sweeter name than His.

So, while our days are filled with words, let's make sure we use them in worship. For He is worthy.

Thank you, Father, for the indescribable gift of Your Son, our Saviour. And thank you, Jesus, that Your name is the balm that soothes the most troubled soul. Amen.

19 December

There was no place for them in the inn.
Luke 2:7

Reading: Luke 2:1–7

Have you ever felt misunderstood or misrepresented? Has your reputation been blackened? Were you made out to be a villain when nothing could be further from the truth? If any of the above is true for you, perhaps you can identify with the innkeeper in the Christmas story. So much has been built on very few words; so many sermons delivered on the man who refused Jesus entry. But did he? Was he an unkind, money-grabbing businessman? Was it his fault that the Saviour of the world was born in a smelly stable?

Truth be told, we don't have enough textual evidence to answer either way, but we do have other historical and social information to help us fill in the blanks.

Caesar Augustus – a greedy man – had dictated that every family return to the place of their birth to be counted. He aimed to squeeze as much tax as he could from Rome's conquered nations. Can you imagine the turmoil such an order caused? People were moving around all over Israel. While inns and places of hospitality were to be found in every town and city in Israel, there was no way they could have accommodated the huge numbers who needed a place to stay.

It's a simple fact: the innkeeper had no room for the young couple when they arrived at his door. All his rooms were booked ... probably *over*booked ... crowded ... beyond standards of safety! And, contrary to a multitude of sermons, the innkeeper had no idea who Mary and Joseph were, or that the Messiah was looking for a place to be born. No angel had visited him to reserve the best room in the house, where the Son of God could be born.

Carols have been written about the gifts of the Magi, and even about the poor shepherds. But might it be that the innkeeper gave what he could? Was a stable His gift to the King? Perhaps it was even more peaceful there than in his over-crowded home.

And have we recognized that we are the innkeepers of our own hearts? But now we know who Jesus is, what is our response to His knock?

Lord, may I always respond quickly to Your knock, and may I continually treat others with grace. Amen.

20 December

'In his name the nations will put their hope.'

Matthew 12:21, NIVUK

Reading: Matthew 12:18–21

The consultant's words have stayed with me throughout the years. As a first-year student nurse, I had somewhat insolently challenged him on not being honest with a family about the impending death of their loved one. 'Hope is all they have left,' he replied. 'If we take that away from them, we confiscate what is still here.'

Hopelessness strangles life. It removes our ability to see the sunshine, deprives us of a reason to get up in the morning, counts us as worthless. And worse still, it denies God's faithfulness and blinds us to His love for us. Hopelessness is like a blackout blind, holding back the light and preventing us from seeing beyond where we are. There is no darker place to sit.

Unfortunately, Christmas often magnifies these feelings, especially as those in pain watch others enjoy what they no longer have, or have no possibility of ever achieving. And thoughts of a new year ahead bring forward the hope that next year will be better. But for many, hope is nothing more than wishful thinking. I mean, I hope to cruise the Caribbean this Christmas . . . but there's absolutely nothing certain about it!

However, there is nothing uncertain about biblical hope. It's neither wishful thinking nor looking for a silver lining. The hope that Jesus brought into the world that first Christmas offers certainty – a confident expectation that what God has promised in His word is true, and will happen, because He cannot lie. 'Now faith is being *sure* of what we hope for and certain of what we do not see' (Hebrews 11:1 NIV, emphasis mine). What makes hope certain? The very Person in whom our confident expectation lies: Jesus.

Biblical hope brings life. It enables us to see the sunshine, gives us a reason to get up in the morning, counts us as of worth. Best of all, it confirms God's faithfulness and demonstrates His love for us. Hope is the frame through which His light comes, allowing us to see what lies beyond the now. There is no brighter place to sit.

'May the God of hope fill [me] with all joy and peace in believing . . . that . . . [I] may abound in hope'.[42] *Amen.*

21 December

'Behold, the virgin shall conceive and bear a son,
and they shall call his name Immanuel'
(which means, God with us).

Matthew 1:23

Reading: Philippians 2:5–8

'What are you doing for Christmas?' is a frequent question on our lips these days. No one likes to be alone over the festive season. Joy should be spread, not kept to ourselves . . . or from others, for that matter. Often the response is: 'The family will be with us.' What could be better than to celebrate the Saviour's birth than with those we love most?

The term 'with us' indicates a physical presence. Modern Zoom communication may bring family or friends into our homes in a virtual way, but remarkable as it is, it will only ever be virtual.

Back in Isaiah 7:14, God promised to send His Son to be 'with us', and some 700 years later that promise was realized. A virgin did indeed give birth to God's Son, and He was given the name – along with other titles – of 'Immanuel', the Hebrew meaning of which is 'God with us'. 'With us' . . . Jesus took on human flesh in order to be physically part of the world He had created. The wonder of the incarnation had happened, and multitudes were privileged to benefit from Christ's physical presence while He lived among them.

Jesus is still Immanuel. We were not born at the wrong time. We have not missed Him. He is still with us. But the reality of His presence happens through the Holy Spirit, given to Christ's redeemed people after He had returned to the Father. And Jesus promised that the Holy Spirit will never leave us (John 14:16). He is not some virtual visitor. He doesn't disappear or freeze when the signal isn't good. He is with us forever . . . until we get the opportunity to meet Jesus, face to face. And 'we know that when he appears we shall be like him, because we shall see him as he is' (1 John 3:2)!

Hallelujah! God is with us. And not just at Christmas!

Lord Immanuel, I am so thankful that I can enjoy Your presence every day, but I can't wait to meet with You, up close and personal. Amen.

22 December

THINK ON THIS

And the Word became flesh and dwelt among us,
and we have seen his glory,
glory as of the only Son from the Father,
full of grace and truth.

John 1:14

- Read through this verse a number of times – including out loud.
- Write it out, stick it on the fridge, have it on your phone.
- Meditate on the words, then respond in praise.
- Take steps to allow God's word to change you: perhaps . . . repent, forgive, love.

23 December

And Joseph also went up from Galilee . . .
to . . . Bethlehem . . . to be registered with Mary,
his betrothed, who was with child.

Luke 2:4–5

Reading: Luke 2:1–7

Christmas is the most wonderful time of year, or so says the music playing on a loop in the shopping centres. Friends meeting for coffee, shopping bags piled around their feet. Bright lights cutting through the darkness. School nativity productions. Family returning home from far and near . . . and the smell of turkey cooking. Ahh . . . It's hard to beat, isn't it?

Yet, it's possible that this isn't what comes to your mind when you hear the word 'Christmas'. For you it's the empty seat at the table. One less gift to wrap. Laughter that stopped long before you were ready. Rather than being hard to beat, it has become hard to bear.

However you feel, come with me, and let's sit in a story – a true story – for a little while. Shh . . . do you hear it? There's a baby crying. You can't help but smile . . . because there's something wonderful about the sound of a baby's first cry. It signals both a completion and a beginning all rolled into one. And even in this stark birthing room where we sit, more joy and hope than you could ever imagine is being delivered. And as the man with calloused hands fumbles with the strips of cloth he is using to swaddle this precious little bundle, the sheep bleat in the corner, unable to feed from the trough now covered in homespun wool.

The bustling streets of Bethlehem don't see what we see in that stable, as a young mother holds her little son close for the first time. This is the baby that the angel had said would 'be called holy – the Son of God' (Luke 1:35). But sadly, those outside are too busy to notice that God has come to earth. Too busy to recognize that by this child salvation will come. Too busy to see that, in Jesus, 'the hopes and fears of all the years' are being met in their dark streets this night. Too busy to see prophecy fulfilled . . . or God's love born in their very midst.

Slow me down, Saviour, that I might see what truly matters this Christmas. Amen.

24 December

And the angel said to them,
'Fear not, for behold,
I bring you good news of great joy
that will be for all the people.'
Luke 2:10

Reading: Luke 2:8–14

What are these rather scruffy men gathered around the campfire talking about? Come close . . . listen in. They're laughing. Joking that being out on the hills might be better than having to bunk up with the cousins who had come to town for the census. But there's a sadness in this bunch that a joke can't cover. The truth is, out here they don't have to look into the eyes of their hungry children or watch the Pharisees turn up their noses as they walk past . . . or wonder why their fathers didn't send them to school with the other boys in Bethlehem.

Shepherds. That's why. It's what they are, all they'll ever be. You don't need to read and write to be a shepherd. You only need to count! Looking after someone else's sheep doesn't amount to much. Even preparing the lambs for the temple sacrifice doesn't bring these men any glory. On the hillside, those on four legs are of more value than those on two. And a gloom fuelled by tiredness hangs over the little band.

'There's that strange light in the sky again tonight,' one of them says as he pulls his blanket up under his chin. 'Brighter than ever,' his friend replies. 'I tell you, there's something afoot,' the oldest of their party interjects. 'That sky's different tonight, and I should know . . . I've been staring at it for too many years!' 'Oh, go to sleep, old man,' the youngest chips in. 'Your head is up in those stars!'

But the old man is right. Tonight *is* different, and it's about more than an unusual star. It's a night they will never forget. For God has chosen them – the uneducated, the poor, the society rejects – over the king, the priests and the wealthy. God chose shepherds in a field – not dignitaries in a temple or a palace – to be the first to hear that the Saviour has been born. The Messiah has arrived!

Father, thank you that You chose, on that night of nights, to give the best news the world has ever heard to those willing to believe. Amen.

25 December

'For unto you is born this day in the city of David
a Savior, who is Christ the Lord.'

Luke 2:11

Reading: Luke 2:15–20

Shepherds would never have been on the guest list for a party. But what a light show they are witnessing for the King of kings in His otherwise muted arrival! Can you hear that angel choir sing? Roll over New Irish ... stand back Belfast Community Choir. Heaven's chorus is in full swing ... GLORY! GLORY! 'Glory to God in the highest!' they're singing. But wait, that's not all ... 'and on earth peace, goodwill toward men' (Luke 2:14, NKJV). PEACE – the longing of our hearts ... and a tear falls from the old shepherd's weather-beaten cheek. PEACE – the calm that is missing from every life. PEACE – freedom from all that disturbs.

Glory to God, and peace to them. That's not a message they ever thought they would hear, but the greatest privilege of all was that the message had been given to them. That's what topped this cake of delight with JOY unspeakable!

It is unlikely that thirty years later any of the shepherds would have heard Jesus declare that the reason He came was 'to proclaim good news to the poor ... liberty to the captives ... sight to the blind ... liberty [to] those who are oppressed ... to proclaim the year of the Lord's favor' (4:18–19). But they certainly experienced it that night in the darkness above Bethlehem. And as we watch them rush down the hill towards the stable in an overcrowded Bethlehem, God is guarding their sheep ... for the simple shepherds are off to meet 'the Lamb of God, who takes away the sin of the world!' (John 1:29). Including theirs ... and ours!

So, it is okay to shed tears over the empty place at the Christmas table today, or to miss the laughter of that friend, or to have one less gift to unwrap, but let's never forget where we've been ... for 'we have seen and testify that the Father has sent his Son to be the Savior of the world' (1 John 4:14).

Come on, let's join the celebration!

You are the greatest gift I could ever receive, Lord, on this day or any other. Thank you isn't enough, but I give it with my love. Amen.

26 December

For to us a child is born,
to us a son is given;
and the government shall be upon his shoulder,
and his name shall be called
Wonderful Counselor, Mighty God,
Everlasting Father, Prince of Peace.

Isaiah 9:6

Reading: Isaiah 9:2–7

Sharing the birth of your new baby with others is something very special, but for me the wonder finally struck when, for the first time, I was left with her on my own.

In the quietness, I was captivated by her little face and how she wrinkled up her tiny nose as she slept. But when she tightly grasped my finger in her tiny hand she stole my heart. This seven-pound baby was mine! The mixed emotions of nine months of pregnancy now had a face . . . a wrinkly, squashed-up, beautiful face. And she had a name. A name that I tried out repeatedly as I held her close. Cheryl. It was her daddy's choice. 'Cheryl,' he'd said. 'It means "darling".' He chose well . . . for that is exactly what she was.

I have the feeling that after the unexpected visitors from Bethlehem's fields, Mary did the same as every mother has done from time immemorial. She counted her little Son's fingers and toes, held Him close, and tried out His name. Jesus. That's what the angel had told Joseph to call Mary's Son. Jesus. 'For he will save his people from their sins' (Matthew 1:21).

Yet, both Mary and Joseph would have known the other names given to the Messiah, as prophesied by Isaiah (9:6). And as Jesus grew, His earthly parents would have seen them fulfilled before their eyes:

- Wonderful Counsellor . . . full of wonder and great in wisdom.
- Mighty God . . . omnipotent, omniscient and omnipresent.
- Everlasting Father . . . all that we need, eternally provided for in Jesus.
- Prince of Peace . . . dispenser of peace and rest to our souls in a mixed-up world.

And while she thought about all these things (Luke 2:19), Mary held her new-born close to her heart, unaware of all that lay ahead.

Jesus . . . my heart thrills at the mention of Your name, for in You salvation has not only come to the world but also to my heart. Amen.

27 December

'I am coming soon. Hold on to what you have,
so that no one will take away your crown.'

Revelation 3:11, NLT

Reading: Ephesians 2:1–7

Once upon a time there were seven churches. Each was a bright jewel in the crown of early Christendom. In fact, such was their commitment that Jesus sent individual letters to each one, to commend them for their faithfulness.

But wait, that's not the end of the story, for this is no fairy tale. It is the reality of seven churches described in the book of Revelation. Only two of the seven could continue to bask in the risen Lord's commendation. For the other five, the Saviour had something more to say, and it wasn't pretty. 'But I have this against you,' He charged (Revelation 2:4), with a cringe factor of seismic proportions.

I wonder, did their smiles disappear, their heads hang low? Were any tears shed as Jesus pointed out the sinful practices they were tolerating within the church, and in their own lives? Yet even in this, God offered mercy for repentance; reward for perseverance. But we don't read of any change of heart. Instead, the light went out.

How could this happen to these vibrant churches – these communities of Jesus' followers? We are not told. My guess is that their problem mirrors much of ours today. Little by little, we allow that first fiery passion for Jesus to be diminished by the 'everyday' of our lives. Then, slowly, the time we make for Jesus dwindles, resulting in a nodding acquaintance with Him rather than warm devotion for 'him whom my soul loves' (Song of Solomon 3:4). How awful that it's possible to drift effortlessly from the Ephesian problem – leaving our first love (Revelation 2:4) – to the Laodicean one: becoming so lukewarm that we make Him sick (3:16)!

Perhaps, like me, your longing is to remain faithful like the Smyrnans (2:8–10) or the Philadelphians (3:7–8), but that responsibility remains firmly with us (Hebrews 10:23). And so, Jesus' words ring loudly in my ears: 'Hold on to what you have, so that no one will take away your crown' (Revelation 3:11, NLT).

Lord Jesus, You have also said that You are returning soon. May I be found faithful on Your arrival. Amen.

28 December

'He will wipe away every tear from their eyes,
and death shall be no more,
neither shall there be mourning, nor crying,
nor pain anymore, for the former things
have passed away.'

Revelation 21:4

Reading: Revelation 21:1–7

Jesus is coming back again! Just as His first coming fulfilled a multiplicity of prophetic utterances (Micah 5:2, for example), so His second coming is equally certain. Did Jesus Himself not say: 'I will come again and will take you to myself' (John 14:3)? He has proved Himself a trustworthy promise keeper . . . and He will continue to be faithful to His word.

When Jesus left the earth, He didn't hide the fact that, because we live on a planet cursed by sin, we would continue to suffer (Genesis 3:14–19) – particularly in relation to our faith in Him (John 15:18). However, everything will be different when Christ returns as King of kings, and reveals to us the new heaven and the new earth (Revelation 21:1).

Today's verse is a favourite of mine. The promises it contains are wonderful, and truly perfect for the broken-hearted.

I lost two daughters – you can imagine the tears shed. The standing joke was that I should have bought shares in Kleenex! Yet, these words of Jesus have frequently brought healing to my soul. Because in heaven there will be:

- No more tears – ever! They will have been wiped away by His nail-scarred hands;
- No more death – humanity's last enemy will finally have been defeated!
- No mourning – for we will see Jesus and be reunited with our loved ones;
- No crying – sadness is not allowed through the gates of His kingdom!
- No pain – our bodies will never succumb to disease again.

Imagine, if you possibly can, that 'all these things are gone forever' (Revelation 21:4, NLT)! Now, think of the year that will soon pass into eternity, and meditate on this: 'I consider that the sufferings of this present time are not worth comparing with the glory that is to be revealed to us' (Romans 8:18).

Returning Saviour, thank you for pouring Your promises of healing and peace into my life. Help me to remember that now is not all there is. Amen.

29 December

THINK ON THIS

So Christ, having been offered once
to bear the sins of many,
will appear a second time,
not to deal with sin but to save those
who are eagerly waiting for him.

Hebrews 9:28

- Read through this verse a number of times – including out loud.
- Write it out, stick it on the fridge, have it on your phone.
- Meditate on the words, then respond in praise.
- Encourage someone by sharing this verse with them today.

30 December

'You also must be ready,
for the Son of Man is coming
at an hour you do not expect.'

Luke 12:40

Reading: Luke 12:35–40

Bethlehem wasn't ready for Jesus. Surprisingly, neither was the religious hierarchy, nor those who studied the prophets. It seemed as if the infant Son of God slipped quietly from eternity into time; from majesty to pauper; from Spirit to flesh, with little notice except to a bunch of shepherds with choirs of angels on their minds, and some Magi from a faraway land.

But wait. What about that relative, born six months before Mary's Son? John was his name, and he had spent his life preparing the way for the coming Messiah (John 1:6–9). He was ready to meet Jesus. And then there was that elderly, unrelated couple belonging to a strange group the Bible refers to as 'waiting for the redemption' of Israel (Luke 2:25, 38) – Simeon and Anna. Godly Simeon, guided by the Holy Spirit, instantly recognized the Christ child and 'took him up in his arms and blessed God' for the fulfilled promised of His coming (2:27–28). Anna quickly joined her old friend in praising God (2:38). They were ready to meet Jesus. And oh, how they were rewarded!

Some years later, the Saviour was encouraging His followers to 'be ready, for the Son of Man is coming at an hour you do not expect' (12:40). This Son of Man was more than flesh – He was God. While among them, He was the Suffering servant, but one day He will come again and break through the clouds as the conquering King (Matthew 24:30–31).

Jesus asked then, as He does now: 'Are you ready?' Are we dressed for action – ready to respond should the trumpet sound? Is the light of our faith burning brightly should He come in the night hours? Does a sense of anticipation for His coming grip our hearts? Is our spirit awake with expectation in this dull, dark world? For 'blessed are those servants whom the master finds awake when he comes' (Luke 12:37).

Conquering King, You will come when we do not expect it. May my life and soul be ready for Your glorious appearing. Amen.

31 December

Together, for this past year we have 'consider[ed] him who endured from sinners such hostility against himself, so that [we] may not grow weary or fainthearted' (Hebrews 12:3). I hope you have discovered, as I have, that there is no one more worthy of our praise and thanks than our Lord Jesus. He truly is God's 'indescribable gift!' (2 Corinthians 9:15, NIVUK). I have been lost for words on too many occasions this past year when I have tried to describe the inimitable Jesus. His words have always said it better than I can.

I pray that as you walk into a new year you will do so with Jesus as your companion. Life's journeys are too difficult without Him. We have barely scratched the surface as we have tried to get to know Him better. I warmly concur with the beloved disciple, John: 'Now there are also many other things that Jesus did. Were every one of them to be written, I suppose that the world itself could not contain the books that would be written' (John 21:25). As we part company, I graciously pray the benediction of Jude over your life:

Now to him who is able to keep you from stumbling and to present you blameless before the presence of his glory with great joy, to the only God, our Savior, through Jesus Christ our Lord, be glory, majesty, dominion, and authority, before all time and now and forever. Amen.

Jude 24–25

Notes

1 J. Piper, 'Who Is Jesus to You?': www.desiringgod.org/interviews/who-is-jesus-to-you (accessed 22 May 2023).

2 Barna Group, 'Perceptions of Jesus, Christians & Evangelism in the UK' (2015): https://talkingjesus.org/wp-content/uploads/2018/04/Perceptions-of-Jesus-Christians_UK_FINAL.pdf (accessed 22 May 2023).

3 Ligonier, 'The State of Theology Survey: 2020 Results': https://www.ligonier.org/posts/state-theology-survey-2020-results (accessed 22 May 2023).

4 Adapted from my book *God Isn't Finished With You Yet* (London: IVP, 2022), pp. 175–6.

5 C. Wesley, 'Jesus, Lover of my Soul', (1740, public domain).

6 E. Elliot, *A Lamp for my Feet* (Ada, MI: Revell, 2021), p. 40.

7 Augustine cited in D. Bast, 'The Compassion of Jesus' (2008): https://www.woh.org/2008/04/20/the-compassion-of-jesus (accessed 22 May 2023).

8 R. A. Jarvie, 'With a Soul Blood-bought' (1918, public domain).

9 Adapted from my book *God Knows Your Name* (Oxford: Monarch Books, 2010), pp. 56–7.

10 R. Burns, 'Man Was Made to Mourn: A Dirge': http://www.robertburns.org/works/55.shtml (accessed 22 May 2023).

11 R. Kitchen, J. Martin, Jr., 'Broken Pieces': https://gospelchoruses.wordpress.com/2020/04/18/broken-pieces (accessed 22 May 2023).

12 C. S. Lewis, *Letters to Malcolm: Chiefly on Prayer* (Boston, MA: Mariner Books, 2002), p. 93.

13 'Was Jesus being rude to Mary when He referred to her as "woman" in John 2:4?': www.gotquestions.org/Jesus-Mary-woman.html (accessed 22 May 2023).

14 C. T. Studd cited by G. Stannard, 'If Jesus Christ be God and Died for Me …': https://understandingthegospel.org/explore-the-gospel/short-articles/if-jesus-christ-be-god-and-died-for-me (accessed 22 May 2023).

15 J. H. Keathley, 'The Uniqueness of Jesus Christ': www.bible.org/article/uniqueness-jesus-christ (accessed 22 May 2023).

16 My adaptation of Luke 6:6–11.

17 R. Ramsey, 'Good Friday in Real Time': https://www.thegospelcoalition.org/article/good-friday-in-real-time (accessed 22 May 2023).

18 J. Bridges, *Transforming Grace: Living Confidently in God's Unfailing Love* (Carol Stream, IL: NavPress, 2008) p. 213.

19 J. Piper, 'God's Sustaining Grace': www.desiringgod.org/messages/gods-sustaining-grace (accessed 22 May 2023).

20 Adapted from my book *God Knows Your Name* (Oxford: Monarch Books, 2010), pp. 179–80.

21 W. E. Henley, 'Invictus': https://www.poetryfoundation.org/poems/51642/invictus (accessed 22 May 2023).

22 Adapted from my book *God Isn't Finished With You Yet* (London: IVP, 2022), pp. 95–97.

23 Adapted from my book *God Isn't Finished With You Yet* (London: IVP, 2022), pp. 95–100.

24 'Prayer of St Francis', Wikipedia: https://en.wikipedia.org/wiki/Prayer_of_Saint_Francis_Peace': https://hymnary.org/text/make_me_a_channel_of_your_peace (accessed 22 May 2023).

25 Adapted from my book *God Isn't Finished With You Yet* (London: IVP, 2022), pp. 166–68.

26 Adapted from my book *God Knows Your Name* (Oxford: Monarch Books, 2010), pp. 158–60.

27 Adapted from my book *When We Can't, God Can* (Oxford: Monarch Books, 2015), pp. 88–90.

28 L. W. Johnson, 'How to pray for our children': www.focusonthefamily.ca/content/how-to-pray-for-our-children (accessed 22 May 2023).

29 A. B. Simpson, 'What Will You Do With Jesus': https://hymnary.org/text/jesus_is_standing_in_pilates_hall_friend (accessed 22 May 2023).

30 Adapted from my book *God Knows Your Name* (Oxford: Monarch Books, 2010), pp. 42–44.

31 Adapted from my book *Journey With Me* (London: IVP, 2018) p. 376.

32 M. Horton, 'Christians and Demonic Activity Today': www.corechristianity.com/resource-library/articles/christians-and-demonic-activity-today (accessed 22 May 2023).

33 Adapted from my book *God Knows Your Name* (Oxford: Monarch Books, 2010), pp. 158–60.

34 T. Keller, *Prayer: Experiencing Awe and Intimacy with God* (New York, NY: Viking, 2014), p. 28.

35 Revelation 4:11.

36 J. Donne, 'Devotions Upon Emergent Occasions' (public domain 1624).

37 W. Wiersbe, *Be Mature* (Colorado Springs, CO: David C. Cook, 1978), p. 128.

38 Psalm 66:16.

39 'World in Brief', *Evangelicals Now* (December 2022).

40 Adapted from my book *Journey with Me* (London: IVP, 2018) p. 376.

41 G. Morse, 'Indescribable: The Many and Marvelous Names of Jesus': https://www.desiringgod.org/articles/indescribable (accessed 22 May 2023).

42 Romans 15:13.